D1235543

Edmund

In memory of
J. B. H. *and* M. C. H.

Edmund Spenser: Protestant Poet

ANTHEA HUME

Senior Lecturer in English
University of Reading

CAMBRIDGE UNIVERSITY PRESS

Cambridge

London   New York   New Rochelle
Melbourne   Sydney

CAMBRIDGE UNIVERSITY PRESS
Cambridge, New York, Melbourne, Madrid, Cape Town, Singapore, São Paulo, Delhi

Cambridge University Press
The Edinburgh Building, Cambridge CB2 8RU, UK

Published in the United States of America by Cambridge University Press, New York

www.cambridge.org
Information on this title: www.cambridge.org/9780521258074

First published 1984
This digitally printed version 2008

A catalogue record for this publication is available from the British Library

Library of Congress Catalogue Card Number: 83-14308

ISBN 978-0-521-25807-4 hardback
ISBN 978-0-521-09160-2 paperback

Contents

Acknowledgements

I am grateful to the editors of *The Review of English Studies* for permission to use in Chapters 1 and 2 material which originally appeared in my article entitled 'Spenser, Puritanism, and the "Maye" Eclogue', *Review of English Studies*, n.s., xx (1969). I am also much indebted to friends who by asking me to give lectures or papers encouraged me to crystallise my thoughts on aspects of *The Faerie Queene*: Professor Jean Bromley, then of Southampton University, invited me to lecture on the subject of Britons and Elves, and Dr Cedric Brown, then of Cardiff University, now of Reading University, asked me to talk about Nature and Grace in the poem. The fact that these events took place some years ago is evidence that the book has been a long time in the making. As a result many other debts acquired over the years cannot now readily be listed; but it is a particular pleasure to record the help I have received from my colleagues in the Renaissance Research Group at Reading University. Challenging and at times alarmingly sharp-sighted discussion on a variety of Renaissance topics including Spenserian ones has been a source of constant intellectual stimulus.

The text of Spenser used throughout is that in the Oxford Standard Authors edition of *The Poetical Works of Edmund Spenser* ed. J. C. Smith and E. de Selincourt (1912). Biblical quotations are taken from the second edition of the Geneva Bible (1562). The original spelling and punctuation of all works quoted have been preserved, but contractions have been expanded.

1

Introduction

In *A Theatre for voluptuous Worldlings* the young Spenser translated
the French of Marot, itself a version of the Italian of Petrarch, with
an enjoyment which is obvious despite the rhythmic stiffness of
inexperience:

> Then heauenly branches did I see arise,
> Out of a fresh and lusty Laurell tree
> Amidde the yong grene wood. Of Paradise
> Some noble plant I thought my selfe to see,
> Suche store of birdes therein yshrouded were,
> Chaunting in shade their sundry melodie.

But elsewhere in the *Theatre*, following his Flemish model, he
sounded with equal conviction the note of Protestant fervour:

> I saw a Woman sitting on a beast
> Before mine eyes, of Orenge colour hew;
> Horrour and dreadfull name of blasphemie
> Filde hir with pride.

Spenser was only sixteen or seventeen when he made these verse
translations for Jan van der Noodt, but in a number of ways they
anticipate his preoccupations of later years. Throughout his writing
life the poet continued to reveal in his work both an enthusiasm for
the humanist inheritance and a zealous, even militant Protestantism.
His knowledge of the literature of antiquity and of Renaissance Italy
and France has received sympathetic critical study during our own
century – his debts to Virgil and Ovid, to Petrarch, Ariosto and
Tasso, to Marot and du Bellay, to Renaissance Neoplatonism,
mythography and iconography, have been admirably scrutinised –
but the impact of his Protestantism on his imaginative writing has
been treated with more reserve. Certainly the Elizabethan Protestant
milieu of the 1570s and 1580s is not on the face of it the most
congenial area for enquiry; yet if we neglect this part of his mental

world we are likely to find ourselves in possession of views of his poems which indicate more about our own assumptions than about his. The present study starts from the wish to redress an imbalance in Spenser scholarship by adding a fuller awareness of Protestant culture to our sense of his Renaissance humanist inheritance. No doubt the occupational hazard implicit in looking into sermons and biblical commentaries in order to increase appreciation of a poet's work is that the poems may be reduced to sounding like treatises. There must be a way, however, of doing justice to the role of Protestant thought and vocabulary in Spenser's writings without minimising the equally important role of classical, mediaeval, Ariostan and Neoplatonic components. Spenser's peculiar genius, after all, was for synthesis. What seems now to be necessary is that the reader should be willing to give as much imaginative attention to the Elizabethan Protestant elements in the synthesis as to the classical or Italian.

If indefinite space were available, most or all of Spenser's poems would call for examination, but in the interests of brevity the book confines itself to *The Shepheardes Calender* and *The Faerie Queene*. Perhaps this is the moment to explain that an intention to study the Protestant aspects of Spenser's art in these two poems does not necessarily imply a resolve to identify the various pastors in *The Shepheardes Calender* with Elizabethan bishops, or to interpret each of the fountains in *The Faerie Queene* as an image of baptism. I am working from the assumption, discussed in Chapter 8, that Spenser's poems are not so much enigmatic as richly suggestive, and hence that if read carefully they have a notable power to explicate themselves; but in cases where words and images have lost their force through twentieth-century remoteness from an Elizabethan Protestant milieu, I shall try to re-animate the relevant context.

My approach as far as possible will be through a reading of the poems, rather than through an account first of 'the tradition' and then of the works. All the same, it seems a good idea in this introductory chapter to consider some of the cross-currents in Elizabethan Protestant religion and politics, and to attempt to establish a satisfactory theory about Spenser's position within that world. In the second chapter more detailed, internal evidence for the theory will be supplied from *The Shepheardes Calender*. I shall be maintaining that Spenser's Protestantism was of the militant variety associated with the Leicester circle, and that in the late 1570s, the

years of *The Shepheardes Calender*, his religion requires the label
'Puritanism'. Definitions of course will be essential to the argument,
but they will gain in substance and intelligibility if they emerge from
discussion of specific doctrines, factions and personalities in the
Elizabethan world.

The case for Spenser's Puritanism has not been fashionable in
recent decades. Nevertheless it received the support of a number of
scholars in the early years of this century: by 1914 Lilian Winstanley,
J. J. Higginson, and F. M. Padelford had all argued that Spenser was
a Puritan or that he held beliefs near to those of the Puritans.[1] In
1930 W. L. Renwick included some useful Puritan material in his
commentary on *The Shepheardes Calender*.[2] But opinion was moving
the other way. Higginson's book in particular, with its speculative
identification of figures in the *Calender* with historical individuals
and its neglect of the fact that Spenser had been secretary to Bishop
Young of Rochester in 1578, rightly carried little weight. Spenser's
evident belief in episcopacy, indicated by his service under Young,
his praise of both Grindal and Young in *The Shepheardes Calender*,
and probably reflected in E. K.'s 'Maye' gloss which supported
'fatherly rule' in the church, seemed to undermine any 'Puritan'
reading of his work. In 1950 Virgil K. Whitaker argued that
Spenser's sympathies lay with 'the conservative party in the
Anglican church', and that he spoke for those who were attempting
'to preserve as much as possible of its Catholic heritage'. The poet
was to be seen 'as the religious fellow of Hooker and ancestor of
Herbert'.[3] Paul E. McLane in his book on *The Shepheardes Calender*
described Spenser as 'a faithful, if conservative, son of the English
Church', who was 'clearly anti-Puritan'. He remarked that 'Spenser's
dislike of Puritanism is, of course, obvious enough in his poetry.'[4]
Subsequently William Nelson warned readers against assuming that
Spenser necessarily shared the religious opinions of the Leicester
party, which 'inclined rather to the left than to the right in the
religious controversy'. Spenser, he claimed, 'was not one of those
who wrote polemical essays on the subject of the religious disputes
of his day...He was a moderate Protestant of the kind of Richard
Hooker, the great apologist of the religious compromise.'[5] Peter
Bayley, for his part, acknowledged that Spenser attacked church
corruption in *The Shepheardes Calender*, but stated that 'this does not
make him a Puritan'.[6]

It is possible that behind the modern consensus on the subject of

Spenser's religious beliefs lie some quite understandable personal preferences. These can reveal themselves through the tone in which points are made. A certain satisfaction, for example, is audible when a critic speaks of 'the re-capture of Spenser from the ranks of the Calvinists and his return to a more ordinary and unobtrusive place among the usual Anglicans of his decades'.[7] The tone of relief hints at the tastes of liberal-minded scholars, who are naturally reluctant to link Spenser with what appears to be an intemperate zeal, let alone with the doctrine of predestination. Yet it would not, in actual fact, prove easy to 're-capture' the Protestant Spenser of the 1570s and 1580s from the Calvinists, so far as the theology of salvation is concerned. The doctrine of the Elizabethan church in this period was predestinarian and, in effect, Calvinist, regardless of the position taken up by individuals in the controversy about the 'apparell', ceremonies, and church government. Whitgift, official voice of the hierarchy in these years for the rebuttal of Cartwright's Presbyterianism, was a Calvinist in his theology of salvation. As he himself often reiterated, he was not disputing with Cartwright about 'the doctrine of the Gospell' which both accepted, but about 'externall matters'.[8] Inevitably his discussion was punctuated by endorsements of the concept of 'the electe'.[9] Article XVII of the Thirty-nine Articles asserted the doctrine of predestination, while the Book of Homilies underlined that of natural depravity ('of our selues, and by our selues we haue no goodnesse, help, nor saluacion: but contrarywyse, sinne, dampnation, and death euerlasting').[10]

One must not neglect the fact that in the 1590s new emphases and new directions in English Protestantism began to claim attention, for example, Baro's rejection of reprobation, Bancroft's and Whitgift's arguments for the apostolic foundation of episcopacy,[11] above all Hooker's stress on natural law and the capacities of human reason. And it is true that these ideas had received some expression in sermons of the 1580s. But their impact was not felt until the 1590s, while their consequences belonged to the following century. The doctrine of the Church of England in the Elizabethan period remained 'Calvinistic'[12] and Spenser cannot be rescued or 're-captured' from the theology of his times.

But we have still to consider the ways in which Puritans differed from their fellows. In part it was a matter of the special intensity of their commitment: Protestants of 'the hotter sort' were 'called

Puritans'.[13] However, more specifically, the central concerns for Puritans may be summarised as a desire for 'further reformation' of the Church of England in the light of the scriptures, a preoccupation with the need for an educated, preaching ministry, a hatred of episcopal pomp and wealth, and a particularly fervent opposition to Roman Catholicism. The omission from this list of any reference to theories of church government is crucial: modern historical scholarship has uncovered the extent to which Puritans differed among themselves on the question of the acceptability of episcopacy. After 1570 some of them campaigned for a Presbyterian polity (the abolition of archbishops and bishops, the election and equality of ministers). This formed the subject of Field and Wilcox's *Admonition to the Parliament* (1572) for which the authors were imprisoned, and of the anonymous *Seconde admonition*. Cartwright expounded the same polity in his Cambridge lectures of 1570, and in his *Replye* and *Second Replie* to Whitgift. Travers's *Ecclesiasticae disciplinae...explicatio* (1574) was also an exposition of the Presbyterian system. Nevertheless, by no means all Puritans endorsed the aims or methods of the Admonitioners. Veteran and much respected Puritan leaders such as Laurence Humphrey, Thomas Sampson, John Foxe and Anthony Gilby withheld their support from the Presbyterian campaign. Humphrey believed that 'in some points and terms' the Admonitioners 'are too broad and overshoot themselves'.[14] Gilby, a former Genevan exile and now preacher at Ashby de la Zouch, exercised a moderating influence from the provinces,[15] although he remained in sympathetic contact with the younger Puritan leaders. He did not denounce episcopacy as such, but sent reminders to bishops about the true conduct of their office. He urged Bishop Cooper of Lincoln to

come amongst us sometimes in Christian humility, laying aside all popish lordliness, and so exercise your good gifts amongst your brethren that we of your great light may receive some light.[16]

With the advent of Grindal to the throne of Canterbury in 1576 the future looked promising for 'moderate episcopalian Puritans' (a useful phrase I have borrowed from the historian M. M. Knappen)[17] since the new archbishop was known to be favourable towards their cause. His efforts were directed towards the reform of the ecclesiastical courts, the encouragement of an educated, preaching ministry, and the severer punishment of recusancy. Above all he supported the prophesyings, which were a product of Puritan zeal without being inherently Presbyterian activities.[18] It was his refusal to agree to their suppression despite the Queen's command which led to his fall in June 1577. For a time it had looked as though the moderate Puritan programme might have been carried through under archiepiscopal leadership, but now it was clear that the struggle would have to continue.

Especially relevant to the present discussion is the position taken up by members of the governing class towards individual Puritans – particularly the stance of the Earl of Leicester's so-called 'progressive' party, which included Sir Francis Walsingham, Leicester's brother the Earl of Warwick and his brother-in-law the Earl of Huntingdon, the Earl of Bedford, Sir Francis Knollys and others. The foreign policy of this group was marked by a vehement spirit of opposition to Spain and to Roman Catholicism, which explained their advocacy of an expedition to aid the Netherlands and their hostility to the projected marriage between the Queen and the Catholic Duke of Alençon. Evidently the concerns of the Puritans and of 'progressive' nobles coincided to a remarkable extent. Leicester provided support and patronage both for moderate Puritans such as Laurence Humphrey, and for more extreme figures including Presbyterians like Field and Wilcox. He seems to have assisted these two in obtaining their release from prison in 1573; he used his influence to procure Field a preaching licence from Oxford University in 1579, and he accepted dedications of two works by Field in 1579–81.[19] He bestowed the Mastership of his Hospital at Warwick on Cartwright in 1586. Leicester's personal religious convictions may have been a good deal less than fervent, but discretion and self-interest disposed him to assist Puritans of various shades, while the same motives deterred him from promoting the Presbyterian movement as such.[20] Walsingham's private beliefs seem to have been more committed. His household, for example, was 'a perfect hotbed of Puritanism';[21] and Robert Beale, who wrote against the inquisitorial methods of the bishops, was his brother-in-law and intimate friend. He gave Cartwright £100 towards a confutation of the Rheims New Testament, and provided funds to establish a lectureship at Oxford for the Puritan John Reynolds. Yet it is noticeable that he resisted rebellious tactics, looking instead for religious reforms to be achieved with royal consent, as he made plain in a letter of 1578 to William Davison: 'I would have all reformations done by public authority.'[22] The Earl of Huntingdon gave protection and patronage to Anthony Gilby, the Puritan lecturer mentioned in a previous paragraph, to his son Nathaniel Gilby, fellow of Emmanuel College, Cambridge, Thomas Sampson (who became Master of Wyggeston Hospital at Leicester), John Stockwood, schoolmaster at Tonbridge, and innumerable others, while the funeral sermon of another of Leicester's brothers-in-law, Sir Henry Sidney, was delivered at Penshurst in 1586 by the moderate episcopalian Puritan Thomas White.

We have now come to a point at which we may attempt to place Spenser in this Elizabethan ecclesiastical world. The salient facts from his biography are perhaps the following. When he was sixteen or seventeen the young poet contributed to Jan van der Noodt's *A Theatre wherein be represented as wel the miseries and calamities that follow the voluptuous Worldlings, As also the greate ioyes and plesures which the faithfull do enioy. An Argument both profitable and delectable, to all that sincerely loue the word of God*, printed by Henry Bynneman in 1569. Van der Noodt was a Protestant refugee from Antwerp, who had fled from the Low Countries to England in the year of the Duke of Alva's arrival with an army to stamp out heresy. His Protestantism was of a fiercely committed kind, though the man was also, we should remind ourselves, a poet and a humanist. The *Theatre* was clearly intended to have a wide circulation, since van der Noodt put it out separately in Flemish, in French and in English. Spenser's part was to translate into English the twenty-one 'Epigrams' and 'Sonets' which opened the volume. After the sonnets came van der Noodt's impassioned prose exposition of their meaning. This starts as an exhortation against worldliness, rapidly develops into a full-scale attack on the Church of Rome, then modulates into a discussion of the meaning of the vision of the New Jerusalem and ends with an account of the temperate life of the faithful. Spenser's part in this volume might be brushed aside as youthful hackwork; but the continuing importance to him of the 'vision' form, which he used later in *The Ruines of Time* and *Visions of the Worlds Vanitie*, and of the themes and images contained in the lines quoted at the start of this chapter, suggests an affinity with van der Noodt's intellectual and religious world rather than the mechanical fulfilling of a commission.

After the *Theatre* came the Cambridge years, 1569–76. These were years which coincided with Cartwright's Presbyterian preaching, followed by his removal from his chair, and with the Admonition controversy. In 1572 reports of the St Bartholomew massacre crossed the Channel. Some awareness of the issues of religious controversy was inevitable – and obviously was not lessened when he attained, in 1578, the secretaryship to a bishop who was a friend of Grindal.[23] In 1579 Spenser entered Leicester's service, visiting Leicester House during months of high drama produced by the Alençon marriage negotiations. While still in the Earl's service he published *The Shepheardes Calender*, dedicated to Leicester's nephew, Philip Sidney, and selected for his poem the printer Hugh Singleton, who was well known for his allegiance to the Puritan cause. He had been printing works for Foxe, Bale and Coverdale in the 1540s and 1550s, and had issued some reprints of Coverdale in the 1570s. In the summer of 1579 Singleton printed an attack on the projected French marriage, *The Discoverie of a Gaping Gulf* by John Stubbs, Cartwright's brother-in-law, for which both Stubbs and Singleton were condemned to lose their right hands; but Singleton escaped the penalty, apparently through a last-minute pardon.[24] *The Shepheardes Calender* was the next work to come from his press.

Spenser's move to Ireland meant, of course, a new patron and employer, Lord Grey of Wilton. Grey was a committed Protestant, whose horror at the St Bartholomew massacre is recorded in one of his letters, while a letter which he received from Sir Henry Sidney on the subject of the role of lord deputy expressed confidence in Grey's religious beliefs:

But nowe to beginne, and that with Godde Almightie. As I knowe you are relidgious, so I wishe your lordshippe to frequent sermons and praier in publique places; it would comforte the fewe protestants you have there, and abashe the papistes, wherof you have many.[25]

Spenser admired Grey and endorsed his stern efforts to suppress rebellion in Ireland, including the slaughter of foreign soldiers at Smerwick. Years later, in *A View of the Present State of Ireland*, he praised 'that right noble Lord' who ruled the troubled country 'like a most wise pilot'.[26]

It seems to me that Spenser's contribution to van der Noodt's radically Protestant book, his choice of the Puritan Hugh Singleton as the printer for his first adult published poem, his loyalty to his patrons, Leicester and Grey – and in particular his continuing allegiance to the memory of Leicester after the Earl's death, to which *Prothalamion* bears striking witness – together suggest rather strongly that he shared in the militant Protestantism of the circle in which he moved. In addition to this, I think that a close reading of the ecclesiastical eclogues of *The Shepheardes Calender*, which will be undertaken in Chapter 2, reveals that in the late 1570s the poet's religious position must be described as that of a 'moderate episcopalian Puritan'. Spenser supported episcopacy as did many other Puritans; but his management of the arguments in the *Calender*, I shall claim, indicates that he participated during those years in the zealous Puritan search for reform of ecclesiastical abuses. Parts of *Mother Hubberds Tale* were written at this time also, in the same spirit. This was an historical moment at which Puritanism possessed a keen intellectual and spiritual appeal to idealistic minds. A. G. Dickens has remarked that 'the vast majority of Elizabethan Englishmen who cared deeply about religion' were in fact either Roman Catholics or Puritans.[27]

Identifying Puritans with any certainty in the 1590s, however, is more difficult than recognising them in the late 1570s. The reason for this is that the Puritan movement – as distinct from Puritan religion – to some extent disappeared from view in the 1590s as a result of the death in 1588 of its 'patron-general', the Earl of Leicester, and the deaths of his brother Warwick and Sir Francis Walsingham in 1590. Moreover, a 'temporary exhaustion of old controversies by the Puritans and their opponents'[28] allowed Puritan energies to be directed now more than ever into sermons, devotional treatises and the cultivation of the Christian life. Hence there is no clear yardstick of controversy by which we can measure whether Spenser in the 1590s retained the Puritan position of his young manhood or not. His poetry was certainly deeply involved with the subject of the Christian life, as we shall show in Chapters 4, 5 and 6; but we do not intend to enter into a discussion as to whether this proves he was still a Puritan. The religion to which he adhered throughout his life was a fervent Protestantism which requires the label 'Puritan' during a specific period. This is the reason why the present study carries the title which it does, rather than the alternative, 'Edmund Spenser: *Puritan* Poet'. I have tried to avoid assertions for which I cannot produce evidence.

Terminology is in any case less important than a recognition of the part played in the making of Spenser's major poems by a Protestant/Puritan vision. Chapters 2 and 3 will consider *The Shepheardes Calender* from this angle, spending more than the usual amount of time on the ecclesiastical eclogues precisely because they often receive less than their due. In Chapter 4 the question of the proper frame of reference for *The Faerie Queene*, originally raised by A. S. P. Woodhouse, will be tackled again in the hope of laying certain notions to rest. We shall not work through *The Faerie Queene* book by book – many excellent studies have already completed that task for the present generation – but Book I will be read rather closely in a context provided by other Protestant writings, while Books II to VI will be treated in a more high-handed fashion. My particular concern is their 'vision cantos'. Two large topics which involve the whole poem will occupy the final chapters: Chapter 7 will put forward a theory about the distinction which Spenser invented between Britons and Elves, and Chapter 8 will examine the basic critical question of whether *The Faerie Queene* is intended, at least in part, to be an esoteric poem.

PART ONE:

The Shepheardes Calender

2

'Maye', 'Iulye' and 'September'

One of the functions of the eclogue, William Webbe reminded readers in 1586, was to give the poet an opportunity to 'enueigh grieuously against abuses'. When he considered the case of the pastoral poem recently published by 'Master *Sp.*', he noted that the 'Iulye' eclogue attacked 'idle and ambitious Goteheardes' and that 'September' exposed 'the loose and retchlesse lyuing of Popish Prelates'. At the same time he was by no means insensitive to the 'delight' which a reader might take at the poet's 'learned conueyance'.[1] Webbe's opinion that purposeful satirical attack was central to the ecclesiastical eclogues is not on the whole shared by recent students of *The Shepheardes Calender*. Instead, Spenser's characteristic stance as a pastoral poet is thought to be one of 'balance' or 'ambivalence' in relation to the opposing views put forward within particular eclogues. Neither the attitudes of Piers on the one side, for example, nor those of Palinode on the other can be taken to carry the poet's endorsement – on the contrary, Spenser exposes the strengths and weaknesses of both. This is the reading briefly proposed by William Nelson in the book mentioned in the previous chapter, and worked out in a full-length study by Patrick Cullen.[2] Nancy Jo Hoffman ends a chapter on the religious eclogues with the claim that Spenser in the *Calender* chose not to 'align himself dogmatically with the Geneva reformers' but envisaged a 'continual, healthy tension' in man's attempt to know a good life in God.[3] 'Balance', 'tension', 'plurality of values', are key terms for the articulation of modern experience of the poem.

Webbe, however, was not alone in his opinion that the ecclesiastical eclogues communicated a telling judgment on the contemporary scene. E. K., from whom Webbe borrowed many of his phrases, took this line; and years later Milton, referring to 'Maye', stated that 'under' the false shepherd, Palinode,

the Poet lively personates our Prelates, whose whole life is a recantation of
their pastorall vow, and whose profession to forsake the World, as they use
the matter, boggs them deeper into the world: those our admired *Spencer*
inveighs against, not without some presage of these reforming times.[4]

Most thought-provoking of all is the fact that Spenser himself linked
The Shepheardes Calender with the poetic invective of a Tudor
forerunner, Skelton, by choosing a name for his fictional representative in the poem from one of Skelton's most biting ecclesiastical
satires, *Colyn Cloute*. To mention this is not to deny that the name
'Colin' was also one of the masks which Clement Marot adopted
for himself in his eclogues of the 1530s; but Spenser implied by
choosing the full name 'Colin Clout' that there was some aspect
of Skelton's work which he wished to affirm and renew. If we are
to resolve the question of whether Spenser's poem can be said to
'enueigh grieuously against abuses' or whether on the contrary it
exhibits that 'mature awareness of a plurality of values'[5] with which
modern criticism feels a particular affinity, the only appropriate
method will be a careful scrutiny of arguments and images within
the ecclesiastical eclogues.

The chief context for *The Shepheardes Calender* is necessarily
provided by pastoral poems from Theocritus to Marot and Barnabe
Googe, but the ecclesiastical eclogues require a more specialised
context, incorporating as they do multifarious allusions to wolves
and foxes, 'conteck' and concord, 'lordship', pedlars, trifles, knacks,
saints and their 'sample', purple and pall, the obligation to 'watch
and ward' in the cold season. In some respects this is simply the
well-established language of attack on religious abuses employed
by Mantuan and Skelton, and given a further lease of life by
Protestant controversialists in the early years of the Reformation.
But in Spenser the traditional vocabulary has become yet more
specialised. Although Mantuan, for example, in his Latin eclogues
of 1498 had referred bitterly to the wolves and foxes which
threatened Christian flocks (Ecloga ix), his 'lupi' and 'vulpes' did
not have the precisely differentiated meanings their English
equivalents have for Spenser. Skelton denounced episcopal 'purple
and paule', but he was not concerned with 'conteck and concord'
nor with pedlars who carry 'trifles'. The idiom of Piers, Thomalin
and Diggon Davie in the ecclesiastical eclogues is in fact that of
Elizabethan Puritan propaganda, as earlier twentieth-century scholars

such as W. L. Renwick remarked. One of the aims of this chapter
will be to strengthen awareness of the Puritan context by producing
further evidence of it, while the chief purpose is to show that Spenser
has organised the dialogues in such a way as to ensure that the
Puritan arguments emerge as the imaginatively persuasive ones.

In the opening speech of 'Maye' Palinode describes the month's
festivities with an eager sensuousness that wins an initial liking for
the speaker:

> Is not thilke the mery moneth of May,
> When loue lads masken in fresh aray?
> How falles it then, we no merrier bene,
> Ylike as others, girt in gawdy greene?
> Our bloncket liueryes bene all to sadde,
> For thilke same season, when all is ycladd
> With pleasaunce: the grownd with grasse, the Woods
> With greene leaues, the bushes with bloosming Buds.
> Yougthes folke now flocken in euery where,
> To gather may buskets and smelling brere:
> And home they hasten the postes to dight,
> And all the Kirke pillours eare day light,
> With Hawthorne buds, and swete Eglantine,
> And girlonds of roses and Sopps in wine.
> Such merimake holy Saints doth queme,
> But we here sytten as drownd in a dreme.
>
> (1–16)

Enjoyment is undoubtedly the order of the day; the only questions
which stir in the reader's mind concern the speaker's attitude to his
role – he apparently dislikes his 'bloncket liuery' or grey coat – and
his assertion at the end of the speech about the preferences of 'holy
Saints'. Piers's brief response takes the form of a discrimination
between two sorts of human beings:

> For Younkers *Palinode* such follies fitte,
> But we tway bene men of elder witt.
>
> (17–18)

The words indicate that Piers and Palinode are middle-aged, and
hence that the games which are indeed 'fitte' for youth are
inappropriate for them. Piers seems also to be reminding his
companion indirectly of another difference between the 'Younkers'
and themselves besides the difference in age: the two speakers are
parish priests, as their 'bloncket liueryes' reveal, committed to a

particular lifestyle by the fact of their calling. That Palinode feels the need to counter this argument is suggested by his reply. Whereas in his first speech he had talked of 'loue lads' and 'yougthes folke', he now refers specifically to a 'shole of shepeheardes' whom he observed this morning. The point for the reader is that 'shepeheardes' in the ecclesiastical eclogues represent Christian pastors or ministers.

> Sicker this morrowe, ne lenger agoe,
> I sawe a shole of shepeheardes outgoe,
> With singing, and shouting, and iolly chere:
> Before them yode a lusty Tabrere,
> That to the many a Horne pype playd,
> Whereto they dauncen eche one with his mayd.
>
> (19–24)

Palinode has seen local clergy sharing in secular sports. The fact that he envies them shows up comically, and not entirely attractively, at the end of his speech:

> (O that I were there,
> To helpen the Ladyes their Maybush beare)
> Ah *Piers*, bene not thy teeth on edge, to thinke,
> How great sport they gaynen with little swinck?
>
> (33–6)

When we realise that Palinode has been watching idle clergy, we have no difficulty in understanding the sharp tone of Piers's retort:

> Perdie so farre am I from enuie,
> That their fondnesse inly I pitie.
> Those faytours little regarden their charge,
> While they letting their sheepe runne at large,
> Passen their time, that should be sparely spent,
> In lustihede and wanton meryment.
> Thilke same bene shepeheards for the Deuils stedde,
> That playen, while their flockes be vnfedde.
>
> (37–44)

I have paused over the opening of this eclogue because it can easily be misunderstood. Patrick Cullen argues that Piers is inconsistent in at first adopting a tolerant tone towards youthful foibles and then launching into 'a tirade' against young people, in which 'he accuses them of irresponsibility in their pleasures and condemns them as "shepeheards for the Deuils stedde"'.[6] But if the love lads and the shepherds are recognised as different groups, Piers's position is found to be a consistently rational one which distinguishes between what is fit for youth and what for age, what is fit for the laity and what for the clergy. An explicit statement of his attitude occurs in a later speech:

> shepheards (as Algrind vsed to say,)
> Mought not liue ylike, as men of the laye.
>
> (75–6)

There is no condemnation of youth nor of May festivities; there is simply a characteristic Puritan emphasis on the peculiar dedication required from the Christian pastor. Among endless expressions of this belief in Puritan sermons and pamphlets we may take one from Edward Dering, the preacher who so rashly told the Queen her business in a sermon of 1569. He deplored the secular occupations and sports all too often practised by clerics:

Looke vpon your Ministery, and there are some of one occupation some of another: some shake bucklers, some Ruffians, some hawkers and hunters, some dicers and carders...[7]

Edmund Grindal, the 'Algrind' to whom Spenser refers, and 'perhaps the prelate closest in his sympathies to the Puritans',[8] had stressed the special obligations of ministers in his *Injunctions for the Clergy* of 1571:

You must travail diligently and painfully to set forth God's true religion, and adorn the same with example of godly life, being circumspect that you offend no man either by light behaviour or by light apparel.

And, by all means ye can, ye shall endeavour yourselves to profit the commonwealth, having always in mind, that ye ought to excel all other in purity of life.[9]

As the argument develops, Piers extends his attack on idle and irresponsible ministers to include a complaint against certain married clergy for their preoccupation with storing up wealth for their offspring. A pastor should be indifferent to such worldly aspirations:

> The sonne of his loines why should he regard
> To leaue enriched with that he hath spard?
> Should not thilke God, that gaue him that good,
> Eke cherish his child, if in his wayes he stood?
>
> (83–6)

The right of the clergy to marry was of course an important Protestant tenet; but it seems that Spenser was particularly aware of the social abuses to which clerical marriage might lead. In *Mother Hubberds Tale* the 'formall Priest' boasts rather lewdly about his married state (475–8). The objection which Piers makes to clerical legacies in 'Maye', however, was not the result of some private prejudice of Spenser's; the same criticism was levied by a Puritan writer in 1572 against Christian ministers who

prouide for their wyfe and children somewhat honestly (I will not say pompously) for fear of afterclaps against a rainye day.[10]

In contrast to the worldly clergy of the contemporary church, Piers invokes the memory of shepherds in the primitive church who showed no desire to accumulate property: 'The time was once, and may againe retorne... When shepeheards had none inheritaunce... But what might arise of the bare sheepe.' The language he uses is that of Puritan pamphlets on the subject, but Spenser gradually adjusts it in such a way that it becomes, also, the language of poetic description of the Golden Age. In *A Full and Plaine Declaration of Ecclesiasticall Discipline* Walter Travers had affirmed that ideally the pastor's income should come from the congregation:

Seinge also ther is nothinge more reasonable then that the shepherd should feede off the milke of his flock should not those shepeherdes be fedde with the milke, and clothed with the flece and wolle of there flockes who susteine for the flockes cause the assaultes of most greeuous wolues...?[11]

Spenser assimilates the familiar images of 'milke' and 'flece'; but by adding a reference to 'honye' he gives the primitive ecclesiastical scene some of the charm which belongs to Ovid's first age of mankind:

> The shepheards God so wel them guided,
> That of nought they were vnprouided,
> Butter enough, honye, milke, and whay,
> And their flockes fleeces, them to araye.
>
> (113–16)

Against this innocent background the subsequent history of the church looks particularly ugly: 'Some gan to gape for greedie gouernaunce...Louers of Lordship and troublers of states.' The reader recognises the familiar Protestant/Puritan conception of the history of the Roman Catholic church as a process whereby the clergy increasingly acquired both power and wealth; but we should also remember that attacks on the 'Lordship' of Roman prelates had, for Puritans, an additional application to certain 'lordly' figures among Anglican leaders. The vocabulary of Field and Wilcox is relevant, although their Presbyterianism is not, when they denounce 'the Lordship, the loyteryng, the pompe, the idlenes' of the English bishops.[12] Piers's historical sketch is devoted to the Roman church, but his words have a way of glancing at current English abuses.

Piers is the moderate Puritan arguing boldly for clerical dedication and unworldliness. Palinode, meanwhile, defends his desire to join in secular sports with some propositions which in their own way also have a familiar ring:

> What shoulden shepheards other things tend,
> Then sith their God his good does them send,
> Reapen the fruite thereof, that is pleasure,
> The while they here liuen, at ease and leasure?
> For when they bene dead, their good is ygoe,
> They sleepen in rest, well as other moe.
> Tho with them wends, what they spent in cost,
> But what they left behind them, is lost
> Good is no good, but if it be spend:
> God giueth good for none other end.

(63-72)

The claim that 'Good is no good, but if it be spend' is one of the traditional libertine arguments which can be heard on the lips of Comus, for example, or, closer in date to *The Shepheardes Calender*, Cecropia in the *Arcadia*. Here is Cecropia addressing Pamela:

No, no sweet neece, let us old folks think of such precise considerations, do you enjoy the heaven of your age, whereof you are sure: and like good housholders, which spend those thinges that will not be kept, so do you pleasantly enjoy that, which else will bring an over-late repentance, when your glas shall accuse you to your face, what a change there is in you.[13]

Good is no good, but if it be spend. If we were in any remaining doubt about the connotations of Palinode's words, it would be removed by E. K.'s comment that lines 69–70 of his speech echo the epitaph of 'ryotous king Sardanapalus', notorious for 'his sensuall delights and beastlinesse'.

In identifying the nature of Palinode's arguments, I certainly do not intend to suggest that he himself attains the stature of some grandly corrupt Sardanapalus or Cecropia. On the contrary, Spenser portrays with more than a little amusement the figure of a middle-aged parson, who enviously watches the pleasures of 'Younkers' and hopefully repeats the opinions of famous sensualists, combining idleness with ineffectuality.

At line 158 the theme of the debate moves slightly, from that of worldliness versus unworldliness to the question of whether clergy should suppress their disagreements for the sake of ecclesiastical concord. Palinode deplores 'conteck' between shepherds (the word is glossed as 'strife contention' by E. K.), and argues for concord:

> Let none mislike of that may not be mended:
> So conteck soone by concord mought be ended.
>
> (162–3)

The question of concord versus contention was of central importance in the debates of the 1560s and 1570s between 'traditioners' and Puritans. Whitgift in his controversy with Cartwright repeatedly attacked Puritan contentiousness:

Wheresoeuer you come, you make contention, and kindle the fire of discorde.

I doe wyth all my hearte hate contention and strife, and especially in matters of Religion.

There were great corruptions in the Church of the Corinthes, and yet the Apostle greatly misliked such as stirred vp contentions for the same: so hath there bin alwayes imperfections in the Church, especially in externall things: and yet such as therfore did breake the peace of it, were alwayes counted as contentious.[14]

The Puritan position in this matter found expression in Anthony Gilby's *A Pleasaunt Dialogue, Betweene a Souldior of Barwicke, and an English Chaplaine.* As we mentioned in Chapter 1, Gilby was the Puritan lecturer at Ashby de la Zouch whose patron was the Earl of Huntingdon. His *Dialogue* seems to have been written in 1566 and published in 1573, although the only edition recorded in the *Short-Title Catalogue* is that of 1581. One of the two speakers, Sir Bernarde Blynkarde the Chaplain, praises ecclesiastical policies which have been created for the sake of 'loue and concorde', whereupon Miles retorts:

Cursed is that concorde that is in falshoode, in hypocrisie, in Idolatrie, or briberie. Yea cursed is that concorde, and cursed is that Policie, that hath not Gods worde to warrante it. For it is darknesse and vanitie. What fellowship hath lighte with darknesse? Righteousnesse with vnrighteousnesse? What concorde hath God with Beliall? Christ and Antichriste, the sincere Gospeller, and the polluted Papist? Wherefore separate your selues from them, touche none of their filthie geare.[15]

Piers's answer to Palinode embodies precisely this attitude, and employs, indeed, part of the same quotation from 2 Corinthians 6.14 ('what communion hathe light with darkenes?') which was regularly used by Puritans in this context:

> Shepheard, I list none accordaunce make
> With shepheard, that does the right way forsake.
> And of the twaine, if choice were to me,
> Had leuer my foe, then my freend he be.
> For what concord han light and darke sam?
> Or what peace has the Lion with the Lambe?
>
> (164–9)

Piers adds that the fable of the Fox and the Kid illustrates the dangers inherent in concord when falsehood is present:

> Such faitors, when their false harts bene hidde.
> Will doe, as did the Foxe by the Kidde.
>
> (170–1)

It is to the fable that we now turn our attention.

As we are going to be concerned with a 'Foxe', I should like first of all to refer to an article written in 1936 by Harold Stein,[16] in which he pointed out that the distinction between Wolves and Foxes in the 'September' eclogue,

> ...the fewer Woolues (the soth to sayne,)
> The more bene the Foxes that here remaine,
>
> (154–5)

is exactly that which is found in William Turner's *The Huntynge of the Romyshe Vuolfe* (1554?). The Wolves in Turner's work represent Roman Catholic priests, while the Foxes are clergy in the Church of England who secretly favour Roman Catholic doctrines and ceremonies. Bishop Gardiner, for example, who had been an Edwardine 'Foxe', had emerged in the reign of Mary as a 'very right Wolfe'. Although Stein's point has been neglected, I believe it is entirely sound, and I shall argue that it has the strongest relevance to 'Maye' as well as 'September'. Stein was not, I think, aware that Turner's Edwardine imagery was subsequently taken up by Elizabethan Puritans as having an application to certain clergy in their own times. Turner's book was reprinted in the Elizabethan period under the title *The Hunting of the Fox and the Wolfe*, with a preface by Anthony Gilby. Although Stein knew of this reprinting, he believed the preface was by John Knox. The new edition of Turner's work formed part of a burst of Puritan propaganda in the mid 1560s. Gilby's preface proved especially useful: it was issued separately as the first of two 'short and comfortable Epistels' addressed 'To my louynge brethren that is troublyd abowt the popishe aparrell'; and it appeared for a third time as a preliminary to Gilby's own attack on 'popishe Traditions in our Eng. Church', his *Pleasaunt Dialogue*. In the course of the *Dialogue* Gilby referred to Turner by name, and mentioned his 'pretie' invention 'of the croppeeared Foxe':

> That olde Doctor Turner (reuerende in other nations abroad for his great learning, and amongste the Godly at home, for his great zeale, his trauailes, his perils so long sustayned, and his great constancie) did almoste thirtie yeares ago espie, and bewray vnto the worlde, the crafte of Satan, that laboured to make poperie policie, and so to goe aboute to cure the wounde of the beast, which being in it self vncurable, shold yet in another beast be cured...His inuention was pretie and pleasaunte, of the croppeeared Foxe, who now was become the Kinges beast, and the Kinges game, that no man might hunt it.[17]

The *Dialogue*'s preface contains a passage which shows that Gilby saw the relevance of Turner's terminology to the contemporary struggle. He is speaking of the 'Popishe' remnants allowed or insisted upon by the authorities:

> Well, by Gods power we haue fought with the Wolues, for these and such like Popishe chaffe, and God hath giuen the victorie: we haue nowe to do with the Foxes, let vs not feare. There is no crafte, cunning, or pollicie against the Lorde.[18]

Turner's Edwardine image of the 'Foxe' was evidently now a serviceable part of the vocabulary of Elizabethan Puritans. Spenser, in borrowing the terminology for 'September', was employing a distinctly Puritan idiom.

Stein did not turn his attention to 'Maye'; but I think the 'Maye' fable moves into focus when an appropriate context of Puritan vocabulary is supplied. The literary model was Aesop's fable 'Of the Wolfe and the Kydde' (number nine in Book Two of Caxton's translation).[19] Spenser, however, made a remarkably interesting alteration when he composed his own version: he substituted a

'Foxe' for Aesop's 'Wolfe'. If we bear in mind the distinction between Wolves and Foxes in 'September', it becomes highly probable that the Fox in 'Maye' is a member of the species attacked by Turner and the Puritans – a secret papist who presents himself as a Church of England pastor.[20]

Whereas in Aesop's fable the Wolf possesses only a disguised voice with which to mislead his victim, and is rebuffed by the Kid through a hole in the door, the Fox in Spenser's fable brings a pack of pedlar's trinkets with which to tempt the youthful creature. Spenser refers to them as 'tryfles' ('bearing a trusse of tryfles'), and subsequently as 'knacks' ('he could shewe many a fine knack'). These words in the 1570s had become part of the distinctive language of Puritans when denouncing the ceremonies and vestments which the authorities permitted or insisted upon, but which to the Puritan mind seemed popish and idolatrous remnants which should be rooted out. 'Trifles' is a loaded word in, for example, An Admonition to the Parliament (1572), where the following passage occurs in the second edition:

Forsothe, [our bishops] be maintainers of trifles, and trifling bishops, consuming the greatest part of theyr time in those trifles whereas they shoulde be better occupied.[21]

The letter from Beza appended at the end of the book urges the English church not to 'fall backe' upon 'the trifles and trashe of mennes traditions'.[22] Gilby's Pleasaunt Dialogue warns repeatedly that the godly should have nothing to do with the popish trifles which secret papists maintain in the Church of England. The painted harlot brings 'shewes, and trifles, to deceiue the world'; 'the foolishe worlde...euer delighteth in trifles'. He lists 'An hundred pointes of Poperie, yet remayning, which deforme the Englishe reformation', and calls them, inevitably, 'popish trifles'.[23]

English Puritans employed a number of well-worn catchwords and catch-phrases to denote these unwelcome remnants in the church. The phrase which E. K. uses in the 'Maye' gloss, the 'reliques and ragges of popish superstition', is perhaps the most familiar of all to students of Elizabethan church history; but 'trifles' is equally recognisable. 'Knacks', less familiar, belongs to the same context. Gilby in his much-reprinted preface styles unwanted ceremonies, 'knackes of Poperie'.[24]

In the Fox's 'trusse of tryfles' are to be found 'bells, and babes, and glasses'. It is an item from the first category, evidently a handbell, which finally causes the fascinated Kid to disappear into the pedlar's basket, while the 'babes' and 'glasses' are interpreted by E. K. as 'Idoles' and 'Paxes'. Gilby's list of 'An hundred pointes of Poperie, yet remayning, which deforme the Englishe reformation' includes 'Ringing of handbels in many places', and also refers to images, or idols, with the entry: 'The Images of the Trinitie, and many other monuments of superstition, generally in al church windowes'.[25] Gilby does not mention paxes – glass tablets carrying sacred pictures – but they were still to be seen in some Elizabethan churches.

The Puritans argued that the relics and rags, the trifles and the knacks, were not things indifferent, as their adversaries claimed, but damaging and even fatal in their effects on specific human groups. On the one hand, the obstinate papists were encouraged by the continuing existence of features from their own church, while, on the other, the 'weak brethren' or 'simple sort' were thrown into doubt, confusion, and even idolatry. The Puritan Robert Crowley gives a characteristic exposition of the case when he says the 'apparell' which the authorities attempt to enforce does not 'edifie the church of Christ' but, on the contrary, 'the blinde, stubborne, and obstinate papistes' will 'by our receiuyng of these things be encouraged'. Meanwhile, 'the simple Christians' are led into superstition:

The simple Christians (ouer whome we shoulde haue the chiefe care) are by these things so grieued, when they see vs receiue them, that they sorrowe and mourne in theyr heartes. And such amongst them as be not altogether so strong, but that they doe yet somewhat depende vpon our example and doctrine (as the nature of man is so long as he is but a Nouice in Christ) those are by vs beaten back to superstition.[26]

Gilby, writing more generally against all popish remnants, accuses those who maintain 'this superstitious shew' of endangering those for whom Christ died. Quoting Bucer, he declares that these things 'hinder the simple', and warns

least the weake brother be boldened, to vse the thinges sacrificed to Idolles. And so thy weake Brother perishe.[27]

The popish trifles endanger the weak and the simple. Spenser's youthful Kid, over whom the Goat 'had a motherly care' as Crowley had recommended, was carried away for ever in the basket of the Fox because of the charm a bell had for him. The Kid, we suggest, represents the simple Christian; and E. K.'s gloss provides direct support for this reading:

By the Kidde may be vnderstoode the simple sorte of the faythfull and true Christians.

Higginson in 1912 declared that 'the Kid stands for the Puritans';[28] but that is not the answer. The Kid, lured to his doom by the Fox's 'tryfles', is an expressive image of 'the simple sorte' of Christians who may perish as a result of the idolatrous remnants retained in the church.

Aesop's Wolf and Kid thus nicely modulate into the foxy priest and simple Christian. One may speculate tentatively about Spenser's presentation of the Fox as 'pedler'. It is possible (but one would not claim more) that his presentation has some affinity with a conception current among Puritans at this period. Gilby sees the 'Neutralles', the semi-papists who belong to the Church of England clergy and urge the retention of popish ceremonies, as 'Chapmen':

The daye shall come, that oure Christe shall scourge oute these Popishe Chapmen, like Dogges, then shall these haltinge Neutralles, hyde their heades, whiche fondly patche Christe his Religion, with the Popes.[29]

And Thomas White, a preacher at Paul's Cross in November 1577 who showed no opposition to episcopacy but was Puritan in his distrust of ceremonies, and in his hostility to 'games and playes, bankettings, and surfettings' on Sundays, described the neutrals, the 'halfe Protestants, halfe Papistes', as 'common pedlers':

How many poysoned Protestants and maymed professours haue wee? (I meane for opinion) for otherwise who is hole and sounde? you shall haue a gospeller as he wil be taken, a ioyly felow to retayne and maintayne such patches of popery and infection of Rome, that me thinkes I see the Serpents sutteltie as playne as by the clawe you may iudge the Lion: one holdeth, faith iustifieth and yet workes doe no harme: an other sayth, prayer for the dead is charitie, and though it doe no good, yet it doth no hurte...some and a large some to, do superstitiously and moste sinfully sweare by Saincts and euery other creature, and thinke it small offence or none at all...But this I read, that they that are nor hote nor colde shall be spued out: that halfe Iewes and halfe Christians, and consequently halfe Protestants, halfe Papistes, are wholy Diuels: that suche Mermaydes as are half fish halfe flesh, or Minotaures, that be halfe men halfe bulles, are all beasts, which thinke that God and Idols, the Sacrifice and the Sacraments, Circumcision and Baptisme, the lawe and the Gospell, nay that fleshe and the spirite, and God and Man may be ioyned togither, are but common pedlers and patchers of Christ coate, which had no seame in deede.[30]

Whether or not these 'Chapmen' and 'pedlers' connect with Spenser's foxy pedlar, White's attack on the superstitious swearing 'by Saincts and euery other creature' which is common among these 'halfe Papistes' has its relevance to the glib oath with which Spenser's Fox greets the listening Kid:

> Ah deare Lord, and sweete Saint Charitee,
> That some good body woulde once pitie mee.

> (247–8)

The identity of the Fox, concealed from the Kid, should be plain to the reader.

Spenser's adaptation of Aesop to the contemporary scene is both ingenious and seemingly effortless. He preserves the homely vigour of manner which belongs to the genre, while introducing subtly pointed allusions to church affairs – allusions which are sufficiently veiled yet sufficiently perspicuous. To underline his sense of the danger to 'the simple' from half-papist clergy he invents a new and ominous conclusion in place of Aesop's happy ending, or, as E. K. puts it, he devises a 'farre different...Catastrophe and end'. The resulting fable can be read by the unsuspicious reader as a warning against Roman Catholic priests who win converts at their secret masses, and this is frequently the way in which E. K. seems to interpret it. But Spenser's substitution of the highly significant term 'Foxe' for Aesop's Wolf, and his allusions to trifles, knacks, and pedlars, reveal the true meaning. E. K.'s position is in fact rather amusing. At times he appears absurdly unaware, or immensely cautious, explaining the obvious anagram 'Algrind' as 'the name of a shepheard'; but at other moments, for instance when he allows the Puritan phrase, 'reliques and ragges of popish superstition', to slip out, his commentary coincides with the meaning of the fable.

After the fable has been narrated, Palinode's response is pleasantly self-contradictory. He denounces the tale, then immediately asks whether Piers will allow him to borrow it:

> Truly *Piers*, thou art beside thy wit,
> Furthest fro the marke, weening it to hit,
> Now I pray thee, lette me thy tale borrowe
> For our sir Iohn, to say to morrowe
> At the Kerke, when it is holliday:
> For well he meanes, but little can say.
>
> (306–11)

Moreover, he fails to see that the satire comes near to touching himself and his Sir John in so far as they themselves are 'neutrals': Palinode, we recall, retains an interest in 'holy Saints', while a 'sir Iohn' is an unlearned and still-popish country parson. A further irony resides in the fact that he considers a frivolous tale (as it seems to him) suitable material for a public sermon. Puritans bitterly complained of ministers who, unable to preach, merely read the homilies, or contented themselves with 'fonde fables to make their hearers laughe'.[31]

Our analysis of Piers's and Palinode's arguments has reached the stage at which we can reconsider the modern view of Spenser as a poet who is poised ambivalently between the two spokesmen in the eclogue. We have shown that in every speech Palinode exposes his own half-comic weaknesses – middle-aged envy, reactionary opinions, uncritical acceptance of libertine arguments, Whitgiftian preference for a concord which the facts of English life show to be perilous, and a foolish allegiance to a local Sir John. Palinode reveals and betrays himself. Although his worldly remarks suggest the local parson's dreams rather than the prelate's opportunities, he is implicated because he is idle and envious.

Piers in contrast takes an austere but consistent line. Clergy have chosen a life of dedication; clerical worldliness endangers the flocks; and, in particular, clergy who retain popish objects in their churches are a spiritual danger to untrained Christians in their congregations. Piers's arguments have the weight which consistency and relevance to acknowledged social facts give them. In passing one may note that there is no austerity in Piers's attitude to the laity. The Kid in the fable is an image of the inexperienced Christian; and it is Piers, not Palinode, who describes the creature in terms of vigorous and attractive natural growth:

> Shee set her youngling before her knee,
> That was both fresh and louely to see,
> And full of fauour, as kidde mought be:
> His Vellet head began to shoote out,
> And his wrethed hornes gan newly sprout:
> The blossomes of lust to bud did beginne,
> And spring forth ranckly vnder his chinne.
>
> (182–8)

The Kid's father, clearly Christ himself, would 'haue ioyed at this sweete sight'.

Are we really to suppose that Spenser was evenly poised between the viewpoints of Palinode and Piers? I suspect that Skelton or Milton would have been surprised to hear it.

'Iulye' is modelled on a section of Mantuan's eighth eclogue, plus a passage from his seventh. Mantuan's eighth opens as a debate between Candidus and Alphus on the rival merits of hills and dales, then moves into further discussion of a topic broached in the seventh, the shepherd Pollux's vision of the Blessed Virgin. Spenser's use of Mantuan, here and elsewhere, combines quite frequent appropriation of detail with bold alteration and inversion in larger matters. The scorching sunshine at the start of 'Iulye' comes from the model; but the decisive alteration which Spenser immediately makes lies in the fact that whereas in Mantuan the rivalry between hills and dales concerns their literal merits, the physical advantages they offer, in 'Iulye' the landscape is regarded allegorically, hills and dales acting as symbols for contrasted modes of clerical life and for contrasted states of mind. Mantuan's is a location debate of a traditional sort: the hills are praised for the streams which flow from them, the marble quarries they contain, the medicinal herbs and the chestnut trees which grow on them, the robust young men who are reared there. This is not allegorical writing, nor, at first, is it associated with religious values, until Candidus goes on to praise hills for their connection with several of the world's most celebrated monasteries. Spenser takes over the device of a location debate, then proceeds to allegorise it from the very first line of his eclogue:

> Is not thilke same a goteheard prowde,
> that sittes on yonder bancke[?]

Because the goatherd is 'prowde' the 'bancke' at once becomes a symbol of his superior social position. Spenser goes on to hint, moreover, that a consequence of the herdsman's pride is neglect of the congregation:

> [His] straying heard them selfe doth shrowde
> emong the bushes rancke.
>
> (3–4)

These hints are indeed only hints; Morrell's cheerful and gregarious tone in response ('What ho, thou iollye shepheards swayne, / come vp the hyll to me') wins the reader's willing suspension of judgment until the arguments on both sides, whether for climbing the hills of power or remaining in 'humble dales', have been heard.

The first half of 'Iulye' contains a good deal of comedy – comedy which derives both from Morrell's bouncing tone and from his use of literal examples to prove an allegorical case. Morrell wishes to defend his own enjoyment of high position, but he does so by citing, in the manner of Mantuan, examples of actual hills which have won renown, including St Michael's Mount and the Kentish hills where the conversation is taking place. His choice of specific examples has considerable charm and immediacy, and in general he earns credit for his high spirits, his knowledge of topography, and his energetic syncretism which, like Mantuan's, allows him freely to mingle mythological and biblical allusions.

But a closer look at his blithe, if essentially irrelevant because mainly literal, examples is necessary. Among the hills he praises are those which are 'holy' because they are 'sacred vnto saints', while another pair of hills receives approval without any explicit reason being given ('Of Synah can I tell thee more, / and of our Ladyes bowre'). Finally he declares that since hills are physically nearer to the sky, the passage to heaven must be easier from hilly positions than from the plains beneath. Thomalin in his forthright and unpolished way has answers for two out of these three arguments, leaving the reader to uncover for himself the significance of the reference to 'Synah' and 'our Ladyes bowre'. Only two lines are required for the lowland shepherd to point out the gross superstition involved in assuming that physical hills are nearer to a spiritual heaven:

> Syker thou speakes lyke a lewde lorrell,
> of Heauen to demen so.
>
> (93–4)

The argument that hills should be honoured because they are 'sacred vnto saints' takes a little longer to deal with because a distinction between different ways of honouring saints and the places associated with them is called for. Thomalin claims that it is one thing to regard hills with affection in memory of the saints who once lived on them, but it is quite another to suppose that the saints left any spiritual powers behind them ('they bene to heauen forewent, / theyr good is with them goe'). Hence the hills are not intrinsically 'holy' or 'sacred' in the sense of conferring magical benefits on those who visit them or their shrines. The saints are important as examples of the good life to those who come after, but not because they continue to intervene on behalf of those who mistakenly pray to them:

> The hylls, where dwelled holy saints,
>   I reuerence and adore:
> Not for themselfe, but for the sayncts,
>   Which han be dead of yore.
> And nowe they bene to heauen forewent,
>   theyr good is with them goe:
> Theyr sample onely to vs lent,
>   that als we mought doe soe.
> Shepheards they weren of the best,
>   and liued in lowlye leas:
> And sith theyr soules bene now at rest,
>   why done we them disease?
>
> (113–24)

Thomalin is uttering classic Protestant doctrine, and his discrimination between the alleged spiritual assistance rendered by saints at their shrines and the true moral example left behind ('Theyr sample onely to vs lent, / that als we mought doe soe') would be felt to be undeniable by any Tudor Protestant believer. Tyndale had made the point familiar in the earliest days of Protestantism, as the following passage, one among many, illustrates:

Let vs therefore set our hartes at rest in Christ and in Gods promises, for so I thinke it best, and let vs take the Saintes for an example onely, and let vs do as they both taught and dyd.[32]

Thomalin, as we remarked a moment ago, does not comment on Morrell's admiration for Mount Sinai and 'our Ladyes bowre', but the alert reader who remembers Mantuan's eighth eclogue is left to enjoy its significance. As a Roman Catholic and prominent

Carmelite Mantuan had naturally included in his debate on the rival merits of hills and dales a reference to the fact that many famous monasteries are situated on the tops of hills:

> hinc divi sanctique patres in montibus altis
> delegere domos tacitas; Carthusia testis,
> Carmelus, Garganus, Athos, Laureta, Laverna
> et Sina et Soractis apex Umbrosaque Vallis...
>
> (50–3)

In Protestant England, on the other hand, one would not expect the presence of monasteries on hills to provide favourable arguments for a clerical speaker who is not a declared papist. In harmony with this expectation Morrell does not openly cite monastic hills as part of his case for the mountainous world, but, to the reader's amusement, he covertly does so. His references to 'Synah' and 'our Ladyes bowre' might simply constitute respectable allusions to the scene of Moses's encounter with God, and to some agreeable spot which E. K. vaguely explains as 'a place of pleasure so called'. But a glance at the lines quoted above from Mantuan reveals that the two places have quite other associations.[33] Just as 'Carmelus', 'Garganus', and 'Athos' were listed by Mantuan for their monastic prestige (Mount Carmel was the site of the first Carmelite monastery, Mount Garganus carried a famous sanctuary of St Michael, Athos was renowned for its twenty-two convents), so too were 'Laureta' and 'Sina'. Loreto was the spot to which the house of the Blessed Virgin at Nazareth had been conveyed by angels, and Mount Sinai was the burial place of St Catherine, included by Mantuan for this reason rather than for its association with Moses.[34] From this list Spenser selects Sinai and Loreto for Morell's approval – a witty selection since neither place, after Loreto has been re-named 'our Ladyes bowre', is openly a monastic site, but both are rich in popish connotations for those able to recognise them. Morrell evidently retains a nostalgic regard for famous shrines and monasteries, but he ingeniously manages to mention them with so much ambiguity that his remarks could be explained away as essentially biblical and Protestant.

After refuting some of Morrell's arguments, Thomalin introduces arguments of his own in favour of 'humble dales'. He is more aware than is Morrell that the evidence he musters should have a moral as well as a geographical relevance to the discussion. Hence the shepherds he names as having lived in the dales are spiritually

31

'humble', 'meeke' and 'lowe', their existence in the valleys serving as an outward expression of their inward humility. For particular examples Spenser raids Mantuan's seventh eclogue, in which Galbula extols the worth of shepherds in contrast to rough ploughmen. From this source come both Abel and Moses, while Spenser adds Aaron, limits Mantuan's 'Assyrians' to the twelve sons of Jacob, and inserts an explicit moral condemnation of the hill-shepherd, Paris, whom Mantuan had mentioned without any moral reservation. The Carmelite's inclusive list of famous shepherds of every sort, both biblical and pagan, is sifted until it becomes an enumeration of dedicated and humble pastors. One notes with interest that Spenser, in balancing Morrell's list of famous hills against Thomalin's list of famous pastors, is using Mantuan against Mantuan – but with this difference: while Morrell's list retains distinct traces of the popish beliefs explicit in the model, Thomalin's excludes any irrelevant or morally dubious shepherds in the Latin source.

Thomalin's speech ends with a passage of invective against ambitious pastors of more recent years. The attack on ecclesiastical pomp and greed applies chiefly to Roman Catholic prelates, but it may also glance at some Anglican leaders, and is couched in a traditional idiom used both by Skelton and the Puritans. This is Skelton, describing the life of certain prelates in *Colyn Cloute*:

> To ryde vpon a mule
> With golde all betrapped,
> In purple and paule belapped;
> Some hatted and some capped,
> Rychely and warme bewrapped,
> God wot to theyr great paynes,
> In rotchettes of fyne Raynes.[35]

And here is Spenser:

> Their weedes bene not so nighly wore,
>   such simplesse mought them shend:
> They bene yclad in purple and pall,
>   so hath theyr god them blist,
> They reigne and rulen ouer all,
>   and lord it, as they list:
> Ygyrt with belts of glitterand gold.

> (171–7)

The invective mounts to a climax of rough-tongued bitterness in some lines explicitly directed at Rome, then turns back to the English scene with a biting irony which is perhaps even more effective:

> Sike syrlye shepheards han we none,
> they keepen all the path.

(203–4)

In the final phase of the dialogue Morrell, for his part, mingles a recognition of the force of Thomalin's arguments ('Here is a great deale of good matter, / lost for lacke of telling') with a continuing allegiance to the world of clerical riches:

> Thou medlest more, then shall haue thanke,
> to wyten shepheards welth:
> When folke bene fat, and riches rancke,
> it is a signe of helth.

(209–12)

But the connotations of the words 'fat' and 'rancke' comically undermine any boast of 'helth'. Again, after he has heard about the recent fate of Archbishop Grindal, Morrell combines a brief expression of pity for the good man with a continuing determination to enjoy the privileges he has achieved for himself.

What kind of figure, then, is Morrell? By no means a complete representative of the arrogant and purple-clad prelates attacked in the key passage of invective, he is none the less a clergyman on the make, who exults in the power he has so far attained, relishes the 'welth' which successful pastors can accumulate, and secretly hankers for the institutions of the Roman Catholic church – the shrines of saints and the famous monasteries. On the other side, Thomalin unites the simplicity revealed by his 'rude' style of speech with a capacity for clear judgment in matters of superstition and church corruption. He is modest, but he is also totally dedicated to the 'shepheard great, / that bought his flocke so deare'. Spenser does not savage his own characters: Morrell is generously treated. But this hardly means that Spenser felt Morrell's claims to be evenly balanced against those of Thomalin.

As the presentation of the rural world in pastoral poetry necessarily involves an implicit or explicit contrast between the country and the town or court, the motif of the traveller from one region to the other has proved recurrently useful. A shepherd may journey to town or palace, then return to the fields and there describe what he has seen, as is the case with Cornix in Barclay's first eclogue or Colin in *Colin Clouts Come Home Againe*. Or a courtier may visit the country – an arrangement which produces valuable developments in the plot of pastoral romance, exemplified in the histories of Pyrocles and Musidorus in the *Arcadia*, Calidore in *The Faerie Queene*, Florizel in *The Winter's Tale*. Another variant is the shepherd who journeys to town and there hears from the lips of a townsman about the uglier aspects of town or court life. This is the device upon which Mantuan's ninth eclogue is based. Candidus, having left his native pastures, has travelled to a barren region inhabited by wolves, foxes, snakes and fighting dogs, which acts as an image of Rome or, more particularly, of the Roman Curia. Faustulus, who lives in Rome, explains and interprets the sinister environment. Spenser used Mantuan's ninth as his model for 'September', but subjected it, as usual, to a decisive alteration. The journey motif is reversed, so that the Spenserian eclogue now resembles Barclay's first, in which the pastoral traveller returns from the city to the country and relates his adventures to a former pastoral companion.

Diggon Davie has returned from his travels physically and emotionally shaken, as his opening speech indicates:

> Her was her, while it was daye light,
> But now her is a most wretched wight.
> For day, that was, is wightly past,
> And now at earst the dirke night doth hast.

> (3–6)

The harsh and difficult diction prepares the reader for the perturbed mood of the eclogue. Hobbinol, as the rural figure who has remained at home, greets Diggon compassionately, showing a very Spenserian understanding of the need for a grieving heart to give expression to its sorrows. He affirms the virtue of contentment with 'tryed state' (68–73) in words which echo some of Faustulus's, and offers his humble cottage as shelter for his companion at the end of the eclogue, again very much in the manner of Faustulus at the start of Mantuan's. Diggon, who in the past has made serious mistakes because of greed ('I dempt there much to haue eeked my store, / But such eeking hath made my hart sore'), has reached through the stress of experience an accurate self-judgment: 'I was bewitcht / With vayne desyre, and hope to be enricht.' Hence Hobbinol and Diggon are in total agreement on the subject of the virtue of contentment. Many critics have emphasised the value of Hobbinol's pastoral doctrine of acceptance, but it would be an error to imply that Diggon, as presented at the time of the dialogue, in any sense disagrees. Hobbinol and Diggon, personal friends, are not radically opposed to each other's viewpoints as are the speakers in 'Maye' and 'Iulye'. The difference between them is subtler – and it certainly does not reside in anything we have discussed so far.

The central section of the eclogue consists of Diggon's description of what he has seen. The question of *where* he has been is left by Spenser in a carefully contrived state of ambiguity. Diggon has visited 'forrein costes' and 'tho countryes', while Hobbinol has the impression, although he may not be well informed, that his friend has 'wandred...about the world rounde'. Whereas Mantuan's Candidus quite explicitly reaches Rome, Diggon has witnessed ecclesiastical abuses in one or many places, and only the details of his description can hint where those places are. The shepherds, 'there', rob one another, look as big as bulls in their self-conceit, are idle or covetous. But since the spiritual claims made by these pastors – 'They saye they con to heauen the high way' and 'They boast they han the deuill at commaund' – reflect a Protestant view of Roman Catholic priestly assumptions, it seems that the invective up to line 101 is directed at Roman Catholic prelates, very probably in Rome itself. It is characteristic that they sprinkle popish 'holy water' as a remedy for conflicts they themselves have created. Diggon, although angered by what he has seen, feels ultimately that these phenomena belong to a territory which cannot be changed, and must simply be left to its own devices:

> But let hem gange alone a Gods name:
> As they han brewed, so let hem beare blame.
>
> (100–1)

Urged by Hobbinol to speak out clearly, Diggon moves on to another section of his report. The fact that it includes discussion of the peculiarly English problem of Wolves and Foxes, analysed earlier in this chapter, suggests that Diggon's travels have brought him into contact with abuses in the Church of England, whether in one English city or many. The mode Diggon chooses for his account is that of reporting what 'men say': 'Their ill hauiour garres men missay', 'They sayne', 'Other sayne, but how truely I note', 'Some sticke not to say, (whote cole on her tongue)', 'Thus chatten the people'. This technique has misled even so well informed a scholar as Renwick, in his invaluable notes to *The Shepheardes Calender*, into supposing that 'the attack changes into defense...of the English clergy', and hence that Spenser 'was less involved in Puritan ideas than some people imagine'.[36] But the device of attributing to others opinions held by the satirist himself, even if with some necessary qualifications, is a familiar one in Tudor satirical poetry. An excellent example is to be found in a poem whose relevance to *The Shepheardes Calender* has already been indicated, Skelton's *Colyn Cloute*. Skelton's poem is an attack on Wolsey and worldly prelates; but it also articulates, in a very moving way, the satirist's own problem in openly expressing these dangerous opinions. During the first part of the poem Skelton's Colin Clout prefers to take refuge in the formula 'men say':

> Laye men say indede
> How they take no hede
> Theyr sely shepe to fede...
>
> What trow ye they say more
> Of the bysshoppes lore?...
>
> I wot neuer how they warke,
> But thus the people barke;
> And surely thus they say...
>
> This is a farly fyt,
> To here the people iangle,
> Howe warely they wrangle...[37]

But as the poem unfolds he uses the formula less and less, so that it becomes plain that the opinions expressed are his own opinions also. It is surely clear that Diggon uses the same device. What he reports about the worldliness of many English clergy, preoccupied with enriching their wives and children, has already been shown to be true in 'Maye'. He adds an especially bitter description, whose accuracy we can hardly doubt, of the way in which prelatical or powerful secular patrons oppress lower clergy by means of financial exactions against which there is no appeal.

The result of pastoral failures, Diggon reports, is that congregations are in immediate danger from Wolves. At this point some analysis of Hobbinol's response to Diggon's revelations becomes imperative. At lines 102–3 Hobbinol had urged Diggon to speak out more plainly; but by lines 136–9 he has become alarmed:

> Nowe Diggon, I see thou speakest to plaine:
> Better it were, a little to feyne,
> And cleanly couer, that cannot be cured.
> Such il, as is forced, mought nedes be endured.
>
> (136–9)

Earlier in the dialogue Diggon had decided that Rome must be left to its own devices; but it is another matter for Hobbinol to advocate 'covering' and 'feigning' in respect of corruptions in his own society. Hobbinol's capacity for contentment evidently can shade at times into passivity and conformism. Moreover, another attribute of Hobbinol is that he is unaware of recent threatening social developments. He knows that there are many 'Foxes' in England – this was a clerical phenomenon which had been noticed as early as the reign of Edward VI – but he denies that there are any Wolves in the country, because he is ignorant of the incursions of Roman Catholic seminary priests during the middle and later 1570s. Hobbinol is willing to have his ignorance corrected, but at each new revelation his response tends to be cautious or slightly complacent: what you say is doubtless true, but 'Better it were, a little to feyne'; doubtless Wolves *are* at large, but 'We han great Bandogs will teare their skinne.' This confident response, at line 163, exposes an ignorance of the subtlety of Wolves and hence of the seriousness of the threat. The fable – probably referring to some actual incident in the diocese of the Bishop of Rochester – illustrates the disturbing wiliness of a proselytising Roman Catholic whose persuasiveness threatens even the godly.

Hobbinol's tendency to look for easy solutions is revealed once more at the end of the eclogue. He asks Diggon how, 'if sike bene Wolues, as thou hast told,' the church is to guard against them; but

when he hears Diggon's answer that pastors are committed to a life
of perpetual watchfulness, he comes back with a characteristic reflex;

> Ah Diggon, thilke same rule were too straight,
> All the cold season to wach and waite.
> We bene of fleshe, men as other bee,
> Why should we be bound to such miseree?
> What euer thing lacketh chaungeable rest,
> Mought needes decay, when it is at best.

(236–41)

These lines of Hobbinol's have found many admirers. Both H. S. V.
Jones and Hallett Smith see Hobbinol's 'philosophy of moderation'
as the 'central doctrine' of the *Calender*.[38] Nancy Jo Hoffman refers
to the line 'We bene of fleshe, men as other bee' as 'a large and
moving gesture of acceptance of himself and others'.[39] But in the
context of the dialogue between Diggon and Hobbinol, with
Diggon's progressive revelation of corruption in the Church of
England and of menacing spiritual attacks from abroad, Hobbinol's
fondness for an easy life is shown to be an inadequate and unrealistic
response to the contemporary scene. Hobbinol's objection that
Diggon's rule 'were too straight' is of a type with which Puritan
controversialists were familiar, and for which they had an uncompromising answer. Walter Travers in 1574 had anticipated precisely
the complaint of Hobbinol, or 'any man', that the Puritan vision
of clerical commitment was too severe:

Neither let any man here complaine that I am more seuere and rigorous then
needethe, seing that which Paule requireth is nothing lesse...

Complaints are irrelevant; the situation demands pastors who

susteine for the flockes cause the assaultes of most greeuous wolues, and watch
for them day and night, suffring the parching heate and chillinge cold for ther
cause, who feede them ouersee them and seeke them and often tymes put ther
life in extreame danger to defend them.[40]

Travers's Puritan vision of the pastor is, clearly, Diggon's also.
Questioned by Hobbinol as to how the attacks of Wolves may be
countered, Diggon answers, in the manner of the Puritans:

> How, but with heede and watchfulnesse,
> Forstallen hem of their wilinesse?
> For thy with shepheard sittes not playe,

38

Or sleepe, as some doen, all the long day:
But euer in liggen in watch and ward,
From soddein force theyr flocks for to gard.

(230–5)

The difference of opinion between Diggon and Hobbinol on modes of clerical life is not resolved. Instead the eclogue moves into its final phase, with Diggon, like Mantuan's Candidus, referring to his personal plight ('Quid faciam? Quo me vertam?' – 'What shall I doe? What way shall I wend?'), and Hobbinol, like Mantuan's Faustulus, offering humble hospitality. Does the lack of an explicit resolution to the debate – a debate essentially about the claims of limited versus unlimited clerical commitment – mean that Spenser is poised ambivalently between the two? Whether we consider 'September' alone, or whether we consider all three ecclesiastical eclogues together, we are led to the conclusion already intimated. In 'September' Hobbinol, compassionate and hospitable, is shown nevertheless to be ill-informed and instinctively ready to retreat from danger or challenge. Diggon, having repented former errors, offers an accurate and consistent critique of existing English corruptions without 'covering' anything. Is this to be 'wild-eyed', as Diggon has been described?[41] Diggon's accusations correspond precisely with those voiced in 'Maye' and 'Iulye'; his conception of the true pastor is shared by Piers and Thomalin, although Diggon expresses it with a special urgency which is appropriate to the facts revealed in 'September'. It is not that Hobbinol himself is under attack; but his very human retreat from unwelcome realities is gently exposed as insufficient.

If all three ecclesiastical eclogues are examined together, some points about Spenser's method emerge. Speakers on both sides are given engaging characteristics – Palinode's capacity for sensuous enjoyment, Morrell's ebullient spirits and love of topography, for example. But as the dialogues unfold, the flaws in one speaker's argument are steadily exposed, while the other speaker builds up a consistent and self-authenticating case. As in any good literary debate there is interest and vitality to be found on both sides; but it is a mistake to suppose that because the medium of pastoral dialogue has been chosen the effect must be one of ambivalence. Barclay's fourth eclogue exposed the errors of Codrus who was one of the two speakers, and Petrarch's sixth had revealed the vices of

Mitio, again one of the two disputants. Spenser quietly accumulates self-betraying images and internal inconsistencies in the speeches of Palinode, Morrell, and to some extent Hobbinol.

The three ecclesiastical eclogues are, we argue, Puritan in their impetus. It is interesting to note that their themes – clerical worldliness in 'Maye' together with an attack, in the fable, on superfluous ceremonies retained in the church; prelatical ambition and 'lordship' in 'Iulye'; the serious menace presented by Roman Catholic missionaries in 'September' coupled with an emphasis on the duties of the true pastor – coincide exactly with the major preoccupations of the moderate Puritan party. Spenser, while handling all speakers with characteristic generosity, gives forceful and, in the context, entirely persuasive expression to the Puritan vision. The pastor is 'taught' to 'feede his sheepe' with the watchful dedication to which he is committed by the fact of his calling.

3

Pastors and Poets

Spenser was not the only Renaissance pastoralist to combine eclogues on ecclesiastical themes with eclogues on love and poetry in a single volume; but no poet besides Spenser had arranged so pointed an alternation of the two sorts of eclogue throughout the middle section of a pastoral work. Petrarch had treated ecclesiastical subjects under the pastoral veil in the *Bucolicum Carmen* as well as political, literary and personal ones, but his sequence was built up over a period of years from 1346 to 1352, and displayed above all the range of interests of an exceptionally cultivated man rather than a concern with patterned alternation. Mantuan had written eclogues about love and eclogues on ecclesiastical subjects; but in his volume six eclogues on love, poetry and town life are succeeded by a final four on religious vision, monasticism, and corruption in Rome – so that the effect is of a decisive shift from the secular to the religious world. Barclay and Googe, for their part, touched on ecclesiastical themes only briefly and with something of the air of a digression, within one or two eclogues. Googe, certainly, ended on an emphatically religious note, but this was not because church affairs had figured largely in his collection, but because the pessimistic vision of romantic love which he had projected throughout the series culminated in the stern advice to renounce earthly love and to love God alone.

In the organisation of its materials *The Shepheardes Calender* differs from all of these predecessors. Spenser's ecclesiastical eclogues are evenly distributed through the central section of the sequence – 'Aprill', '*Maye*', 'Iune', '*Iulye*', 'August', '*September*'. The structure indicates that these church-oriented poems have an important part to play in the creation of the *Calender*'s total meaning, since they evidently are not a digression, nor for that matter do they form a spiritual finale in which the reader is required to turn his attention away from the secular world to the religious one. Instead, the secular and the religious are pointedly and repeatedly juxtaposed throughout the summer months. The effect on the reader encountering the poem for the first time is one of bold contrast, both between lyrical and satirical poetic styles, and between the modes of existence appropriate to songmakers and churchmen respectively. The resonant love-complaint and graceful compliments at the end of 'August', for example, give way to the harsh dialect and bitter mood of 'September'. Variety of mood, of metre, and of theme is clearly a large part of the new poet's aim.

At the same time a number of ingenious methods are employed to bind the eclogues together. Shepherds who on their first appearance seem to belong to one particular and specialised world reappear later in another. Thomalin's preoccupation in 'March' is with the rankling wound inflicted by Cupid, but in 'Iulye' he speaks out in praise of humble and godly pastors. Hobbinol, who in 'Aprill' and 'Iune' explores the subject of Colin Clout's love for Rosalind and its effect on his poetry, discusses church affairs with Diggon in 'September'. Piers in 'Maye' is the zealous spokesman for dedicated clergy, but he re-enters in 'October' to remind Cuddie of the true role of the poet. Moreover, the very name of the dominant shepherd in the *Calender*, Colin Clout, has the effect of linking eclogue to eclogue, since, as we mentioned in the previous chapter, it carries associations of ecclesiastical satire even though Colin does not dispute about church affairs. Piers's name belongs to the same tradition of late-mediaeval and sixteenth-century invective as Colin Clout's, acquiring its suggestion of zeal and plain-speaking not only from Langland's poem but from popular satirical works such as *I plaine Piers which can not flatter* (1555?). Piers is true to his name whether his theme is the life of the clergyman or the life of the poet.

Less immediately visible than the linkage by speakers is the effect created by the recurrence of images from one eclogue to another, something we shall notice as the discussion proceeds. My argument is that linked names, images and words gradually draw seemingly disparate eclogues into a closer relationship until not only a parallelism but even a unity of theme emerges in the final phase of the poem. The effect is not created at the outset – 'Aprill' and 'Maye' seem far apart if we read the *Calender* consecutively – but it becomes increasingly marked as the poem unfolds. Pastors, poets, and their respective roles furnish the subject matter of the work;[1]

Spenser's distinctive organisation of his materials establishes, I think, the significant relationship between those two roles.

The twelve eclogues 'proportionable to the twelue monethes' decorously depict activities which belong to the relevant seasons in the rural world, but they also concern themselves with stages in the life of man. Hence young men and their predicaments occupy the early months, while maturer men, whether sadder or wiser, tend to appear in the later eclogues. The first four months present a number of versions of an experience which connects with youth, that of love or falling in love. The experience, the poem suggests, is nearly inevitable and certainly not culpable,[2] since it is common both to the human and natural worlds as Cuddie's bullock in 'Februarie' ('Weenest of loue is not his mynd?') and Willye's hawthorn in 'March' ('How bragly it beginnes to budde') bear witness. But although the phenomenon is common it evidently produces diverse reactions in different human beings. 'Ianuarye', 'Februarie' and 'March' present three young lovers, Colin, Cuddie and Thomalin, whose similarities and differences are swiftly outlined, while 'Aprill' sums up and makes explicit the questions which have been raised. The theme of church affairs meanwhile remains in the background. Although in 'Februarie' we hear a brief account of misguided ceremonies associated with the Oak, the main interest of the eclogue continues to be the struggle between youth and age, impatience and patience.

Comparison between Colin and Cuddie is invited by the similar openings of their complaints. Colin's demand that the 'Gods of loue' and especially Pan should 'pitie the paines' he suffers, reappears in Cuddie's exclamation at the discomforts of February weather:

> Ah for pittie, wil rancke Winters rage,
> These bitter blasts neuer ginne tasswage?
>
> (1–2)

Both ask for pity, with an amusing self-pity; but where Colin represents the lamenting amorist, Cuddie exemplifies the disgruntled hedonist. Both feel they have a right to complain, but while Colin stands in the line of pastoral and Petrarchan lovers who examine the correspondences between the state of their own minds and that of the natural world around them, Cuddie is a latter-day version of the discontented 'Youth' figure found, for example, in Mantuan's and Barclay's discussions about young shepherds in winter. Hence the opening parallelism quickly develops into contrast: in Colin's case love is presented as not only an overwhelming but even a disabling experience which causes him to neglect his sheep and break his pipe; in Cuddie's it takes the form of a light-hearted game appropriate to his youth, which can be initiated with the gift of a decorated girdle and ended when a fitting number of 'dayes' has passed ('*Phyllis* is myne for many dayes: / I wonne her with a gyrdle of gelt, / Embost with buegle about the belt'). Both shepherds evoke sympathy and both are the objects of a tolerant yet critical judgment. Colin's snapping of his 'oaten pype' is shown to be the somewhat illogical result of his frustration over lack of success with Rosalind: 'Both pype and Muse, shall sore the while abye.' Our impression that we are witnessing a fit of pique is confirmed by the gentle and objective voice of the narrator in the final stanza:

> the pensife boy halfe in despight
> Arose, and homeward droue his sonned sheepe.
>
> (76–7)

Cuddie, also, comes under a mild judgment, not so much in the give and take of his dialogue with Thenot in which each scores points against the other, as through the effect of the fable, which reveals the unwisdom of adopting an impatient attitude towards old age.

But it is the conduct of Thomalin, the third lover, for all his semi-comic naivety of manner, which functions as an implicit critique on the behaviour of Colin. In a sprightly six-line rhyme scheme Willye and Thomalin discuss the mysterious goings-on of the God of Love, Willye proving even less experienced than Thomalin who has suffered the fate prophesied in Bion's fourth idyll. Thomalin's reaction to his new experience is one of increased caution, since he has discovered to his cost that love's 'sorowe' can cause harm to innocent sheep. The sophisticated reader smiles at the shepherd's unpolished phrases about the 'clouted legge' of an 'vnhappye Ewe', but is obliged to acknowledge that the speaker shows a due concern for his flock:

> Nay, but thy seeing will not serue,
> My sheepe for that may chaunce to swerue,
> And fall into some mischiefe.
> For sithens is but the third morowe,

> That I chaunst to fall a sleepe with sorowe,
> And waked againe with griefe:
> The while thilke same vnhappye Ewe,
> Whose clouted legge her hurt doth shewe,
> Fell headlong into a dell.
>
> (43–51)

Thomalin's resolve not to allow love in future to interfere with sheep-keeping contrasts implicitly with Colin's self-abandonment to grief. The diversity of love's 'pageant' in these three eclogues leads into explicit discussion of Colin's case in 'Aprill'. The social consequence of his particular form of lover's melancholy is that it deprives the pastoral community of enjoyment:

> Shepheards delights he dooth them all forsweare,
> Hys pleasaunt Pipe, whych made vs meriment,
> He wylfully hath broke, and doth forbeare
> His wonted songs, wherein he all outwent.
>
> (13–16)

Thenot's dry comment on this indicates that the experience which to Colin seems so overpowering can, in fact, be contained or, in the traditional metaphor, 'bridled':

> What is he for a Ladde, you so lament?
> Ys loue such pinching payne to them, that proue?
> And hath he skill to make so excellent,
> Yet hath so little skill to brydle loue?
>
> (17–20)

It is in the control of passion, which is not the same thing as its elimination, that Colin is seen to fail – a fact which makes him interestingly analogous to another literary lover of the late 1570s and early 1580s, Astrophel. In the case of Astrophel the metaphor of the bridle or 'the raines' takes on an especially ironic significance: as a skilled horseman Astrophel dominates his mount, but 'by strange worke' he finds that he himself is mastered by Cupid:

> I on my horse, and *Love* on me doth trie
>   Our horsmanships, while by strange worke I prove
>   A horsman to my horse, a horse to *Love*;
> And now man's wrongs in me, poore beast, descrie.
> The raines wherewith my Rider doth me tie,
>   Are humbled thoughts, which bit of Reverence move,
>   Curb'd in with feare, but with guilt bosse above

45

Of Hope, which makes it seeme faire to the eye.
The Wand is Will, thou Fancie Saddle art,
Girt fast by memorie, and while I spurre
My horse, he spurres with sharpe desire my hart:
He sits me fast, how ever I do sturre:
And now hath made me to his hand so right,
That in the Manage myselfe takes delight.[3]

Astrophel's capacity for self-analysis is greater than Colin's, but both figures are brought at the close to a similar state of helpless subjection to unrequited love, in which fulfilment of their social obligations seems almost impossible. Thomas Nashe's description of Sidney's sonnet sequence as 'the tragicommody of love'[4] gives a hint, I think, of the attitude appropriate to Colin's plight also.

The 'Aprill' encomium of Elizabeth testifies, of course, to Colin's former poetic skill, and hence to the 'pittie' and folly ('Ah foolish boy') of his present condition. In the 'laye' the poet while still in command of his creative gift had combined a ceremonial richness worthy of the Queen with rustic details suitable to a pastoral singer. The procession of celebrants which follows the Exordium and Blazon includes both the illustrious figure of Phoebus and the local shepherds' daughters; the plants which adorn the Queen's coronet include formal bay leaves and green primroses. The song reveals the extraordinary contribution which a pastoral poet might make to his community by both delighting his listeners and imaginatively instructing them in the worth of the monarch.

The transition from 'Aprill' to 'Maye' particularly merits scrutiny. With the first of the four months which occupy the middle of the year Spenser widens the scope of the *Calender* by introducing a new theme, the obligations of the Christian pastor, alongside his earlier investigation of the lives of lovers and poets. Moreover he exploits the reader's half-conscious sense of the passage of time in a poem about the months of the year by shifting his attention from youths to maturer men. The problems implicit in the experience of love remain the theme of 'Iune' and 'August', but Colin has acquired more self-knowledge in 'Iune' than he showed in 'Ianuarye', and the Willye of 'August' is more experienced and more sardonic than the Willye of 'March' who had never personally met Cupid. The two speakers of 'Maye' are both middle-aged. Much, then, is new in the fifth eclogue, with its stress on the austerity of life to

which Christian pastors are called, but at the same time it is deftly
tied to its predecessor and to the appropriate month of the year by
Palinode's opening description of May festivities. Some of the
flowers which play a part in the 'Aprill' encomium – roses and
Sops-in-wine – reappear in the traditional games of the 'loue lads' in
'Maye', adding to their legitimate charm. Spenser ensures continuity
with the previous eclogue, yet prepares the way for difference,
because there is a distinction between the lives of love lads and of
middle-aged parsons, as we showed in the last chapter. The 'Maye'
eclogue as it unfolds reveals ever more clearly the validity of Piers's
arguments that the clergy should labour for their flocks rather than
for their families' material advancement, and that 'concord' with
treacherous Foxes can only lead to disaster.

The life of the poet and the life of the pastor at this stage seem
to have little in common; but the sixth and seventh eclogues which
jointly occupy a position at the centre of the *Calender* are significantly
bound together by a common metaphor, that of the hills and the
dales. Colin's state of mind is reflected by the landscape he has chosen
in his misery – 'those hilles, where harbrough nis to see, / Nor
holybush, nor brere, nor winding witche' – in contrast to the fruitful
dales where the flocks graze serenely and the Muses are frequent
visitors. By choosing the hills Colin has cut himself off from his
friends and from the opportunity of contributing to the rural world
through poetry. The opening of 'Iulye', in a different mood and
less elegant verse-form, makes an analogous point: Morrell by
choosing the hills has cut himself off from his congregation, who
now are found 'straying' among 'the bushes rancke'. Morrell
boisterously enjoys his hilltop existence, but, as I suggested in the
last chapter, Thomalin's fervour and freedom from superstition win
the argument on behalf of the dales. Spenser's use of the hill–dale
contrast in two juxtaposed poems, although the hills have specialised
meanings within their own eclogues, hints at a single underlying
theme, that of wilful isolation from the community as opposed to
willing involvement in its needs.

The meaning of 'Iune', however, is complicated by the fact that
half-way through it, from line 65 onwards, Colin takes up a new
position, and instead of dismissing pastoral poems as 'weary wanton
toyes' indicates that he still writes them although his passion for
Rosalind has destroyed his eloquence ('since I am not, as I wish I

were'). This change of stance causes the reader some difficulty; nevertheless the climax of the eclogue remains the comparison between Colin and his predecessor, Tityrus. Whether Colin refuses to make poems (lines 1–64) or simply fails to make eloquent ones (lines 65–120), the comparison illustrates two different ways in which a poet can respond to the experience of unrequited love. Colin exemplifies the poet disabled by romantic passion, while Tityrus, Chaucer, in his own era revealed a self-mastery which allowed him to 'slake' the flames in his heart and redirect personal emotion into public poems, which might take the form of love-complaints or merry tales:

> He, whilst he liued, was the soueraigne head
> Of shepheards all, that bene with loue ytake:
> Well couth he wayle hys Woes, and lightly slake
> The flames, which loue within his heart had bredd,
> And tell vs mery tales, to keepe vs wake,
> The while our sheepe about vs safely fedde.
>
> (83–8)

Chaucer, evidently, demonstrated in his own life that ability 'to brydle loue' to which Thenot referred in 'Aprill'.

At a humbler level, Perigot in 'August' demonstrates the same power. He joins the *Calender*'s gallery of lovers, clearly resembling Colin in his neglect of his sheep and his recent failure 'to make the iolly shepeheards gladde / With pyping and dauncing'; but he unexpectedly reveals, in unassuming fashion, the Chaucerian ability to redirect his emotion into poetry. The singing match, with its bouncing rhythms and neat juxtaposition of Perigot's love-formulae with Willye's amused and sometimes deflating comments, brings evident relief to 'paynefull loue' even while it expresses it. When the match is over, Colin's sestina sung by Cuddie surprisingly illustrates the same phenomenon: that is to say, despite Colin's declared belief that the anguish of love must silence him as a poet, we find he has written a resonant love-complaint which through its Italianate rhyme scheme and bold enjambment gives considerable aesthetic satisfaction to its hearers. Not only do Thomalin, Chaucer, and Perigot in their different ways and at different stages in the sequence indicate that lovesick shepherds need not neglect their sheep or their task of songmaking, but the actual practice of Colin Clout temporarily contradicts his own theory about himself.

Set within the world of 'August' are the small but vivid scenes engraved on the drinking cup which is one of the prizes for the singing contest. Alongside the representation 'of Beres and Tygres, that maken fiers warre' is to be found a scene in which a lamb in mortal peril from a wolf is saved by a shepherd.

> Thereby is a Lambe in the Wolues iawes:
> But see, how fast renneth the shepheard swayne,
> To saue the innocent from the beastes pawes:
> And here with his shepehooke hath him slayne.
>
> (31–4)

In one sense this is a wholly conventional image: a carved cup forms a traditional reward in singing matches, and bears, tigers, and wolves are frequent if unwelcome visitors in the pastoral landscape – witness *The Faerie Queene* VI. x. 34 and *The Winter's Tale* III. iii for the tiger and the bear. But, occurring as it does quite late in the pattern of *The Shepheardes Calender*, the scene has a more than conventional force. It necessarily stirs in the mind of the reader memories of predatory wolves and devoted shepherds in 'Maye' ('There crept in Wolues, ful of fraude and guile') and 'Iulye' ('Wolues, that would them teare'). Those two eclogues were, of course, concerned with ecclesiastical matters and might seem to have no connection with 'August's' world of rustic singers; but the presence of an image of shepherd, lamb and wolf, which by this stage in the sequence carries inescapable religious connotations, on the mazer which is a prize for poets suggests that there is a significant analogy between the roles of pastor and poet. The incised image functions as an exemplar for either profession or both: the poet as well as the pastor is called upon to defend the local community against spiritual attack. 'Iune' and 'Iulye' were linked by the motif of a culpable withdrawal from the dales to the hills, relevant both to poet and to pastor; in the same way 'Iulye' and 'August' are linked by an image which reveals a common responsibility to play a part in spiritual warfare.

The four summer eclogues certainly point up the difference in lifestyle between poets and pastors (pastors 'mought not liue ylike, as men of the laye') yet at the same time they hint at similarities of obligation and purpose. In the final four eclogues of the *Calender* the analogy which until now has been obliquely suggested by metaphors becomes the dominant factor in the organisation of ideas:

two adjoining eclogues, 'September' and 'October', respectively sum up the poem's ecclesiastical and literary themes, while 'Nouember' fuses the two themes into one. The concern of the summer eclogues with maturer men continues in the final group, now coupled with an autumnal recognition of consequences and repercussions. 'September' brings a darkening of mood reflected in the change of weather, the harsher diction, and the gravity of Diggon's worldview. Diggon sees more comprehensively than any other pastor the full range of evils afflicting the church. He describes both the Roman Catholic and the English churches; he understands not only about English Foxes, as Piers did in 'Maye', but about the newly arrived Wolves (missionary priests trained abroad) 'priuely prolling two and froe'. With an urgency which is appropriate to the context he defines the pastor's duty of continuous watchfulness. The eclogue sums up, we have suggested, all that the *Calender* has revealed about the vocation of the Christian pastor; but at the same time it is overshadowed by the melancholy consequences of Diggon's former pursuit of monetary 'gayne'. The theme reappears in 'October'.

Like 'September', 'October' gathers up themes and images from preceding eclogues, in this case the eclogues which have dealt with poets, poetry and the experience of love. It is modelled on Mantuan's fifth eclogue although with a characteristically bold adjustment. The neo-Latin eclogue consisted of a debate between the poet Candidus and the rich but selfish Silvanus, who wanted to hear Candidus's songs without providing him with the necessary financial support. Spenser does away with the niggardly Silvanus and inserts in his place the idealistic Piers. Cuddie echoes much of Candidus's pessimism about the contemporary world of patronage, and earns some sympathy from the reader; but the energy and zeal of his companion, Piers, make Cuddie's consistently negative responses seem defeatist. Moreover, Cuddie's refusal to pipe arises basically from a resentment at the lack of material 'gayne' to be achieved through poetry ('Yet little good hath got, and much lesse gayne'). A significant parallel with the previous eclogue is established. Diggon had allowed his sheep to starve because of his desire for gain, and Cuddie neglects his role as piper for the same reason. Evidently neither pastor nor poet will fulfil his vocation if his interest is in the accumulation of material rewards. Gain should not be the goal of either.

Piers not only draws attention to the true reward of poets, but even more importantly gives the *Calender's* climactic statement about the function of poetry:

> Cuddie, the prayse is better, then the price,
> The glory eke much greater then the gayne:
> O what an honor is it, to restraine
> The lust of lawlesse youth with good aduice:
> Or pricke them forth with pleasaunce of thy vaine,
> Whereto thou list their trayned willes entice.

> Soone as thou gynst to sette thy notes in frame,
> O how the rurall routes to thee doe cleaue:
> Seemeth thou dost their soule of sence bereaue,
> All as the shepheard, that did fetch his dame
> From *Plutoes* balefull bowre withouten leaue:
> His musicks might the hellish hound did tame.

> (19–30)

The reference to the delight which the 'rurall routes' receive from the poet's music echoes earlier statements in 'Aprill', 'Iune' and 'August'; but Piers carries the subject further, to reveal that the poet instructs his listeners as well as delighting them, in accordance with the vital Horatian formula. The poet incites the wills of his hearers to virtue by means of the pleasure which his art gives them: he can 'pricke them forth with pleasaunce of his vaine'. Moreover, Piers's allusion to Orpheus, the world's first poet, not only gives appropriate dignity to later poets, but through the reference to the taming of 'the hellish hound' suggests the spiritual power of the writer's art. The analogy between poet and Christian pastor has never been clearer; both poet and pastor share the goal of victory over spiritual evil, although their modes of existence and of expression differ. A sensitive critic, discussing the allusion to Orpheus, has argued that it must imply the limitations in poetry's power, since 'in spite of his "musicks might", Orpheus did not succeed, finally, in reversing the course of nature, and Eurydice's ultimate fate would, one imagines, have been present in the minds of Spenser's readers'.[5] Certainly the modern reader may call to mind Orpheus's failure; but on the whole it seems that for English sixteenth-century readers Orpheus was essentially a figure of triumph – the ideal artist, lover and civiliser – whether his example was cited by Barnabe Barnes, Thomas Watson, Sidney, or Spenser himself in *The Faerie Queene* and elsewhere.[6]

Cuddie's gloomy responses continue throughout the eclogue. He manages to find a reason for rejecting each of Piers's suggestions about available poetic genres, with the result that his resourcefulness in pessimism becomes amusing. That Spenser endorses Piers's Horatian view of the poet's role, and his belief that after exploring the pastoral genre the writer should turn to heroic accounts 'of wars, of giusts', cannot really be doubted. The eclogue's summation of the *Calender*'s themes concerning poets and poetry would not be complete, however, without a discussion of the effect of unrequited love on the aspiring poet. Cuddie's opinion that the tyrant Love prevents the imagination from working was certainly Colin's in 'Ianuarye' and 'Iune', but the *Calender* has also presented important contrary evidence. Thomalin in 'March', although no poet, refused to allow love to interfere a second time with sheep-keeping; Thenot in 'Aprill' indicated that love could be bridled; the telling example of Chaucer in 'Iune' illustrated how a major poet fashioned songs out of his 'Woes'; in 'August' Perigot channelled his grief into a singing match, while the elaborate sestina in the same eclogue surprisingly revealed that Colin himself could write effective love poems despite his avowals to the contrary. Hence Piers's statement that love can inspire a shepherd to poetry and, indeed, to true imaginative ascent, has the weight of the *Calender* as a whole behind it, although his language takes on a Neoplatonic colouring which is new for this work:

> Ah fon, for loue does teach him climbe so hie,
> And lyftes him vp out of the loathsome myre:
> Such immortall mirrhor, as he doth admire,
> Would rayse ones mynd aboue the starry skie.
> And cause a caytiue corage to aspire,
> For lofty loue doth loath a lowly eye.
>
> (91–6)

Cuddie rejects Piers's Neoplatonism, just as he has rejected his view of the function of poetry and the possibility of epic, but the theory of inspiration which he offers in its place — the creative stimulus contained in 'lauish cups' of wine — though vigorously expressed collapses even while he formulates it. His 'corage' grows cool rather rapidly.

The 'October' debate is not explicitly resolved, any more than are the other debates in the collection, but as in the rest of the cases we have discussed one speaker progressively builds up a position which demands assent. If the reader remains in doubt, however, the following eclogue, the culmination of *The Shepheardes Calender* from every point of view, settles the question. The poet tormented by love, exemplified by Colin Clout, has the power to write a pastoral elegy which moves the listener both to delight and tears ('I ne wotte, / Whether reioyce or weepe for great constrainte'). Colin's private grief is redirected into public utterance for the sake of a patron, the 'greate shepheard *Lobbin*', and the other mourners for Dido. But 'Nouember' not only settles the debate between Cuddie and Piers about whether a victim of love can achieve 'famous flight' in poetry, it forms the culmination of another, equally important, enquiry in the *Calender*, the implicit investigation of the relationship between the roles of the pastor and the poet. 'September' had summed up the tasks of the committed pastor, and 'October' those of the aspiring poet. In 'Nouember' Colin creates a poem which is both a finely shaped artifact and a religious consolation in the face of death: aesthetic and spiritual preoccupations are fused. The poet's art serves the same invisible end as the art of the preacher.

Formally, the elegy is a considerable achievement, incorporating the established topoi of the genre and finding room for deft allusions to previous eclogues. The second stanza refers to the breaking of pipes, here a gesture of sorrow not of petulance; in the eighth and ninth stanzas all nature mourns Dido's death with the characteristic exception of 'the Wolues, that chase the wandring sheepe'; in the tenth stanza Muses 'that were wont greene bayes to weare' (as they did in 'Aprill' – 'Bene they not Bay braunches, which they doe beare?') now 'bringen bitter Eldre braunches seare', a decorous transformation. The complex stanza-form is used with great dexterity too. In the eleven stanzas of lament the slowly diminishing line-lengths contribute to the sense of decline and loss, with one final burst of emotion in the penultimate line, before the downward movement is confirmed in the closing two-foot line:

> Whence is it, that the flouret of the field doth fade,
> And lyeth buryed long in Winters bale:
> Yet soone as spring his mantle doth displaye,
> It floureth fresh, as it should neuer fayle?

> But thing on earth that is of most availe,
> As vertues braunch and beauties budde,
> Reliuen not for any good.
> O heauie herse,
> The braunch once dead, the budde eke needes must quaile,
> O carefull verse.
>
> (83–92)

But in the four stanzas of rejoicing the line-lengths are exploited in a wholly different way, to suggest in the latter half of the stanza a new lightness, an unbodied freedom:

> Why wayle we then? why weary we the Gods with playnts,
> As if some euill were to her betight?
> She raignes a goddesse now emong the saintes,
> That whilome was the saynt of shepheards light:
> And is enstalled nowe in heauens hight.
> I see thee blessed soule, I see,
> Walke in *Elisian* fieldes so free.
> O happy herse,
> Might I once come to thee (O that I might)
> O ioyfull verse.
>
> (173–82)

As this stanza itself illustrates, after the 'turn' from grief to consolation, Spenser mingles pagan and Christian vocabularies with happy confidence. Dido reigns simultaneously as a 'goddesse' and a 'sainte'; 'heauen' and the Elysian fields are synonymous. A strongly biblical reference to the 'gates of hel' which will not prevail (Matthew 16.18) fits easily between the Fates and the Furies:

> But maugre death, and dreaded sisters deadly spight,
> And gates of hel, and fyrie furies forse:
> She hath the bonds broke of eternall night,
> Her soule vnbodied of the burdenous corpse.
>
> (163–6)

We have argued that the whole elegy represents a fusion of aesthetic and spiritual preoccupations, or, to put it another way, is an example of the poet's art employed for the same ends as the Christian pastor's. The eclectic vocabulary of the final stanzas confirms this union of visions. So, in a different medium, does the woodcut scene which prefaces the eclogue. As in two other of the *Calender*'s woodcuts a shepherd is found piping in a rustic landscape; but in the present case his music accompanies a procession of mourners who carry a coffin towards a village church. Previous woodcuts have included a variety of background buildings, ranging from an ideal Renaissance city, a palace, and a classical temple, to rural cottages and huts, but none has presented quite so explicit an image of a Christian church. November's piper, receiving the laurel crown from his companion, contributes his music to the local church's needs.

Colin's achievement in the 'Nouember' eclogue is a temporary phenomenon, however. The tragicomic presentation of his life-story ensures that the lovesick poet falls back into complaint and ultimate silence because of his mistaken view of his own predicament – his belief that love must inevitably destroy his poetic gift. The model for 'December' is Marot's third eclogue, which portrays the life of the speaker in terms of the four seasons of the year, but Spenser's highly significant addition is the Colinesque theme of disabling love, not to be found in Marot. The English poet interweaves passages imitated from the French with new passages in which Colin laments his love-sufferings. The metaphor which occupied a key position in 'Aprill', that of the bridle needed for the control of passion, now reappears in Colin's account of his experience:

> Forth was I ledde, not as I wont afore,
> When choise I had to choose my wandring waye:
> But whether luck and loues vnbridled lore
> Would leade me forth on Fancies bitte to playe.
>
> (61–4)

The use of the adjective 'vnbridled' for a moment half admits the speaker's failure to control his mount; but at the same time the passive verb in 'Forth was I ledde' and the equation of 'loues vnbridled lore' with mere 'luck' indicate that he chiefly regards himself as the victim of forces which he could not possibly master. He had no 'choise', he tells us; but the *Calender* has shown that there are other options for the poet in love. Believing himself irreparably damaged by love, denying his own evident capacity for poetic creation, Colin hurries into a premature old age.

The Shepheardes Calender, which gradually reveals the vital relationship between the roles of poet and pastor, ends ironically with the failure of its chief poet. Nevertheless the Epilogue confirms

that the work's purpose has been 'To teach the ruder shepheard how
to feede his sheepe':

> Loe I haue made a Calender for euery yeare,
> That steele in strength, and time in durance shall outweare:
> And if I marked well the starres reuolution,
> It shall continewe till the worlds dissolution.
> To teach the ruder shepheard how to feede his sheepe,
> And from the falsers fraud his folded flocke to keepe.

The poem as a whole has prepared the reader for this use of a single
metaphor to summarise the obligations of both pastors and poets.
Despite lively differences in modes of existence and of utterance,
both groups are committed to the moral and spiritual nourishment
of their hearers.

PART TWO:

The Faerie Queene

4

Nature and Grace reconsidered

Although critical understanding of *The Faerie Queene* has developed
strongly in recent years – especially in relation to the separate books
of the poem – the work remains one which is not easily kept in focus
as a totality. Its unfinished state is a factor here, as are its sheer scale
and inclusiveness; but in addition there continues to be scholarly
disagreement about the nature of the ideas which underpin its
structure. Is the poem to be regarded as a treatise on the powers
of the imagination? is it shaped above all by the requirements of
encomium? are its books arranged to form Neoplatonic triads? or
does it pluralistically affirm the existence of three distinct value-
systems?[1] Perhaps one reason why A. S. P. Woodhouse's theory
about the poem's frame of reference had such lasting influence was
that it seemed to offer a clear-cut, well-informed reading of a work
which often eludes definition. According to this theory the
intellectual scheme is quite precise: Book I moves 'on the religious
level' and has 'reference to the order of grace', while 'the remaining
books' move 'on the natural level only'.[2]

The impact made by the theory can be measured by the fact that
the relevant article found its way into at least four separate
collections of essays on Spenser.[3] But at the same time reservations
and qualifications became audible, voiced by Robert Hoopes, Harry
Berger, Jr, Alastair Fowler and others.[4] Nowadays few readers
would accept the Woodhouse theory in an unmodified form, since
Book II clearly includes much more Christian material than
Woodhouse allowed. But the theory has left its mark all the same:
scholarly references are still made to the contrasted 'orders' of grace
and nature, although these usually lead on to suggestions that in
Book II there is a 'merging' or 'reconciliation' of them. Hoopes
paved the way in this respect. A. C. Hamilton in his fine annotated
edition of *The Faerie Queene*, after summarising Woodhouse's
theory, writes: 'Later critics have replied that the two orders of grace

and nature merge when Guyon is reconciled to the Redcross Knight in the opening episode.'[5] Carol V. Kaske, acknowledging a debt to the ideas of both Woodhouse and Hoopes, argues 'that Book I keeps its Christianity pure, even Calvinistic at times, and that Book II alone is truly syncretic, providing a *via media* of Christian humanism, as Hoopes long ago suggested, between the exclusively Christian viewpoint of Book I and the exclusively humanistic viewpoint of Books III–VI'.[6] The poem, she claims, is pluralistic, offering three distinct viewpoints or intellectual worlds.

Nothing could be clearer than the fact that Spenser draws ideas and images both from Christian and from classical culture, and that he follows an extraordinary variety of literary models at one point or another in *The Faerie Queene*. He himself mentions four different models for narrative poems in the *Letter to Raleigh*, quite apart from his glancing allusions in the same letter to the work of Aristotle, Plato, Xenophon and St. Paul. The poet of *The Faerie Queene* is the poet of *The Shepheardes Calender*: his eclectic, inclusive mind gathers ideas and motifs from the maximum number of sources. But the question which still needs to be examined is whether this multiplicity of material involves the poet in one or more changes of frame of reference as *The Faerie Queene* unfolds – a change perhaps from a Christian scheme to a syncretic one, or indeed from a Christian to a syncretic to an exclusively humanistic one. The issues are not simple. If we are to see them at all clearly we must return to Woodhouse with whom the debate began and ask the fundamental question which has never, I think, been put with quite the directness which is necessary: has the pair of opposed theological terms which Woodhouse selected for attention in fact any relevance at all to *The Faerie Queene*? It is not, of course, a matter of questioning the relevance of the concept of grace to the poem, but of asking whether the contrast between the 'orders' of grace and nature has a bearing on the poem's structure. When we have looked at Woodhouse's ideas, we shall go on to Hoopes's.

Woodhouse maintained that the theological contrast, generally accepted in the sixteenth century, between the order of grace and the order of nature was relevant to the internal organisation of *The Faerie Queene*. The 'order of grace' was that to which man belonged 'in his character of supernatural being', while the 'order of nature' was that to which man belonged when unenlightened by revealed religion and guided only by natural law. The distinction was relevant to the poem because Spenser presented the Redcross Knight as an illustration of the Christian doctrine of man's dependence on divine grace for salvation, whereas Guyon, by contrast, served as an illustration of 'natural man', directed by natural ethics and 'realising the potentialities of his nature' by his own effort, without religious motive or supernatural sanction. Hence the two books deliberately portrayed contrasted modes of being.

Obviously Woodhouse was right that Book I dealt with the theme of salvation and operated within a Christian frame of reference, but his view of Book II and later books invited controversy. The only logical way to settle the matter is to establish from the theologians cited by Woodhouse – St Augustine, St Thomas Aquinas, Calvin, Erasmus and Hooker – some definition of the powers or limitations of man in the order of nature, and then to test Sir Guyon, protagonist of Book II and allegedly a 'natural man', against that definition.

Although theologians agreed that natural man, fallen but un-redeemed, could show remarkable ability in handicrafts, in the seven Liberal Arts, and in the creation of a civil society (Augustine and Calvin gave lucid accounts of the subject),[7] there was some difference of opinion about the extent to which natural man could attain moral virtues by his own efforts. Aquinas affirmed that natural principles within man enabled him to achieve for himself the moral virtues defined by human reason, even though the theological virtues were beyond his reach unless infused in him by the power of God:

Human virtue directed to the good which is defined according to the rule of human reason can be caused by human acts, in so far as such acts proceed from reason, by whose power and rule such good is established. On the other hand, virtue which directs man to good as defined by the Divine Law, and not by human reason, cannot be caused by human acts, the principle of which is reason, but is produced in us by the Divine operation alone.[8]

But Calvin, for his part, regarded such moral virtues as the product of externally imposed restraints, while the heart of the natural man remained inwardly uncleansed.[9] Because of this division of opinion about the quality of the moral virtues attainable by a natural man, it is difficult to test Guyon's moral achievements by any agreed criterion.

However, there was an important area where the theologians did not differ, and that was in their statements about the kind of religious faith available to men in the state of nature. Natural men have the law of nature engraved on their hearts, which tells them of the existence of God; but they cannot comprehend or approve without revelation the specifically Christian doctrine of redemption by Christ. Augustine, Aquinas, Calvin, Hooker, all asserted this – and the authority behind them was of course St Paul, especially I Corinthians 1.18–24. To illustrate the consensus it is best to take a passage from Hooker rather than Augustine or Calvin, because it was part of Hooker's purpose to demonstrate the value for mankind of natural reason and natural law, yet he too stated that natural man could not comprehend the crucifixion and resurrection:

> we know that of mere natural men the Apostle testifieth, how they knew both God, and the Law of God. Other things of God there be which are neither so found, nor though they be shewed can ever be approved without the *special* operation of God's good grace and Spirit. Of such things sometime spake the Apostle St. Paul, declaring how Christ had called him to be a witness of his death and resurrection from the dead, according to that which the Prophets and Moses foreshewed. Festus, a mere natural man, an infidel, a Roman, one whose ears were unacquainted with such matter, heard him, but could not reach unto that whereof he spake; the suffering and the rising of Christ from the dead he rejecteth as idle superstitious fancies not worth the hearing.[10]

Here, then, is an agreed statement about what is and what is not within the reach of natural man. Men in the order of nature, by definition, can have no faith in Christ crucified.

Early in Book II, after he has been hoodwinked by Archimago and Duessa, Guyon is shown galloping impetuously towards the Redcross Knight with his spear in position. For a moment the scene is presented from the viewpoint of spectators who cannot understand why Guyon, the aggressor, should suddenly lower his spear:

> They bene ymet, both readie to affrap,
> When suddenly that warriour gan abace
> His threatned speare, as if some new mishap
> Had him betidde, or hidden daunger did entrap.
>
> (II. i. 26)

The moment's bafflement adds drama to Guyon's disclosure of his mind in the following stanza:

> And cryde, Mercie Sir knight, and mercie Lord,
> For mine offence and heedlesse hardiment,
> That had almost committed crime abhord,

And with reprochfull shame mine honour shent,
Whiles cursed steele against that badge I bent,
The sacred badge of my Redeemers death,
Which on your shield is set for ornament.

(II. i. 27)

The allegedly 'natural' man calls upon Christ as his 'Lord' and asks for his mercy with the same personal directness as he uses in addressing the Redcross Knight. He envisages Christ not merely as 'Redeemer' but specifically as 'my Redeemer', and he regards the cross as sacred.

By definition, Guyon clearly cannot be a 'natural man'. His faith puts him outside that category. All the same, Woodhouse might still seem to have a retort available, of a kind which he employed in an article of 1955 written in reply to Hoopes. Hoopes had argued that the phrase, 'God guide thee, Guyon', uttered by the Palmer during the present episode, showed the religious orientation of Book II, and Woodhouse replied that the doctrinal significance of the phrase and the episode resided 'in the ready acknowledgment, prompted by reason, of the superiority of grace to nature'.[11] The point is a legitimate one in relation to 'God guide thee, Guyon', since natural man could indeed 'acknowledge' the existence of God. But our case does not rest on 'God guide thee, Guyon' but on the specifically Christian affirmations in Guyon's speech to the Redcross Knight. The passage we have quoted from Hooker states without hesitation that the suffering and rising of Christ were rejected by natural man as 'idle superstitious fancies'. Calvin had declared that in matters relating to his salvation natural man was blinder than a mole:

Now is to be declared what mans reason seeth, when it commeth to the kyngedome of God and to that spirituall insight, whyche consysteth chyefely in three thynges: to knowe God, and hys fatherly fauoure towarde vs, wherein oure saluation standeth: and the waye to frame oure lyfe accordynge to the rule of hys lawe. Bothe in the first two and in the seconde, proprely thei that are most wytty, are blinder than molles.[12]

Guyon, far from being blinder than a mole in such matters, actively demonstrates his reverence for his redeemer. In addition the Palmer, whom Woodhouse supposed to represent natural reason, refers with warmth to 'that deare Crosse' on the Redcross Knight's shield.

The Palmer's phraseology continues to be illuminating. When, after praising the Redcross Knight, he describes the way ahead for his own companion, Guyon, he employs the notably biblical metaphor of the 'race':

> But wretched we, where ye haue left your marke,
> Must now anew begin, like race to runne;
> God guide thee, *Guyon*, well to end thy warke,
> And to the wished hauen bring thy weary barke.

(II. i. 32)

The 'race' as a metaphor for the Christian life derives from 1 Corinthians 9.24, Galatians 5.7, 2 Timothy 4.7 and elsewhere. Commenting on Galatians 5.7 ('Ye did runne well'), William Perkins, the ablest of Elizabethan Calvinist theologians and an influential preacher in Cambridge in the 1580s and 1590s, carefully spelled out the three main implications of the metaphor:

In these words, Paul sets downe three duties of Christian people. The first is, that they must be runners in the race of God...The second dutie of Christian people is, that they must not onely be runners, but they must runne well. And that is done by beleeuing, and by obeying the true religion...The third dutie is, that wee must runne the race from the beginning to the end, and finish our course, so as wee may apprehend life euerlasting.[13]

The Palmer, in praying that Guyon may run the race, may run it well, and run it to its end, reveals a distinctly Pauline vision of human life. Such a vision is beyond the powers of natural man, who not only regards the crucifixion as 'foolishness' but also, as Calvin indicated, has a very imperfect grasp of the process of moral renewal which follows justification by faith.

It is not only in the episode to which we have been referring (II. i. 5–34) which functions as a link-passage with Book I, but in the subsequent Mordant and Amavia episode that Guyon's words expose his metaphysical status. The episode brings together an extraordinary variety of motifs from classical antiquity and Italian romantic epic, including a Circe-like or Alcina-like enchantress, a poisoned cup, a grave adorned with classical cypress boughs, and a fountain which might be thought to have baptismal associations.[14] Amidst all this variety, and despite his distress at the death of Amavia, Guyon alludes with sober confidence to the doctrine of the Last Judgment:

> Palmer (quoth he) death is an equall doome
> To good and bad, the common Inne of rest;
> But after death the tryall is to come,
> When best shall be to them, that liued best.
>
> (II. i. 59)

The word 'tryall' in this context certainly refers to the Last
Judgment, as a brief passage from William Perkins confirms ('But
how shall this triall be made? *Answ.* By workes: as the Apostle saith,
We must all appeare before the iudgement seate of Christ').[15]
Another Elizabethan Protestant, John Woolton, Bishop of Exeter,
made quite plain that the doctrine of the Day of Judgment was one
of those about which the pagans knew nothing:

They knew nothing of the resurrection of the dead; nothing of the day of
doom; nothing of the eternal bliss and immortality which the faithful shall
enjoy in body and soul in the heavenly kingdom.[16]

Guyon and the Palmer by definition cannot be natural men. Their
faith and their spiritual knowledge are beyond the reach of pagans –
hence they are Christians participating in the order of grace in the
same way as does the Redcross Knight. The Woodhouse theory is
evidently not valid: the contrast between the order of grace and the
order of nature has no relevance to the structure of *The Faerie Queene.*

We come then to Robert Hoopes's answer to Woodhouse.
Hoopes quite rightly saw that Spenser presents Guyon as a Christian,
although as we showed earlier he used defective evidence to make
out his case (he cited 'God guide thee, *Guyon*' where he should have
cited 'my Redeemer'). But instead of announcing boldly that
Woodhouse was mistaken, Hoopes described his ideas as an
'overstatement' rather than a 'fundamental misstatement', and
argued that the contrast between Books I and II was not 'so absolute'
as Woodhouse claimed. 'The two ideals', Hoopes suggested, were
'imaginatively, if not philosophically, harmonised' in Book II,
where there was evidence that Spenser had 'tried explicitly to
reconcile them'.[17] If we are to assess this statement we must go back
to definitions: the orders of grace and nature are not 'ideals' but
alternative metaphysical states in which a man may exist, in the sense
that he may either be enlightened by revealed religion or he may
be unenlightened by revealed religion and guided only by natural

ethics. Both logic and theology insist that a man cannot simultaneously *be* and *not be* a natural man. To look for a 'reconciliation' of these two states can only lead, I think, to confusion.

If it does not make a great deal of sense to talk about the 'merging' of the orders of grace and nature – and we should remember that we are only involved in formulating such odd propositions as a result of Woodhouse's mistaken view of Guyon – we need to identify some other frame of reference for the poem. That framework must be one which takes account both of the markedly theological concerns of Book 1 and of the copious use of classical motifs and classical ethics in the presentation of the adventures of Guyon and subsequent knights. I don't think Elizabethan readers would have been in much doubt about the sequel to justification *sola gratia, sola fide*, the theme explored in Book 1. After Christian belief came the Christian life, the pursuit of perfection. This is such a central tenet of Tudor Protestantism that an almost excessive amount of evidence comes to hand, but the first Book of Homilies has the necessary representative character. There, a sermon on 'the saluation of mankynde, by onely Christ' is immediately followed by two sermons on the way in which a true faith expresses itself in a life of good works:

this fayth doeth not lye dead in the heart, but is lyuely and fruitfull in bringing forth good workes.[18]

Richard Rogers, a Puritan preacher in Essex from the mid 1570s onwards, made the characteristic point when he devoted the first of his *Seven Treatises* to justification by faith, and the second to showing 'what the life of the true beleeuer is'. The opening paragraph of this second treatise indicates how essential is the connection between faith and the virtuous life:

Hitherto I haue shewed, who are they whom the Scripture calleth beleeuers, and the sonnes, and daughters of the Lord Almightie. Now, it is necessarie, and followeth in order, to shew what the life of the true beleeuer is: and how he, who hath faith, must behaue himselfe throughout his whole conuersation: for as yet nothing hath been said of that...[The believer] must ioyne with his faith, vertue, knowledge, temperance, patience, godliness, brotherly kindnes, and loue, etc.

(2 Peter 1.5–7)[19]

A single sentence crystallises the issue:

faith bringeth alwaies with it new life.[20]

The new life took the form of a gradual transformation of the mind, the heart, and even the body. Rogers, certainly, included a mention of the body in his extensive discussion of the subject:

> Here therefore vnderstand and know, that the heart which is the fountaine from whence the practise of godlines must growe and come, ought to be purged and clensed: and consequently, the bodie it selfe, ought to be first made a fit instrument for the same (to the accomplishing of that which is good, and to the well ordering of the life) in which two, consisteth the sanctification of the whole man.[21]

These processes occurred 'by little and little' (p. 89), we are told, and would not be completed 'vntill the life to come' (pp. 114–15). Hence a favourite metaphor among preachers and devotional writers for the new life after conversion was that of a journey, 'from virtue to virtue'. The Puritan lecturer at St Clement Danes from 1587, Henry Smith, put it like this:

> Thus a Trauailer passeth from towne vnto towne, vntill hee come to his Inne: so a Christian passeth from vertue to vertue, vntill hee come to Heauen, which is the iourney that euery man must endeuour to goe till death.[22]

Thomas White, delivering the sermon at the funeral of Sir Henry Sidney, employed similar phrases, while making explicit the always-understood proviso that perfection could never be achieved during the present life:

> And because we can neuer come neere vnto perfection in this life, and yet we ought to presse hard, and to followe after it, what else doth the Apostle meane by these words, but that there should be in vs a continuall indeuour to proceede from vertue to vertue, and neuer to desist, vntill we come into the brightnesse of his presence?[23]

My argument is that these concepts provide the appropriate frame of reference for *The Faerie Queene*, which dramatises first of all the need for salvation by grace and then the process of growth in moral virtue which necessarily follows it. Despite modern critical argument, there is no change in the poem's frame of reference after Book I, since the idea of a new life of virtue belongs to the same Christian scheme as does the concept of conversion. A single vision propels the poem forward, a vision of how to live well, or, in Spenser's own words, a vision of the 'XII Morall vertues'. The structure of the work informs us that the acquisition of these virtues depends first and foremost on a divine act of grace, and then consists of a lengthy process of individual development in which the mind increases in comprehension, the heart in self-mastery, and to which – or so the Castle of Alma episode suggests – the well-ordered body has a contribution to make. Spenser's choice of a narrative structure composed of a sequence of linked quests allows for a clear analysis first of justification *sola gratia* and then of the successive virtues one by one. The protagonist of each book starts at the point at which his predecessor leaves off, 'taking up the baton', and continuing the journey.[24] As readers of the poem have often noticed, the first three books present virtues which especially involve the individual's private or inner world of experience, the second three, virtues of a social kind which are necessary to life in small and then larger social groups. The poem's subject is nothing less than the spiritual, moral, emotional and social life of man.

One difference, though, between Book 1 and subsequent books needs to be clarified. In the process of conversion or justification man's own will can play no part. It is grace alone which intervenes in the life of a sinner to save him from helpless bondage to evil. William Perkins explained:

the worke of preparation is Gods and not ours; vnlesse it be possible for a man dead in his sinnes to prepare himselfe to his owne spirituall viuification: by nature we are seruants of sinne, and our libertie beginnes in our iustification. Therefore before we are iustified, we cannot so much as will that which is good.[25]

A couplet in Book 1, Canto x, which may seem problematic to some ears, becomes quite intelligible when placed in this doctrinal context:

> If any strength we haue, it is to ill,
> But all the good is Gods, both power and eke will.

> (I. x. 1)

The final sentence quoted from Perkins – 'Therefore before we are iustified, we cannot so much as will that which is good' – reminds us that Spenser's lines represent classic Protestant doctrine with reference to unregenerate man. Perkins went on to affirm, however, that *after* justification the regenerate human will could turn towards goodness and co-operate with God in the process of moral development:

without this gift of regeneration (which is the true preuenting grace) all externall motions and excitations to that which is good, are of no effect. For the cause must goe before the effect. Now that the will may affect and doe that which is good, the cause is the regeneration thereof: in which is giuen to the will, not only a new action, whereby it wils wel, but also a new qualitie, whereby it is able and can will well.[26]

Spenser's unselfconscious acceptance of this established doctrine is reflected in Books II to VI where the protagonists' wills strive for the attainment of moral good. Even in the combat of the Redcross Knight with the dragon, which takes place after his justification, his will or 'goodwill' is able to co-operate to some extent with the divine grace which so powerfully aids him: 'More then goodwill to me attribute nought' (II. i. 33).[27] The important point is that this difference in the role of the human will does not make Book I a 'Christian' poem and the subsequent books 'humanistic'. The regeneration of the will after justification is part of the Protestant worldview just as is the doctrine of the bondage of the will prior to justification. As we remarked earlier, there is no change in the poem's frame of reference after Book I, since both conversion and the new life of virtue form part of the same Protestant vision.

In depicting the journey from virtue to virtue, many Protestant writers, and indeed some preachers, felt free to draw on classical literature, classical history and classical ethics. The Protestant controversialist for whom Spenser made his first verse translations, Jan van der Noodt, announced that his prose exposition of the poems included in the *Theatre* would be 'taken out of the holy scriptures, and dyuers Orators, Poetes, Philosophers, and true histories'.[28] In his account of avarice he called upon Seneca, Plato, Aristophanes, Martial and Plutarch for support; in his discussion of carnal love he cited the example of the followers of Ulysses, entangled by love, who forgot their native country. He explained that he had included woodcuts in the volume in order to give 'delight and plesure' as Horace advised.[29] Some Protestant preachers, too, referred to the ethical wisdom of the ancients and included mythological allusions in their sermons: Henry Smith was a case in point, and so indeed was Grindal himself. Above all, Protestant poets, with their task of delighting, instructing and moving the wills of their hearers to the love of virtue, drew freely on the whole body of art and of nature to create 'images' or 'examples' of virtues, vices and passions which would, in Sidney's words, 'strike, pierce', and 'possesse the sight of the soule'.[30] Spenser's immediate predecessor among French poets, the Protestant Guillaume du Bartas, amplified his biblical subject in *La Semaine* and *La Seconde Semaine* with contemporary science and pseudo-science, geography, history and classical mythology. The point I am making is that an unperturbed mingling of Christian and classical material was common to many Protestant writers and does not need to provoke us into an explanatory theory that Spenser was concerned to illustrate the contrast between the order of grace and the order of nature, or to achieve some special and individualistic reconciliation of them.

An important objection to this chapter's thesis remains to be answered. I have suggested that the poem possesses a unified frame of reference and that its protagonists all share the same Christian status. The intriguing distinction between Britons and Elves will be discussed in Chapter 7; but meanwhile a seeming difference between the Redcross Knight and later protagonists requires attention. If, as a critic remarks, his story 'ends in the exalted bliss of sainthood' whereas the knights encountered in subsequent books are 'good men...but they are not saints',[31] the protagonist of Book I may represent a very specialised type of human being. But the meaning of the word 'saint' for committed sixteenth-century Protestants rebuts this view. All the elect were saints and would be saints in heaven. Actually the language of Book I, Canto x itself makes this plain, I think, but the vocabulary of the Puritan George Gyffard writing in the 1570s reinforces the point. God sent an angel to St John to reveal

what subtiltye and cruell tirannye, the deuill by the ministry of Antichriste woulde practice against the sainctes the true seruauntes of Christ.[32]

The saints are the servants of Christ, evidently; and Canto x uses the word in the same way. When the Redcross Knight is shown the New Jerusalem by Contemplation, he learns that God's chosen people who dwell there are all termed 'Saints':

> Faire knight (quoth he) *Hierusalem* that is,
>   The new *Hierusalem*, that God has built
> For those to dwell in, that are chosen his,
>   His chosen people purg'd from sinfull guilt,
>   With pretious bloud, which cruelly was spilt
> On cursed tree, of that vnspotted lam,
>   That for the sinnes of all the world was kilt:
> Now are they Saints all in that Citie sam,
> More deare vnto their God, then younglings to their dam.
>
> (I. x. 57)

Soon afterwards Contemplation tells him that 'thou emongst those Saints, whom thou doest see, / Shalt be a Saint'. The meaning of the word has been clearly established: George will be one among the 'chosen people' who have been washed 'with pretious bloud...of that vnspotted lam'. However, he will also acquire another role: he will be his 'owne nations frend / And Patrone', with the result that the word 'Saint' will preface his name ('thou Saint *George* shalt called bee, / Saint *George* of mery England, the signe of victoree'). But the sequence of stanzas has ensured that his sainthood resides in his kinship with all the other believers in heaven and not in the inspirational role which subsequent generations of Englishmen will bestow on him. There is no difference in status between the Redcross Knight and those who dwell in the New Jerusalem, and no difference between him and his chivalric successors in the poem except that his adventures furnish an image of the first stage of the Christian life.

5

Book 1: *Sola Gratia*

When the themes of Book 1 of *The Faerie Queene* are discussed in isolation from the poem which contains them, they seem particularly unpromising material for an imaginative fiction. Spenser's remarkable achievement is the embodiment of these themes in a finely constructed and psychologically penetrating romance narrative. Through an account of the adventures of two romance persons, whom iconography makes quite recognisable at their first appearance, he communicates a range of moral and spiritual meanings which the reader assimilates from the suggestions implicit in word or image. Interpretations need not be imposed from outside; Spenser is a poet who can be trusted to indicate by his language what moral, spiritual or ecclesiastical ideas are relevant from moment to moment in the narrative. Moreover, the dense accumulation of detail is controlled by a strong design, in which all the episodes concerning the protagonist derive from the initial defects in his own nature. A small amount of necessary romance interlacing is provided by the adventures of Una in Cantos iii and vi.

As in other books of the poem, the eclectic poet made use in Book 1 of an extraordinary variety of sources and models, although two in particular have central importance for this book – the St George legend and the Revelation of St John. The latter reached Spenser, as Josephine Waters Bennett showed in 1942,[1] profoundly coloured by the interpretations of sixteenth-century Protestant commentators such as Bale, Bullinger, Fulke and van der Noodt. In the present chapter I shall build on that insight of hers, but I shall also make an analogous point about Spenser's other major source, the life of St George. Book 1 depends, I think, not only on a Protestant reading of Revelation, but also on a Protestant re-creation – effected by Spenser himself – of the St George legend. The version which he presents of the familiar story of knight, lady and dragon has been shaped by a Protestant vision.

The best place to start our study is with the key word on the title page, 'Holinesse', because in this book as in others what the poet offers the reader is an imaginative exploration of a term which seems mainly abstract in character until he dramatises and exhibits its meaning. He creates a sequence of physical, emotional and intellectual experiences which work to replace the abstraction by a new and specific awareness. It is not simply a matter of re-animating traditional wisdom: by his organisation of his material Spenser unofficiously but decisively guides the reader to a particular view of holiness. In the same way in Book III he exhibits and celebrates a number of different forms of chastity – Belphoebe, Amoret, Florimell and Britomart are all praised for chaste affection or for chastity itself – but the progress of the narrative gives special emphasis to that chastity which takes the form of faithful love, embodied in Britomart. In Book I Spenser hints in the very first Argument stanza, where he refers to the Redcross Knight as the 'Patron of true Holinesse', that he will gradually reveal what that virtue really is. His re-working of the traditional saint's life will point up the nature of the only *true* holiness.

St George had been associated with the virtue of holiness before Spenser took up the story, as the third stanza of Lydgate's poem on the subject shows:

> This name George by Interpretacioun
> Is sayde of tweyne, the first of hoolynesse,
> And the secound of knighthood and renoun.[2]

Lydgate's St George both possesses and demonstrates holiness in his successive adventures, above all in his first exploit, the killing of the dragon. Spenser's 'Patron of true Holinesse' interestingly possesses little or nothing of the requisite virtue. Despite a couple of early and perhaps somewhat ambiguous victories the defects in his human nature grow more and more apparent: over-confidence, lust, pride and sloth carry him with a kind of inexorability into Orgoglio's dungeon in the central cantos of the book. The patron of true holiness paradoxically demonstrates man's bondage to sin – but this is the whole point. In the Protestant conception of human nature the only 'true' holiness is that of Christ, imputed to the sinful human being *sola gratia, sola fide*. The human individual, meanwhile, must discover his own unholiness. It is only after his justification that he will begin to show traces of the virtue in his life and actions. A definition of the word 'Holy', from the Lutheran theologian, David Chytraeus, focuses the issue:

Holy, Halowed by the holy Ghost, pure, and cleane, that is too wit, by imputation of Chrystes holynesse, and by beginning too bee holy.[3]

John Bale, the vehement Protestant propagandist of the mid-century who became Bishop of Ossory, remarked that the holiness even of the very elders in heaven was the gift of God and not their own achievement:

They confessed their own good works, merits, and deservings to be nothing at all; but their whole health, wisdom, knowledge, virtue, holiness, righteousness, and redemption to be only of his liberal gift and undeserved goodness.[4]

Spenser's Protestant conception of 'true Holinesse' caused him to transform his inherited fiction in the most radical way. Whereas in Lydgate's, Caxton's and Mantuan's versions of the legend St George's first act, in the first section of the work, was the successful slaying of the dragon, in Spenser's romance it is his last. The knight reaches a state of readiness for the dragon-fight only after the long process of spiritual education which the fiction portrays. Nevertheless, with ingenious formal artistry Spenser shows the Redcross Knight killing a kind of dragon in the presence of the princess as his 'first aduenture', so that his legend is framed in monster-slayings; but already in that opening episode numerous details indicate how far the knight is from being equipped for the task for which he is famous. Spenser's version of the St George legend steadily unfolds the facts of man's proneness to sin, his self-imprisonment, his need for rescue by a more-than-human power, the psychological crises he will pass through after grace has begun to work in him, and his ultimately victorious struggle with Satan.

As there was no equivalent for this educational process in the legend, Spenser incorporated images from other sources to define the protagonist's descent into sin. The chief of these he took from Revelation, above all the Whore of Babylon with her ability to seduce and destroy, and the Seven-headed Beast upon which she rode. These images necessarily carried with them a whole cluster of attendant meanings. If the sinister romance mistress is progressively endowed with the characteristics of the Whore of Babylon, whom

Protestants interpreted as the Roman Catholic religion or the Roman Catholic church, the knight when he succumbs to her allurements must typify not only the morally imperfect warrior but also the spiritually imperfect believer beguiled by false religion. Spenser's characteristic method of revealing more and more aspects of his key figures[5] means that the true ugliness of Duessa is steadily exposed between her first appearance in Canto ii and her stripping in Canto viii. In the same way, Spenser enlarged and enriched the significance of St George's princess by gradually bestowing on her some of the traits of the apocalyptic Woman clothed with the Sun, invariably interpreted by Protestants as true religion or the true church. As the book unfolds, Una's connection with true religion becomes more and more evident. Hence the romance which portrays human sin and divine rescue, also portrays a lapse into seductive irreligion and a return to the true faith.

But the reader has to reckon with yet another possibility. The presence of images from Revelation may indicate that Spenser has a further enterprise in hand, the delineation of some specific phase in the history of the church between the apostolic age and the Last Day. Protestant commentators on Revelation saw the work as a prophecy of the conflicts which would be endured both by the individual Christian throughout his life and by the church throughout her history. Hence the presence of apocalyptic images in Book I makes it quite possible that Spenser is including, among his other strands of meaning, the history of a particular sequence of ecclesiastical conflicts in England or more generally in Europe – the notorious 'historical allegory'. The possibility has called forth, as the Variorum edition shows, a large number of mutually incompatible readings. In such a critical impasse the cautious reader hardly knows where to turn, but it may be that the sixteenth-century commentators themselves can provide us with some assistance. While some of them argued that the images of Revelation foretold a specific sequence of historical events, others saw the images as a timeless representation of the continual struggle – a struggle which would last until the end of time – between Christian and Antichristian powers.[6] John Bale, for example, read parts of Revelation in one way, parts in another.[7] These divergences among the commentators should encourage the reader, I think, to approach Book I with an open mind in this respect. There may indeed be a consistent historical allegory embedded in the narrative, which no-one has yet satisfactorily uncovered, or there may be a more general warning to Christians of the dangers to which both individuals and the church are perennially subject as a result of the activities of Antichrist. Since, as we suggested at the beginning of the chapter, Spenser is an artist who can be trusted to signal the presence of his various meanings by pointed phrase or relevant allusion, the poem itself may be expected to contain indications about how an episode should be read.

The Error episode, well stocked with both psychological and allegorical interest, reveals the high potential of the book's protagonist together with his significant limitations. His physical appearance is suitably martial, but his inexperience coupled with a naive over-confidence frequently attracts our attention. The Redcross Knight is optimistic about the 'great aduenture' which he supposes to be imminent, but a benign irony plays over his eager anticipation that the battle will be 'braue' and that his 'new force' will be fully adequate to the ordeal:

> And euer as he rode, his hart did earne
> To proue his puissance in battell braue
> Vpon his foe, and his new force to learne;
> Vpon his foe, a Dragon horrible and stearne.
>
> (i. 3)

The same combination of inexperience and over-confidence is audible in the knight's blithe declaration at the mouth of Error's den that 'Vertue giues her selfe light, through darkenesse for to wade.' His style of action, too, has a youthful precipitancy:

> But full of fire and greedy hardiment,
>   The youthfull knight could not for ought be staide,
> But forth vnto the darksome hole he went,
> And looked in.
>
> (i. 14)

The knight's deficiency in self-knowledge is not hard to recognise. Rather more elusive is the nature of Spenser's poetic statement about the Wandering Wood and the Redcross Knight's and Una's presence in it. Some readers may feel that the pair should never have entered a grove whose 'loftie trees' seem arrogant in their determination to shut out 'heauens light'. On the other side, there is no denying

that the sudden storm compels 'euery wight' to take shelter, and
that Una is as ready as is the Redcross Knight to regard the wood
as 'faire harbour'. The wood, in fact, like many other of Spenser's
imagined locations, is at first presented with an ambiguity which
warns that both the characters and the reader will need to scrutinise
the fictional world with care. The episode introduces the theme of
deceptive appearances which will emerge again in the Archimago
episode, the Fradubio episode, and to some degree in the early stages
of the House of Pride episode. But Spenser's position is a tolerant
one: the fact that the virtuous Una cannot immediately recognise
the Wandering Wood for what it is, any more than she can discern
the true nature of Archimago when he presents himself as a hermit
or when he masquerades as the Redcross Knight, suggests that no
human being, however well intentioned, can immediately penetrate
hypocrisy, falsehood, or the initial stages of erroneous argument. It
is as the observer moves from the periphery towards the centre of
the phenomenon – in this case, from the edge of the Wandering
Wood inwards to the monster's den to be found at its centre – that
the true nature of the place is revealed to the wary eye. Una becomes
alert to the significance of the too numerous 'turnings' in the forest
paths, the 'beaten' track, and the 'hollow caue' in the middle. The
warning she utters, 'Be well aware', is central to Book I. The
Redcross Knight both in the present instance and in several
subsequent episodes fails to acquire that wariness which Spenser sees
as essential to life in a misleading world.

The sequence of events within the episode suggests the ease with
which the traveller can be drawn into the place of error, through
initially attractive propositions which gradually become more
problematic and more suspect until the full ugliness of erroneous
argument or erroneous doctrine is finally discovered. The repulsive-
ness of Error manifests itself in her appearance, her dangerous
'traine', and climactically in the flood which she emits at the feet
of the knight and the lady. Josephine Waters Bennett rightly noted[8]
that this flood derived from the flood emitted by the Dragon in
Revelation to stop the passage of the beautiful Woman, mentioned
at 12.15 and 16.13: 'the serpent cast out of his mouth water after
the woman lyke a flood' and 'I sawe thre vncleane spirits like frogges
come out of the mouth of the dragon.' Nevertheless, the biblical
verses fall a good deal short of suggesting the peculiarly disgusting

character of the Spenserian flood; and here I think Bale's exposition of the theme has made its mark on the poet's imagination. Bale, more than any other commentator, grew prolix and impassioned on the subject of the Dragon's flood, which he took to be an image of the 'hypocrisy, errors and lies' continually promulgated by the members of Satan:

And the dragon (saith St John) did cast out of his mouth water after the woman. A doctrine of hypocrisy, errors and lies, hath always passed from the synagogue of Satan. None other fruits hath gone from them, than wavering superstitions, idolatry, and heathen ceremonies: these hath flowed forth like a great river; daily have they augmented, and continually increased. Innumerable are the cumbrous and unprofitable burdens of their fantasies and dreams, wherewith they noy men's consciences, drown their small faith, and overload their souls.

This stinking water did the serpent vomit by his ravenous antichrists, which are his insatiable mouth, to stop the passage of the woman. He poured it forth in abundance, that he might cause her to be caught of the flood. Such is always the mischievous nature of the devil and his angels. Vengeable assaults have they, and innumerable crafts to deceive the innocent, not knowing them. Our first mother Eve was thus trapped in the beginning, and so had been drowned with Adam her husband, had they not had faith in the promised Seed. An innumerable multitude had been, and are yet to this day, swallowed up of this flood, and without great difficulty none escapeth it. Exceeding is the compass, study, and practice of this false generation. Evermore pour they out their poison; they dispute matters with errors and lies, with counsels and customs, having upon their side the darkened powers.

Yet is the Lord merciful to his poor congregation, that they are not drowned with all this filthy flood. None of it once toucheth their hearts. No part of their faith doth all this riffraff hinder. This dirty baggage accumbreth not their souls. Only are they satisfied with the wholesome doctrine of Christ's Spirit.[9]

The biblical water has become 'stinking'; the serpent 'vomits' it forth; it is described as 'poison' and a 'filthy flood'; it 'noys' men's consciences; the burdens are 'cumbrous'. Nevertheless, ultimately it cannot drown, touch or hinder the faithful. Spenser, I think, has assimilated this vocabulary into his version of the monster's flood:

> Therewith she spewd out of her filthy maw
> A floud of poyson horrible and blacke,
> Full of great lumpes of flesh and gobbets raw,
> Which stunck so vildly, that it forst him slacke
> His grasping hold, and from her turne him backe:
> Her vomit full of bookes and papers was,

With loathly frogs and toades, which eyes did lacke,
And creeping sought way in the weedy gras:
Her filthy parbreake all the place defiled has.

The same so sore annoyed has the knight,
That welnigh choked with the deadly stinke,
His forces faile, ne can no longer fight.
Whose corage when the feend perceiu'd to shrinke,
She poured forth out of her hellish sinke
Her fruitfull cursed spawne of serpents small,
Deformed monsters, fowle, and blacke as inke,
Which swarming all about his legs did crall,
And him encombred sore, but could not hurt at all.

(i. 20, 22)

Bale's generalised account is focused into an immediate and nauseating experience for the Redcross Knight and the reader. In particular, Bale's sense that in the last resort the flood of Satanic errors and lies is harmless to members of the congregation comes through in the final line quoted above ('but could not hurt at all') and in the simile which follows:

As gentle Shepheard in sweete euen-tide,
When ruddy *Phoebus* gins to welke in west,
High on a hill, his flocke to vewen wide,
Markes which do byte their hasty supper best;
A cloud of combrous gnattes do him molest,
All striuing to infixe their feeble stings,
That from their noyance he no where can rest,
But with his clownish hands their tender wings
He brusheth oft, and oft doth mar their murmurings.

(i. 23)

Spenser, like Bale, indicates the triviality of the swarming creatures, while at the same time he takes the opportunity to refresh the reader with a glimpse of a world of unassuming service to which the knight will eventually return.

If Bale's description of the Dragon's flood has influenced Spenser's language in these stanzas, it is possible that Bale's opinion of its meaning may assist in the search for an accurate interpretation. The incident, with its apocalyptic overtones, is necessarily one of those which invite speculation about a concealed historical allegory. Perhaps Error constitutes an allusion to a particular religious heresy at a specific historical moment, such as fourth-century Arianism.[10]

However Bale, for one, saw the Dragon's flood as an inclusive image of all the errors and lies with which the Devil has 'evermore' afflicted the world from the time of Eve up to 'this day'. The battle against such errors is continuous. Bale's commentary in this way reinforces the supposition that the opening episode of Book I announces a major theme of the book in broad and inclusive terms, in the manner which is characteristic of the opening episodes of subsequent books of the poem, rather than in narrowly historical ones. Amavia and Mordant prefigure the irascible and concupiscible passions which are thematically central to Book II; Malecasta embodies the unchastity which will be variously dramatised in Book III. The placing of the monster Error in the opening episode of Book I indicates that the protagonists are at large in a world which will repeatedly present them with misleading appearances and with exponents of false religions.

Each of the enemies of the Redcross Knight in the first half of Book I is a false religionist. Two are papists (Archimago and Duessa) while two are adherents of Mahomet (Sansfoy and Sansjoy); all four share with each other a hatred of 'highest God' (i. 37, ii. 18), although they differ in the methods by which they seek to advance their cause. Archimago and Duessa work by means of fraudulent 'shewes' whereas the Saracen brothers operate through physical violence. The appropriate frame of reference is provided by Bale when he declares that Antichrist appears in two main guises in human history – the Pope with his followers and Mahomet with his:

For no doubt of it, this fierce temptation and cruel handling of the boisterous antichrists, Mahomet standing in the way of sinners, and the Romish pope sitting in the most pestilent seat of errors, will come upon all the world by execrable sects of false prophets, liars, hypocrites, blasphemers, and teachers of devilish doctrine, to tempt and allure them which dwell here upon earth, sometime by flattering promotions, sometime by threatenings and penalties, to renounce that verity, and deny that word, to the utter damnation of their souls.[11]

'All the world' will suffer from such assaults, which will take the form either of 'flattering promotions' or of 'threatenings and penalties'. This is the representative fate which Spenser imagines for the Redcross Knight in the first half of Book I and, indeed, also for Una, who is deceived by Archimago and attacked by Sansloy, although she has other problems to cope with in addition. The theological conception of the two Antichrists is assimilated into the romance world with a characteristically Spenserian appearance of ease: the guileful papists are presented as familiar hermit or tempting mistress, the violent followers of Mahomet as Saracen knights, frequent participants in mediaeval romance as well as Italian romantic epic (Sir Beves killed fifty on a single day).[12] Significantly, Spenser draws attention to the underlying connection between the two sorts of religious error by creating narrative links between them. When Duessa, the Whore of Babylon, makes her first appearance, it is in the company of the 'faithlesse Sarazin' Sansfoy, whom she entertains with 'faire disport and courting dalliaunce'. In Canto iv she conducts a promising flirtation with Sansjoy, and in the following canto intervenes to save his life. The connection becomes unmistakable when the common ancestry of the two forms of false religion is revealed in Canto v: both Duessa and the Saracen brothers are direct descendants of darkness, grandchildren of Night.

The Redcross Knight can deal comparatively easily with the physical assaults made by the followers of Mahomet. The papist enemy works in subtler ways, creating or promoting ambiguous spectacles for the inexperienced knight to contend with: a 'lowly Hermitage' (i. 34), a 'goodly Lady' (ii. 13), 'two goodly trees' (ii. 28), a 'goodly building, brauely garnished' (iv. 2). 'Goodly', of course, is that equivocal adjective which in Spenserian descriptions can precede what is truly valuable or treacherously deceptive. In these episodes, as in the Error episode itself, the knight is not, I think, to blame for his initial mistake in reading his deceptive world, but for his persistence in error after warning signals have clearly indicated that the phenomenon on hand ought to be rejected. His persistence in error is inseparably linked with his surrender to sinful impulses. After each adventure his mind is more clouded and his heart more tainted by the nature of the experience he has passed through.

Archimago's hermitage at first seems to offer a true pastoral simplicity of life, and neither Una nor the Redcross Knight can discern its true meaning. The reader, on the other hand, is guided from the surface to the reality beneath the surface in the way which is characteristic of Spenser's handling of deceptive places or people, whether we look at the present case, or the two stanzas which describe Lucifera (iv. 8–9), or the technique used in portraying the

Bower of Bliss (II. xii. 42–3). A single stanza or pair of stanzas forms a unit which opens attractively but gradually exposes sinister preoccupations and purposes:

> Arriued there, the little house they fill,
> Ne looke for entertainement, where none was:
> Rest is their feast, and all things at their will;
> The noblest mind the best contentment has.
> With faire discourse the euening so they pas:
> For that old man of pleasing wordes had store,
> And well could file his tongue as smooth as glas;
> He told of Saintes and Popes, and euermore
> He strowd an *Aue-Mary* after and before.

> (i. 35)

The 'little house' appears in the opening lines to be dedicated to humble contentment. It is the quietly managed shift in the character of the adjectives used to describe the hermit's discourse during three consecutive lines – from the neutral 'faire' to the suspect 'pleasing' to the fatal 'smooth' – that reveals the old man's hypocrisy, while the last two lines identify him as a papist. By means of this stanza the reader is prepared for the discovery that the hypocritical hermit is in fact a sorcerer who deals in 'mighty charmes, to trouble sleepy mindes', and for the possibility that his sorcery may have an ecclesiastical significance. Bale had denounced papist clergy as 'conjurors' who 'daily deceive the ignorant multitude with their sorceries and charms'.[13]

The activities of the Enchanter have a twofold interest, therefore. He shows remarkable cunning in disturbing his visitor's equilibrium first of all with an erotic dream which provokes an 'vnwonted lust' in the dreamer, and then by the spectacle of the seeming-Una in 'lewd embracement' with a squire. The sight creates a painful confusion of feelings in the young man: his jealous and lustful 'burning' at the spectacle quickly transforms itself into moral indignation:

> Which when he saw, he burnt with gealous fire,
> The eye of reason was with rage yblent,
> And would haue slaine them in his furious ire.

> (ii. 5)

The undoubtedly lustful 'fire' becomes 'rage' which in turn becomes a more righteous and respectable 'ire'. Although the knight escapes from the hermitage, he cannot escape the newly stirred but unadmitted desires which he carries with him. The episode has great psychological interest; moreover, viewed in retrospect, it also possesses an ecclesiastical significance, in so far as the papist sorcerer with his 'mighty charmes' and his intense hostility towards Una ('For her he hated as the hissing snake') has succeeded in separating the wayfaring knight from the woman who more and more will be revealed as the embodiment of true religion.

Faced with the 'faire' Duessa, and subsequently with the promise of shade offered by two spreading trees, the knight responds with characteristic eagerness. When the warning signals reach him – in the form of Duessa's self-explanation with its lack of faith in Christ's resurrection and its patent lie about the Saracen having led her against her will, not to mention Fradubio's account of his own history with its pointed resemblance to the Redcross Knight's recent adventures – the young man neglects them because of his increasing abandonment of himself to his desires. He does not listen to what is being said because of his growing lust:

> He in great passion all this while did dwell,
> More busying his quicke eyes, her face to view,
> Then his dull eares, to heare what she did tell.
>
> (ii. 26)

At the opening of the House of Pride episode the Redcross Knight is again faced with ambiguous appearances whose meaning the reader immediately understands but whose ominous elements quite escape the youth's notice. As usual, Spenser leaves engagingly uncertain the question of whether a newly arrived traveller would or could have noticed the lack of mortar between the bricks of the palace or the sandy foundations on which it is built. When the knight does begin to show a dislike of the society in which he now moves, that dislike, comically, springs from the fact that he himself is infected with the prevailing vice:

> Yet the stout Faerie mongst the middest crowd
> Thought all their glorie vaine in knightly vew,
> And that great Princesse too exceeding prowd,
> That to strange knight no better countenance allowd.
>
> (iv. 15)

What seems to be an accurate perception of the nature of the House of Pride proves to be evidence of his vanity and lack of self-knowledge.[14] In the nicely equivocal opening stanza of Canto v the narrator teases the reader with the possibility that the knight may still be concerned with the 'glorie excellent' which is the reward of virtuous action; but the character of the 'doughtie turnament' which is about to ensue – a competition for a pagan shield in the grounds of a House dedicated to self-advancement – suggests that the lines modulate towards an irony which is both amusing and sad:

> The noble hart, that harbours vertuous thought,
> And is with child of glorious great intent,
> Can neuer rest, vntill it forth haue brought
> Th'eternall brood of glorie excellent:
> Such restlesse passion did all night torment
> The flaming corage of that Faery knight,
> Deuizing, how that doughtie turnament
> With greatest honour he atchieuen might;
> Still did he wake, and still did watch for dawning light.
>
> (v. 1)

The true meaning of the 'honour' the Redcross Knight seeks is exposed when he chooses to present his victory to Lucifera and to join the procession of the deadly sins from which earlier he had held aloof.

In Cantos i, ii, iv and v, then, Spenser depicts a moral fall, a surrender to sinful impulses, which is also and simultaneously an ecclesiastical apostasy, an abandonment of true religion and a choice of 'whoredom in the spirit' with Roman Catholicism.[15] The narrative method allows the reader to respond either to the first of these two meanings or to both at once – a peculiar feature of Spenserian allegory which does not so much demand that a 'literal level' should be 'translated' on to another plane, as offer the reader simultaneous meanings of which he can register one or more as he wishes. The narrator's tone, the expression of his attitude towards the sinning knight, deserves mention at this point, also. He combines a clear-sighted awareness of the Redcross Knight's faults with an affectionate sympathy which continues to label him 'that good knight' when his follies or vices are most obvious (ii. 29, iv. 37). The adjective 'heroicke' is first used to describe the traveller at the moment when he is surrendering to the charm of Duessa's flattering manners:

> She turning backe with ruefull countenaunce,
> Cride, Mercy mercy Sir vouchsafe to show
> On silly Dame, subiect to hard mischaunce,

And to your mighty will. Her humblesse low
In so ritch weedes and seeming glorious show,
Did much emmoue his stout heroicke heart.

(ii. 21)

The resulting tone is wry and ironic, but sympathetically ironic. Spenser has taken care to make the Redcross Knight into the representative erring man, subject to familiar sins in which every reader can imaginatively share. Hence the narrator's attitude is not censorious but full of fellow-feeling.

Interlaced with the adventures of the representative sinner are those of Una, contained in Cantos iii and vi. Una's meaning unfolds and expands throughout Book i, from the princess traditionally linked with St George but unexpectedly wearing a veil, and riding on an ass of humility and purity, through the Error episode where her grasp of religious doctrine emerges in her exhortation 'Add faith vnto your force', to our present concern, the opening of Canto iii, in which Spenser's imagery reveals her identity:

From her faire head her fillet she vndight,
And laid her stole aside. Her angels face
As the great eye of heauen shyned bright,
And made a sunshine in the shadie place;
Did neuer mortall eye behold such heauenly grace.

(iii. 4)

The truth-speaking woman of Canto i is evidently the apocalyptic Woman clothed with the Sun and hence an embodiment of the true church. In Cantos iii and vi Una suffers the characteristic fate of the true church, a period of 'exile' spent in the 'wildernesse'. The motif comes to Spenser from Revelation 12.6, which commentators took to refer either to one particular exile suffered by the little flock of true believers, or to a recurrent predicament of the faithful from the biblical era right up to the sixteenth century. Bale, for one, assumed that a recurrent phenomenon was foreshadowed, claiming that 'evermore, when dangerous persecution is', the members of Christ's congregation have authority to flee into the 'wilderness' or the 'desert'.[16] Hence the two cantos may contain an allegorical representation of particular events in the history of the church, or they may suggest recurrent sufferings in the life of the congregation. I incline to think that the latter interpretation is the correct one, for reasons which will emerge as we go on.

Our first concern, as always in *The Faerie Queene*, is with the romance fiction itself. Words and images will gradually suggest what additional meanings we should take into account. Una, the forsaken princess wandering in the 'woods and wastnesse', receives the attentions of animals, remote cottage-dwellers, and lawless travellers appropriate to these uncultivated regions. That a lion should pay homage to an innocent virgin is a literary motif the reader might anticipate, although here it gains poignancy from the contrast between the animal's devotion and the Redcross Knight's infidelity towards her. But as the episode unfolds, the insistent references to the 'lordly' and 'kingly' qualities of the beast signal the presence of an allegorical dimension in which the lion represents royal power acknowledging and serving true religion. The interpretation is confirmed when the lion, acting on Una's behalf ('From her faire eyes he tooke commaundement'), intervenes to punish the abuses practised by Abessa and her lover Kirkrapine. Sister Mary Falls rightly showed in 1953 that the scene is concerned not with abbesses and monasticism but with the diversion of church funds away from the needs of parishes into the pockets of absentee clergy who are personified in Abessa, absenteeism.[17] To add a relevant passage to those already provided by Sister Mary Falls, I will quote from a sermon published in 1581:

Liuinges are not geuen, they are solde as common as oysters at Byllinges-gate...this is the cause why doltes, ignorant Asses, idle, and idole Shepheardes haue the liuinges. I call them Idols: I wil proue it. They haue eyes and see not, eares and heare not, handes and minister not, tongues and speake not: I was about to say, they haue mouthes and eate not, but then I shoulde haue slaundered them: In this I confesse they are not Idols. A good scholer, and an honest godlie minister, will rather beg, then buy your liuinges, O yee robbe Churches, whose portion shalbe fire and brimstone too drinke: for you are the causes, why many thousands of soules haue perished.[18]

Idle, non-resident clergy are indifferent to the needs of their congregations: 'they haue eyes and see not, eares and heare not, handes and minister not, tongues and speake not'. Nothing could explain more clearly why Abessa, absenteeism, is presented by Spenser as both deaf and mute: 'She could not heare, nor speake, nor vnderstand.' Non-resident clergy, Bisse declares, in effect 'robbe Churches' by absorbing ecclesiastical wealth for their own use while leaving souls to perish. Spenser presents a deaf, indifferent absenteeism which has never seen the face of the true church (iii. 11) and which is the product of spiritual blindness, Corceca. Such absenteeism might almost be pathetic were it not for its corrupt relationship with church robbery: the non-resident grows fat on money stolen from the congregation. Kirkrapine brings his booty to Abessa:

> With whom he whoredome vsd, that few did know,
> And fed her fat with feast of offerings,
> And plentie, which in all the land did grow.

(iii. 18)

The gross images tellingly reflect on the evil conduct. By a grim pun the 'offerings' which Kirkrapine makes to his mistress were originally the offerings of devoted parishioners to the church. Church robbery could only be punished by royal authority, and Spenser enforces the point when he shows the lion holding Kirkrapine 'vnder his Lordly foot' before destroying him. Since the abuse was common before the Reformation, after the Reformation, and in Spenser's own decades as Bisse's sermon shows, the episode probably constitutes an image of a frequently occurring problem and its potential solution rather than of a specific occasion.

Canto iii contains three sections, in the first of which the true church is seen in a corrective role, while in the second and third she is subjected to the characteristic assaults of her enemies. The subtle Archimago attempts to deceive her under a new disguise, after which the pagan Sansloy attempts to rape her with brutish violence. Interestingly, Canto vi is constructed in the same way: in her dealings with the satyrs and Satyrane Una is seen in a teaching role, but in the second half of the canto she is once more deceived by Archimago, now in the disguise of a pilgrim, and caused to flee by the ferocity of Sansloy. In both the cantos which portray Una's adventures Spenser seems to envisage certain characteristic tasks and recurrent dangers for the Woman clothed with the Sun.

Una's encounter with the satyrs has called forth at least one very precise historical interpretation which we can perhaps test against the facts of the poem. Frank Kermode supports the view first put forward by Upton: 'The rescue of Una from Sansloy by satyrs, as Upton noticed, means the succour of Christianity by primitivist movements such as the Waldensian and Albigensian.'[19] The question is whether the poet's presentation of the satyrs does or does not suggest a community of Christian believers, however primitive.

Satyrs for Spenser can carry various connotations, depending on the context and the theme to be explored, as the satyrs whom Hellenore joins so contentedly in Book III, Canto x, illustrate. In the present case the 'Faunes and Satyres' function first of all as a delightful example of the unexpected ways in which Eternal Providence can come to the rescue of a lady in distress, and secondly demonstrate the characteristic response of savage people to religion. Rude and ungainly though they are, with their 'rough hornes' and 'backward bent knees', the satyrs recognise in Una something which deserves worship. They possess a religious instinct, but all too soon it passes over into idolatry. Calvin in his chapter on natural religion had remarked on the universality of a belief in some kind of God, even amongst the most savage people, although it might often manifest itself in idolatry:

But (as the heathen man saith) there is no nation so barbarous, no kind of people so sauage, in whom resteth not this persuasion that there is a God. And euen they that in other parts of their lyfe, seme very litle to differ from brute beastes, yet do continually kepe a certain sede of religion... Yea and ydolatrie it selfe is a substanciall profe of the persuasion. For we know how vnwillingly man abaseth himself to honour other creatures aboue hymselfe. Therfore when he had rather worshyp a blocke and a stone, than he would be thought to haue no god: it appeareth that this imprynted persuasion of God is of most great force, which is so impossible to be raced out of the minde of man, that it is much more easie to haue the affection of nature broken: as in deede it is broken, when man from his own natural swellyng pride of his own wyl stoupeth down euen to the basest creatures, to honour God.[20]

The words provide not a source but a relevant backcloth to Spenser's episode. The 'saluage nation' (vi. 11) with their 'barbarous truth' (vi. 12) have a strong impulse to worship ('The woodborne people fall before her flat / And worship her as Goddesse of the wood'); but since they are baffled by revealed religion, the 'trew sacred lore' (vi. 30) which Una teaches them, they stoop instead to worshipping even the basest creature, her ass. Spenser's rendering of the subject is genial and tolerant, but he is fully aware of the satyrs' limitations:

> Glad of such lucke, the luckelesse lucky maid,
>   Did her content to please their feeble eyes,
>   And long time with that saluage people staid,
>   To gather breath in many miseries.
>   During which time her gentle wit she plyes,
>   To teach them truth, which worshipt her in vaine,

And made her th'Image of Idolatryes;
But when their bootlesse zeale she did restraine
From her own worship, they her Asse would worship fayn.

(vi. 19)

In contrast to the satyrs, Sir Satyrane, whose parentage and training
give him higher potential, is capable of responding to Una's religious
instruction:

Thenceforth he kept her goodly company,
And learnd her discipline of faith and veritie.

(vi. 31)

The fictional vehicle richly expresses the theme of the relationship
between natural religion, revealed religion, and idolatry. What the
satyrs do not in any way suggest are the Christian communities of
the Waldensians and the Albigensians. Spenser even at his most
difficult gives hints through key words and images of the areas of
meaning with which he is concerned. In the present case he explores
the question of what may happen when Christianity is preached to
a 'saluage nation'. Once again, we are faced with an episode which
depicts a characteristic experience of the true church rather than a
particular historical moment.

It is just possible that Canto viii, the narrative and thematic centre
of the whole book, constitutes an exception to the general procedure
for which we have argued. Some words and images in it do seem
to point to a great historical event; but even if this is the case such
a reading must be subordinate to the first interest of the poem, that
is to say the romance fiction and the adventures of an individual
knight or lady. Book I is chiefly concerned with the attainment of
a 'true' holiness by the Redcross Knight, which paradoxically means
a discovery of his own sinfulness and of his dependence on divine
grace for personal transformation. In Canto vii the knight who at
the start of the book so confidently expected to perform heroic deeds
but lacked the self-knowledge which would warn him of his own
proneness to sin, and who since then has grown ever more subject
to his own corrupt impulses, sinks finally into total bondage. Sloth
is added to lust as he lies down without his armour and drinks from
the fountain of the nymph who resembles himself in her wish 'to
rest in middest of the race'. The dungeon of Orgoglio is the
necessary destination of a knight who is in several senses 'disgrast,
and inwardly dismayde'.

In the opening stanza of Canto viii the narrator meditates on human readiness to fall into sin, while he also introduces the theme of deliverance by heavenly grace:

> Ay me, how many perils doe enfold
>   The righteous man, to make him daily fall?
>   Were not, that heauenly grace doth him vphold,
>   And stedfast truth acquite him out of all.
>   Her loue is firme, her care continuall,
>   So oft as he through his owne foolish pride,
>   Or weaknesse is to sinfull bands made thrall:
>   Else should this *Redcrosse* knight in bands haue dyde,
> For whose deliuerance she this Prince doth thither guide.
>
> (viii. 1)

The tone combines deep sympathy for the plight of the average man with a sober confidence in the divine power which is ready to intervene on man's behalf. This does not mean that Arthur, the future British king and, of course, a 'mortall wight' (viii. 18) becomes Christ during the canto. He acts as an agent of heavenly grace without ceasing to be himself. The point is enforced when we witness the collapse of the human champion at the very moment that his shield, uncovered 'by chaunce', releases a light of astonishing brilliance:

> The stroke vpon his shield so heauie lites,
>   That to the ground it doubleth him full low:
> What mortall wight could euer beare so monstrous blow?
>
> And in his fall his shield, that couered was,
>   Did loose his vele by chaunce, and open flew:
>   The light whereof, that heauens light did pas,
>   Such blazing brightnesse through the aier threw,
>   That eye mote not the same endure to vew.
>
> (viii. 18–19)

The spectator registers both the brightness and the energy (the shield 'open flew') of this phenomenon; moreover, by means of Spenser's characteristic accumulation of pregnant words and images, the reader grows increasingly aware that the physical light is also a spiritual one.[21] In the lines quoted above the brilliant emanation from the shield surpasses 'heauens light'; in the following stanza the beast is amazed 'at flashing beames of that sunshiny shield', so that a link is established with the sunshine of Una's face in the wilderness; and in the next stanza the spiritual intimations are confirmed by the allusion in the simile to 'th'Almighties lightning brond'. Orgoglio foresees his end

> In that bright shield, and all their forces spend
> Themselues in vaine: for since that glauncing sight,
> He hath no powre to hurt, nor to defend;
> As where th'Almighties lightning brond does light,
> It dimmes the dazed eyen, and daunts the senses quight.
>
> (viii. 21)

Arthur's rescue of the Redcross Knight from prison forms a magnificent romance episode while also reverberating with spiritual meaning. When he hears the laments of the miserable voice within, the prince tears down the door with heroic fury; his foot feels giddily for the floor and finds none:

> Where entred in, his foot could find no flore,
> But all a deepe descent, as darke as hell,
> That breathed euer forth a filthie banefull smell.
>
> (viii. 39)

The way leads down into a literal prison which, the simile indicates, is also a psychological hell: the stench from it is both physically 'filthie' and spiritually 'banefull'. In Spenserian allegory, as we have already noted, it is not so much a matter of 'translating' from one 'level' to the other, as of a narrative whose suggestions progressively expand to encompass both realms, the physical *and* the moral or spiritual. The prisoner's bodily weakness is described in a style of unassuming realism: 'His bare thin cheekes for want of better bits...Could make a stony hart his hap to rew', but the simile at the end of stanza 41 implies that he has lost not only his physical but also his spiritual beauty: 'all his flesh shronk vp like withered flowres'. The wretched man needs food (viii. 43); and he also needs to master the spiritual lesson of his imprisonment (viii. 45).

The central theme of the episode is the central theme of sixteenth-century Protestantism – the radical dependence of the individual on unmerited grace for his conversion or justification. This intervention of free grace in the life of a sinner was taken to be the most important event of his spiritual history. Lost in sin, he could not make any effort or any preparation for renewal. As William Tyndale had put it in the earliest years of the Reformation, describing his own experience,

well I wot, I neuer deserued it, nor prepared my self vnto it, but ranne an other way cleane contrary in my blyndnesse, and sought not that way, but he sought me, and found me out, and shewed it me, and therwith drew me to him.[22]

Hence the whole of Spenser's episode insists on the inability of the man 'to sinfull bands made thrall' to bring about his own release from Orgoglio's dungeon. 'Else should this *Redcrosse* knight in bands haue dyde' (viii. 1) if Prince Arthur had not 'found the meanes that Prisoner vp to reare' (viii. 40). Spenser dwells again on the theme of sin and grace in the uncompromising stanza that opens Canto x:

> What man is he, that boasts of fleshly might,
>   And vaine assurance of mortality,
>   Which all so soone, as it doth come to fight,
>   Against spirituall foes, yeelds by and by,
>   Or from the field most cowardly doth fly?
>   Ne let the man ascribe it to his skill,
>   That thorough grace hath gained victory.
>   If any strength we haue, it is to ill,
> But all the good is Gods, both power and eke will.
>
>   (x. 1)

The last two lines sum up the knight's predicament and at the same time express classic Protestant doctrine with regard to unregenerate man.

Subject to Orgoglio, the Redcross Knight is also subject to Duessa, a fact which reminds us that he is not only the slave of sin but also an apostate who has surrendered to false religion. A further dimension of meaning opens up when the reader notices the significant part played by Orgoglio in clothing false religion in 'purple pall' and placing the triple crown on her head. It is he who has mounted her on the Seven-headed Beast:

> From that day forth *Duessa* was his deare,
>   And highly honourd in his haughtie eye,
>   He gaue her gold and purple pall to weare,
>   And triple crowne set on her head full hye,
>   And her endowd with royall maiestye:

Then for to make her dreaded more of men,
And peoples harts with awfull terrour tye,
A monstrous beast ybred in filthy fen
He chose, which he had kept long time in darksome den.

(vii. 16)

The commentators on Revelation in the second half of the sixteenth century usually interpreted the Seven-headed Beast as Rome with her seven hills, and hence as the power of the Roman Empire which had been transferred to the Pope. Spenser's addition to the bible and the commentators is the figure of Orgoglio. Through his fiction the poet communicates his sense of the part played by monstrous human pride in the growth of ecclesiastical pomp and power since the time of the early church. He had made the same point in another way in the 'Maye' eclogue (117–25). Orgoglio represents both the pride of the individual Christian and the pride which has operated so damagingly in the history of the church. The manner of his death – his body vanishes, leaving only 'an emptie bladder' behind – confirms his identity, if this is necessary. Abraham Fleming's words on the subject of pride in a moral treatise of the 1580s sufficiently illustrate the traditional vocabulary. He exhorted the Christian reader to 'spue out all swelling loftines, which puffeth vs vp like wind blowne into a bladder'.[23]

The task of wounding one of the heads of the Seven-headed Beast was bestowed by Spenser on Prince Arthur. The wounding was, of course, an apocalyptic motif (Revelation 13.3), and one which particularly interested the commentators. In the Geneva Bible a note declared that the wound referred to the death of Nero, who slew himself after persecuting the church. William Fulke, on the other hand, remarked that interpreters disagreed about the historical moment at which the wounding occurred, but he himself believed that Constantine the Great, in granting peace to the church, effectively wounded the Beast.[24] In *A Theatre for voluptuous Worldlings* van der Noodt saw the wound as a prophetic image of the present situation in Germany, England, France, Scotland, and Poland, where the Pope's bulls, pardons, purgatory and masses had suffered a considerable blow to their reputation:

Which thing is come to passe since the time of Iohn Hus in *Boheme*, and after that in *Germanie*, and is since (God be praised) daily more and more, that the head of the Beast is wounded, in places where gods word is preached. As in

England, Fraunce, Scotland, Poland, and else where, as euery one may wel perceiue, except he will needes be blinde. For it is euident to al men, that in most places, Buls and Pardones of the Pope are little set by, hys power and might troden vnder feete, hys name blotted out, his Purgatory, Masses, Pilgrimages, Idols, and other like trumperies, cried out vpon. If this be not a deadly wound on the head of the beast, I think it to haue none at all. If this be not a manifest token of his fall to come, there is none to be looked for.[25]

Spenser's use of the British prince in this context – Arthur 'stroke one of those deformed heads so sore, / That of his puissance proud ensample made' (viii. 16) – has important imaginative consequences: it necessarily suggests that British monarchs have played a major part in fulfilling the biblical prophecy by their actions against the power of Rome. Where van der Noodt refers to several nations in which reformation is on the way, Spenser celebrates the achievements of British monarchs in particular, whether Henry VIII, Edward VI, Elizabeth I, or all three. The royal descendants of Arthur have wounded the head of the Beast in England itself.

Details of the Beast's activities in the poem reinforce my feeling that here, in Canto viii, Spenser is concerned not only with general or recurrent activities of Antichrist but with a specific historical moment. The Protestant commentaries drew attention to the Beast's persecution of faithful Christians in the days of the Roman Empire and again in the days of the Pope. Spenser's handling of the subject indicates how very recently these ecclesiastical murders have taken place. The Seven-headed Beast is 'bloudie mouthed with late cruell feast' (viii. 6) and 'swolne with bloud of late' (viii. 12). The allusion seems to be to persecutions fresh in the reader's memory and ended by a British monarch, as Elizabeth I had ended the Marian persecutions. The full horror of these recent events is realised in the poem when Arthur searches the castle and finds evidence of what has been going on within while Orgoglio, Duessa and the Beast have been dwelling there. The juxtaposition of walls arrayed with gold and a floor defiled with 'bloud of guiltlesse babes' is sufficiently poignant whether the episode is read historically or not; but the images have an even greater power to move when they are apprehended as referring to real and recent happenings. The narrator's intense involvement is audible in his appalled comments, and especially in the final line:

There all within full rich arayd he found,
  With royall arras and resplendent gold.
  And did with store of euery thing abound,
  That greatest Princes presence might behold.
  But all the floore (too filthy to be told)
  With bloud of guiltlesse babes, and innocents trew,
  Which there were slaine, as sheepe out of the fold,
  Defiled was, that dreadfull was to vew,
And sacred ashes ouer it was strowed new.

And there beside of marble stone was built
  An Altare, caru'd with cunning imagery,
  On which true Christians bloud was often spilt,
  And holy Martyrs often doen to dye,
  With cruell malice and strong tyranny:
  Whose blessed sprites from vnderneath the stone
  To God for vengeance cryde continually,
  And with great griefe were often heard to grone,
That hardest heart would bleede, to heare their piteous mone.

(viii. 35–6)

The apocalyptic image of the souls under the altar (Revelation
6.9–10) has been absorbed into the description: 'I sawe vnder the
altar the soules of them, that were killed for the worde of God, and
for the testimonie whiche they mainteined. And they cryed with
a lowde voyce saying How long, Lorde, holie and true! doest not
thou iudge and auenge our blood on them that dwell on the earth?'
A British prince discovers and terminates this slaughter of innocents.

    Arthur's final act in Canto viii is the stripping of borrowed robes
from Duessa. The account of the event derives from the prophecy
in Revelation 17.16 that the Whore of Babylon will become desolate
and naked, and from the exposure of Alcina in *Orlando Furioso*,
Canto vii. I think Spenser's vision has also been influenced by the
commentators on Revelation, who expounded the verse as a
prophecy of the time when the Roman Catholic church would be
deprived of her possessions. William Fulke had written:

And they which before committed fornication withe the Churche of Rome
and her abhominable religion, after that the light of the gospell is spronge
vp, they shal clearely see and perceiue her deformitie, they will hate her with
deadly hatred. So that she which before was inuironed and garded with so
greate a bande of her louers, shall be forsaken of all and shall remaine desolate
and solitary, then whiche nothinge can happen more greuous or sorowfull
to a harlot. For kinges shall bothe withdrawe themselues, and also the people

of there dominions, from her most abominable company. And also they shall spoyle her of hir riches, substance, ornamentes, faier buildinges, large possessions, and all the rest of her goodes, and shall driue her naked forth of the dores.[26]

Spenser ensures that the Redcross Knight, Duessa's former lover, as well as Prince Arthur is present at the stripping, to 'perceiue her deformitie' as Fulke had put it: 'Which when the knights beheld, amazd they were, / And wondred at so fowle deformed wight' (viii. 49). The false church is 'despoild' of her rich 'ornaments':

> that witch they disaraid,
> And robd of royall robes, and purple pall,
> And ornaments that richly were displaid;
> Ne spared they to strip her naked all.
> Then when they had despoild her tire and call,
> Such as she was, their eyes might her behold,
> That her misshaped parts did them appall,
> A loathly, wrinckled hag, ill fauoured, old,
> Whose secret filth good manners biddeth not be told.
>
> (viii. 46)

It would be possible to read the stanza as a vision of some future shaming of false religion, but since the act is carried out by a British prince I think Spenser is alluding to the dispossession of the Roman Catholic church in England by Tudor monarchs. Una's temperate proposal that the witch, having been disrobed, should not be slain but allowed to flee, may well be a Spenserian compliment to the mercy of Elizabeth I.

During Canto viii the Redcross Knight has simultaneously represented the individual sinner rescued by heavenly grace, the unfaithful man brought back from spiritual whoredom, and probably, if our suspicion that the canto contains a series of historical allusions is correct, the English nation released from captivity to the Church of Rome by Spenser's own monarch. The canto is certainly, by any standards, the turning point of the entire book, and contains events which may have one or many meanings. It would not be unfitting if Spenser had chosen this central episode as an opportunity to celebrate the historical Reformation achieved in his own country by Tudor princes.

In the remaining cantos of Book I we return to the moral and spiritual progress of the individual knight who has been rescued from prison but has yet to acknowledge the seriousness of his sins.

Repentance is essential, but Despair is dangerous; and the knight finds himself – partly because he still lacks wariness – at the cave of the latter. Despair takes a hold on his mind by gradual stages. At first he talks in terms of a secular justice which assigns what is 'due' to offenders, then of death as a desired escape from life, and the Redcross Knight remains unmoved except by surprise at the speaker's rhetorical skill (ix. 41); but when Despair begins to engage with theological concepts, including that of the will of God (although he gives it the pagan name of 'strong necessitie'), 'sin', and 'the day of wrath', emotional pressure on the listener increases. The theological argument reaches a climax with a powerful invocation of divine law:

> Is not he iust, that all this doth behold
> From highest heauen, and beares an equall eye?
> Shall he thy sins vp in his knowledge fold,
> And guiltie be of thine impietie?
> Is not his law, Let euery sinner die:
> Die shall all flesh? what then must needs be donne,
> Is it not better to doe willinglie,
> Then linger, till the glasse be all out ronne?
> Death is the end of woes: die soone, O faeries sonne.
>
> (ix. 47)

The rhythmic intensity of the repetitions, 'Is not he iust...', 'Is not his law...', the resonant scriptural echoes, move the feelings of both knight and reader:

> The knight was much enmoued with his speach,
> That as a swords point through his hart did perse,
> And in his conscience made a secret breach,
> Well knowing true all, that he did reherse.
>
> (ix. 48)

The knight needs the experience of repentance for his sins; at the same time the reader is aware that the argument has been subtly yet crucially distorted. The divine law certainly calls for the punishment of iniquity, but Despair supplies only one half of the relevant doctrine. The central Lutheran analysis of Christianity consisted in the proposition that it was made up of both Law and Gospel, both condemnation of sinners and forgiveness of sinners; hence Protestant writers urgently repeated the warning that 'the law and Gospell may neuer be separate', in Tyndale's words.[27] The grim speaker,

however, separates them, dwelling exclusively on the demands of
the Law, and the knight as a result moves quickly past repentance
to the adjacent but fatal condition of despair: 'nought but death
before his eyes he saw, / And euer burning wrath before him laid'.
It is Una, the possessor and at times the embodiment of truth, who
supplies the missing half of Christian doctrine, and preaches the
Gospel to a sinner in despair under the Law:

> Come, come away, fraile, feeble, fleshly wight,
>   Ne let vaine words bewitch thy manly hart,
>   Ne diuelish thoughts dismay thy constant spright.
>   In heauenly mercies hast thou not a part?
>   Why shouldst thou then despeire, that chosen art?
>   Where iustice growes, there grows eke greater grace,
>   The which doth quench the brond of hellish smart,
>   And that accurst hand-writing doth deface.
> Arise, Sir knight arise, and leaue this cursed place.
>
> (ix. 53)

Her brief but fervent reminders of heavenly 'mercies' and 'grace'
are uttered compassionately and yet with an appropriate note of
gentle reproof. The very precise theological instruction contained
in the episode is communicated in terms of the particular romance
relationship.

Spenser describes the dwelling to which Una takes the Redcross
Knight for spiritual recovery as 'an auntient house...Renowmd
throughout the world for sacred lore'. Its inhabitants certainly strike
the reader as personifications of a profoundly traditional kind,
including as they do the three Theological Virtues and, in a nearby
hospital, the seven Corporal Works of Mercy. This house of
instruction feels satisfyingly familiar. At the same time, the poet has
built into the narrative a large amount of distinctively Protestant
detail. The combination of old and new in the episode is of great
cultural interest, although it is probable that Spenser would not have
acknowledged such a distinction and would have felt the Protestant
material to be quite as ancient as the rest. Fidelia's chalice is the
well-established iconographical attribute of Faith, but the particular
way in which she expounds the contents of the bible depends upon
the Protestant conception of Law and Gospel discussed above. The
preacher kills the heart with the rigorous judgments of the Law, then

consoles it with the promises of the Gospel. The experience is given emotional power by the pronounced delay of the grammatical object, a delay which allows the poet to link the words 'kill' and 'raise againe to life' with the maximum closeness:

> For she was able, with her words to kill,
> And raise againe to life the hart, that she did thrill.

> (x. 19)

The knight's conscience, however, remains deeply troubled by the memory of his sins; and Spenser embarks on a theme of great concern to Elizabethan Protestant, or more particularly Puritan, writers, that of the guilt-ridden mind and its appropriate treatment. It seems that a wounded conscience was quite a widespread phenomenon in Puritan circles, a fact to which the poet refers when he points out that Coelia was 'well acquainted with that commune plight, / Which sinfull horror workes in wounded hart' (x. 23). The cure for the condition was regularly described in metaphors from surgery and medicine. Hence Coelia sends for a 'Leach' who has 'great insight' into the 'disease of grieued conscience'. Spenser's imaginative realisation of the theme is best understood against a background of the Puritan writings which defined it, well represented by a work by Richard Greenham, *A Most Sweete and assured Comfort for all those that are afflicted in Conscience*. Greenham, a preacher in Essex, was renowned in Puritan circles for his abilities as a physician of souls.[28] In the treatment of the conscience a vital point was that the consoling words of the Gospel should not be used until a true sense of sin had been attained, just as in surgery the wound had to be thoroughly probed before it was encouraged to heal:

it is farre safer before incarnatiue and healing Medicines, to vse corrosiue and mundifying waters, without which though some sores may seem to cloase and skin vp apace; yet they proue worse, and be rotten still at the coare; they haue aboue a thin skin, and vnderneath rotten flesh. In like manner, wee would cloake, we wold hide and couer our sinnes, as it were with a curtaine; but it is more sound Chirurgerie to pricke and pierce our Consciences with the burning yron of the law; and to cleanse the wound of the Soule by sharpe threatenings, least that skinne being pulled ouer the Conscience for a while, wee lament the rotten corruption, which remaines vncured vnderneath.[29]

At first the Spenserian 'Leach' attempts the too-rapid cure described by Greenham, but then, realising his mistake, resolves to apply the

'corrosiues' which are essential to the complete cleansing of the
diseased soul. The physician

> comming to that soule-diseased knight,
> Could hardly him intreat, to tell his griefe:
> Which knowne, and all that noyd his heauie spright
> Well searcht, eftsoones he gan apply reliefe
> Of salues and med'cines, which had passing priefe,
> And thereto added words of wondrous might:
> By which to ease he him recured briefe,
> And much asswag'd the passion of his plight,
> That he his paine endur'd, as seeming now more light.

> But yet the cause and root of all his ill,
> Inward corruption, and infected sin,
> Not purg'd nor heald, behind remained still,
> And festring sore did rankle yet within,
> Close creeping twixt the marrow and the skin.
> Which to extirpe, he laid him priuily
> Downe in a darkesome lowly place farre in,
> Whereas he meant his corrosiues to apply,
> And with streight diet tame his stubborne malady.

(x. 24–5)

The following stanzas describe the necessary spiritual surgery. Even
in the Protestant treatises the imagery possesses a disturbing quality;
Spenser heightens it with adjective or verb which compels the
reader to participate in the experience of the suffering knight. In the
treatises one meets the phrase 'the burning yron of the law', but
in the poem the senses flinch at the mention of 'pincers firie whot'
which 'pluck' away superfluous flesh:

> And euer as superfluous flesh did rot
> *Amendment* readie still at hand did wayt,
> To pluck it out with pincers firie whot,
> That soone in him was left no one corrupted iot.

(x. 26)

In the treatises the Law pricks the conscience; but the verb 'pricke'
acquires a needle-like sharpness when it is joined with 'nip', the two
actions producing tiny drops of blood which spring as though from
a fountain:

> And sharpe *Remorse* his hart did pricke and nip,
> That drops of bloud thence like a well did play.

(x. 27)

The reader's sympathetic involvement is reflected in the poem by Una's, and then calmed into acceptance through the example of her patience.[30] Finally the completeness of the cure is imaginatively realised by the rapid shift of focus to Charissa and her babies, the knight's 'darkesome' bed giving way to her 'fruitfull nest', his physical and spiritual anguish to her physical and spiritual happiness:

> A multitude of babes about her hong,
> Playing their sports, that ioyd her to behold.

(x. 31)

After a true repentance which frees the sufferer from 'that disease of grieued conscience', the Redcross Knight is ready to receive instruction in the new life of virtuous actions which inevitably follows it. During the visit to the hospital of the seven Bead-men the reader may well be struck again, as in the sojourn at Coelia's house, by the profoundly traditional nature of the materials Spenser employs: the seven Corporal Works of Mercy are a patristic and mediaeval conception. Yet here too the materials have been given a Protestant stamp. Charles E. Mounts pointed out in 1939 that Spenser's seven Works are not the seven which had been enumerated by Aquinas and which had become traditional in the Roman Catholic church, but the seven originally listed by Lactantius and during the sixteenth century reiterated by the Swiss reformer, Heinrich Bullinger, chief pastor of Zurich, in his *Decades*. Mounts at the end of his article wondered why, in 'a canto marked so conspicuously by sympathetic reference to the paraphernalia of mediaeval Christianity', Spenser should have turned from the listing made by the scholastic Aquinas to the list composed by Lactantius which Spenser knew 'not perhaps in the Latin original, but almost certainly in the readily accessible Englished version of Bullinger's *Decades*'.[31] Our discussion of Canto x may have shown that such a mingling of traditional and Protestant materials is not in fact surprising but characteristic.

Book I as a whole depicts a process of spiritual descent and ascent; Canto x in little re-enacts that pattern with the knight's descent into his dark bed and his ascent, at last, of the Mount of Contemplation. His vision of the New Jerusalem is a high spot of his experience; and the poet takes the opportunity to claim a similar power of religious vision for poets, by means of the comparison with Mount

Parnassus, even while he modestly denies that his 'simple song' can describe that 'goodly Citie'. Much of the discussion between the Redcross Knight and the hermit Contemplation, which follows, is concerned with the respective merits of the heavenly and earthly cities. Cleopolis, the noble centre of earthly activity and essential stage on the journey to the New Jerusalem, is necessarily inferior to its heavenly counterpart. Even the most heroic earthly actions are tainted with imperfection, especially when viewed from a divine perspective. For this reason the hermit points to the inevitable human sins involved in acts of war, which may nevertheless be required by conditions on earth: 'For bloud can nought but sin, and wars but sorrowes yield' (x. 60). Spenser is alert to the opportunity for nice clashes of viewpoint in a dialogue between speakers dedicated to action and contemplation respectively. Although the tone of the conversation is serious there is room for a lightly comic disagreement or mutual misunderstanding on the subject of romantic love. The knight regrets that he will have to abandon 'Ladies loue...so dearely bought', whereupon the hermit sternly declares, sounding rather like Thenot, 'As for loose loues are vaine, and vanish into nought' (x. 62). Each has slightly misrepresented himself. St George's reference to 'Ladies loue' ambiguously suggests a series of courtly affairs rather than devotion to one woman, with the result that Contemplation for his part is provoked into a denunciation of all romantic love, when in fact he endorses the service of Una (x. 63) which has a romantic element in it. Spenser's gift for the pleasing juxtaposition of contrasted points of view – equally manifested in the discussion between Mammon and Guyon, or between Meliboe and Calidore – does not mean that his own standpoint is invisible, however. The hierarchical relationship between the earthly and heavenly cities, in which one constitutes the necessary way to the other, emerges sufficiently strongly from the dialogue.

From the vision, and the discovery of his full identity,[32] St George returns to the world of battles, as does Goffredo after the analogous episode in *Gerusalemme Liberata*, Book XIV. The knight who was wholly unready for his allotted task at the beginning of *The Faerie Queene* is now, through the work of grace, fit to undertake the destined role. Spenser, as we have seen, rewrote the St George legend in a most fundamental way by transforming the saint into a representative sinner; but when the dragon fight at last falls due, he makes sure that his account meets the requirements, narrative and iconographical, of the legend. The princess watches the battle at a convenient distance; further away her parents look on anxiously from the walls of their castle; the dragon belches flame and is eventually killed through the mouth, as in Carpaccio's and Crivelli's versions. The fiction is satisfyingly presented, while at the same time particular words and phrases suggest the larger meaning which is also Spenser's concern: that is to say, the Christian man now encounters the Devil his adversary. The dragon is 'that feend' (xi. 2), 'that huge feend' (xi. 3), whose jaws gape 'like the griesly mouth of hell' (xi. 12); the knight for his part is 'this man of God' wearing 'godly armes' (xi. 7). The Argument stanza alludes directly to Revelation 20.2 when it uses the phrase 'that old Dragon'. There is no doubt, therefore, that St George's dragon fight also represents a human being's spiritual combat with Satan; and Spenser gives the episode impressive physical impact and spiritual resonance.

The reader shares with the knight the experience of the daunting size of the beast as it looms above him ('Approching nigh, he reared high afore / His body monstrous, horrible, and vast') and of the choking fumes – an effect created by the insistent repetition of consonants – which pour from the creature's ominous mouth:

> A cloud of smoothering smoke and sulphur seare
> Out of his stinking gorge forth steemed still,
> That all the ayre about with smoke and stench did fill.
>
> (xi. 13)

When the wretched knight's body is scorched by his armour, made red-hot by a blast from the dragon, impassioned rhetorical figures involve the reader closely in his physical and mental state:

> Faint, wearie, sore, emboyled, grieued, brent
> With heat, toyle, wounds, armes, smart, and inward fire
> That neuer man such mischiefes did torment;
> Death better were, death did he oft desire,
> But death will neuer come, when needes require.
>
> (xi. 28)

'Death better were': for a moment we share St George's inmost thoughts. Heroic though he is, the knight remains vulnerably human.

The Well and the Tree which providentially refresh him during the combat possess vivid sensuous qualities in the literal world of the romance – 'a springing well, / From which fast trickled forth a siluer flood' and 'a goodly tree…Loaden with fruit and apples rosie red' – but in the characteristic Spenserian way they quickly show their spiritual significance in addition. Both images derive, it has long been recognised, from Revelation 22.1–2, and the Protestant commentaries throw some light on their meaning, I think. St George rises 'new-borne' from the 'well of life', his 'baptized hands' stronger than ever; yet the reader may be bothered by the thought that the knight must surely have been baptised long before this. Augustine Marlorat in his commentary on Revelation which was translated into English by Arthur Golding (the Elizabethan translator of Ovid) remarked that some interpreters took the 'riuer of water of life' in Revelation 22.1 to represent the sacrament of baptism, but that others 'more rightly' took it to represent Christ's doctrine:

There be whiche referre this ryuer to the Sacramente of Baptism…But more rightly do others vnderstand it to be the force of the doctrine of Chrysts spirit.[33]

Marlorat's hesitation as regards the biblical image may correspond with ours in relation to the poem. The Redcross Knight's immersion in the well of life resembles a baptism, but its meaning seems to be more inclusive. The well has the power to wash which belongs to baptism, but its healing properties seem to go beyond this and to reflect the power of Christ's doctrine:

> For vnto life the dead it could restore,
>   And guilt of sinfull crimes cleane wash away,
>   Those that with sicknesse were infected sore,
>   It could recure, and aged long decay
>   Renew, as one were borne that very day.

> (xi. 30)

Marlorat is in no doubt about the Tree of Life. It represents Christ himself in the midst of the 'whole congregation of the godly' to whom he gives 'euerlasting life':

That wood of lyfe then in the middes of the Citie (that is too wit, of the Church, which is Christs kingdom) is Christ himselfe the destroyer of death, who quickneth whom he listeth.[34]

He does not take the view that it symbolises the Eucharist, and nor does van der Noodt ('that moste pleasant tree of lyfe, namely Christ

Iesus')[35] and nor does Bale ('the most delectable tree of life, Jesus Christ').[36] It is interesting to find that Spenser's protagonist does not feed on the fruit of the tree but instead lies 'besmeard' with its 'pretious Balme' (xi. 50). The tree may indeed incorporate a eucharistic reference, since one of the ways in which Christ gives himself to believers is through the Holy Communion, but, as with the well, Spenser's vision seems to be more inclusive. The tree with its remarkable powers of healing and of actually raising the dead represents, I think, Christ himself, the destroyer of death:

> From that first tree forth flowd, as from a well,
> A trickling streame of Balme, most soueraine
> And daintie deare, which on the ground still fell,
> And ouerflowed all the fertill plaine,
> As it had deawed bene with timely raine:
> Life and long health that gratious ointment gaue,
> And deadly woundes could heale, and reare againe
> The senseless corse appointed for the graue.
> Into that same he fell: which did from death him saue.

(xi. 48)

The often-repeated view that the well and the tree represent the two major sacraments of the Church of England is, in my opinion, rather too schematic and too narrow for the effects created by the poem. Spenser's images are astonishingly abundant and unlimited in their life-giving properties. A reading which responds to them as Christ's doctrine and Christ himself seems truer to their unlimited resonance in the poetry and to sixteenth-century Protestant thought.

On the morning of the third day of the combat the knight, refreshed and renewed by Christ's aid, rises early and slays the dragon – imitating Christ his master who rose on the third day after his victory over sin and death. At once another controversial question presents itself: does the Redcross Knight on the final day of his battle *become* Christ himself? Rosemond Tuve was right, in my opinion, to resist this widely held view and to stress that the life of the true Christian is lived in imitation of Christ.[37] Through the action of the well and the tree Christ's grace supports the Redcross Knight (St Paul's formula at 1 Corinthians 15.10 is illuminating: 'I laboured more abundantly then they all: yet not I, but the grace of God whiche is with me'), but he remains a human being, as several pieces of evidence in the following canto show. For example, when Una's heavenly beauty is at last disclosed, the knight,

engagingly surprised, 'did wonder much at her celestiall sight: / Oft
had he seene her faire, but neuer so faire dight' (xii. 23). Even more
important, the final lines of Canto xi sum up his victory over the
dragon in terms which stress his human nature and his dependence
on God. Una drew near:

> Then God she praysd, and thankt her faithfull knight,
> That had atchieu'd so great a conquest by his might.
>
> (xi. 55)

The couplet first and foremost praises God for divine strength, but by
means of a delicately controlled ambiguity in the phrase 'by his
might' it also registers the fact that the Redcross Knight has made
his own contribution through his faithfulness, and through that
'goodwill' which is mentioned in II. i. 33 (see pp. 68–9 above).

In the concluding episode of the book Una's identity as true
religion and the true church receives its final 'showing'. The
betrothal scene depicts simultaneously the betrothal of St George
and the princess, the Christian man and true religion, and, very
probably, the English nation and the true church. In typical
Spenserian fashion the happiness of the occasion is both earthly and
spiritual. Song, mirth and feasting provide a firm basis to the
enjoyment, while in the midst of it all the sound of angels' voices
is heard (xii. 39). Equally Spenserian, though, is the recognition that
no victory is final, no conclusion conclusive. Each book of *The Faerie
Queene* ends with an indication that there is more to come, whether
further years of service to a monarch, a reunion not yet achieved,
a marriage not yet finalised, a chivalric and social feat overshadowed
by the knowledge that time will undo it. From one angle these are
useful narrative devices to draw the reader into subsequent books:
but more fundamentally they are symptoms of Spenser's deep sense
of process. Because there is no attaining perfection in this life, no
book of the poem ends with uncomplicated repose.

6

Books II–VI: From Virtue to Virtue

In presenting with creative zest as many aspects as he could encompass of human moral, emotional and social experience in Books II to VI of *The Faerie Queene*, Spenser drew on the full range of his eclectic reading. Pagan books and Protestant tracts both proved valuable to him, as did the Renaissance treatises on 'the Ethicke part of Morall Philosophie'. These latter works, of which Giovanni Battista Giraldi's or Pierre de la Primaudaye's will serve as examples, expounded the moral virtues with frequent and even-handed reference to Aristotle and Christ, Plato and St Augustine, Pythagoras, Democritus, Seneca, Cicero and St Ambrose. A late sixteenth-century poet who chose to 'fashion a gentleman or noble person in vertuous and gentle discipline' could turn if he wished to copious stores of ancient and modern thought on the subject.

The Renaissance ethical handbooks certainly made their contribution to *The Faerie Queene*. The division of Book II, for example, into two sections exploring the irascible and concupiscible passions respectively, with the opening of Canto VI acting as a watershed ('A Harder lesson, to learne Continence / In ioyous pleasure, then in grieuous paine'), relies on a distinction which goes back to the *Republic*, Book IX, and can be found in Giraldi's discussion, among others.[1] Similarly, the linking or pairing of virtues within particular episodes often follows a lead provided by the handbooks, as is the case when Guyon's special affinity with Shamefastness is discovered at the Castle of Alma. Spenser's witty rendering of the scene, in which the temperate knight talks politely to the lady beside him without realising either that she is a personification or that she is intimately connected with himself, is entirely the poet's own; but the conceptual linking of Temperance and Shamefastness depends on the ethical tradition. Pierre de la Primaudaye had written:

Neuerthelesse for the finishing of our dayes worke, I thinke we are to consider what shame and shamefastnes are, which, as the Philosophers say, are ioyned with this vertue of Temperance. For the more we loue glory and honor, the more we feare, and labor to eschew shame and dishonor. Now seeing we haue been taught where to seek for true glory and honor, we shal receiue no lesse profit, if we learne wherein we ought to feare shame and dishonor.[2]

Spenser's Shamefastness blushes repeatedly – because blushing was held to be an appropriate expression of true shamefastness in young people. De la Primaudaye had noted on the following page:

I looke for small goodnes of a yong man (saith Seneca) except of such a one as blusheth after he hath offended.

Our brief mention of Giraldi and de la Primaudaye might just as well have been a mention of Sir Thomas Elyot or Francesco Piccolomini,[3] since Spenser's debt to humanist writings on ethics is extensive. But this does not mean that *The Faerie Queene* either suddenly or gradually becomes a secular poem, concerned solely with a scheme of practical ethics which justifies itself on grounds of rationality or moderation alone. Reminders that the new life of virtue has a spiritual dimension recur throughout Books II to VI. Biblical allusions, for instance, do not cease after Book I, although they become less frequent. Artegall's first task in Book V is based on the Judgment of Solomon (to take a random example), while Phaedria's song at II. vi. 15–17 is a subtly distorted version of lines from the Sermon on the Mount. Prince Arthur despite a temporary mood of frustration knows that the children of day will ultimately reach the heavenly kingdom (III. iv. 59), and in making this affirmation he echoes 1 Thessalonians 5.5. The difference between the True and the False Florimell at Marinell's wedding is defined in terms of the Protestant doctrine of images. Artegall places the true woman beside the replica:

> Then did he set her by that snowy one
> Like the true saint beside the image set,
> Of both their beauties to make paragone,
> And triall, whether should the honor get.
>
> (v. iii. 24)

The True Florimell eclipses the False in the same way as the saint's living example eclipses the painted 'image', the material replica, the 'Idole', as False Florimell is called at IV. v. 15.

But above and beyond these sporadic biblical or doctrinal allusions, I shall argue in the present chapter that it is the 'vision cantos' which especially contain reminders both to the protagonists and the reader that the extended process of ethical development possesses a religious meaning. Both protagonists and reader can forget, immersed in the detail of romance adventures, that the moral virtues have a divine origin and a divine destiny. The virtues in the first instance are gifts from God (see, for example, III. v. 52, v. x. 1, VI Proem 3) although the individual by his or her own efforts can play a part in their increase. Moreover, the journey from virtue to virtue will ultimately lead to an eternal kingdom. The 'vision cantos', or more precisely, the 'cantos of instruction and vision', build up an inclusive image of the virtue with which a particular book is concerned, and in the course of this portrayal they offer the spectator a visionary glimpse of the spiritual realm which overarches the entire action.

The cantos to which I am referring are I. x,   II. ix,   IV. x,   v. ix and VI. x. Like every other writer on the subject I am indebted to C. S. Lewis's analysis of the poem's 'allegorical centres' or 'allegorical cores';[4] but it will be evident that the list I have given does not coincide with his. I do not include the Garden of Adonis (III. vi) or the Temple of Isis (v. vii) because there seems to be an advantage in treating as a group episodes which the poet himself has linked formally – each occurs late in the book's pattern, at Canto ix or x – and by his method of presentation – each provides a spectacle which is 'seen' by the protagonist of the book in question. Scudamour, it is true, is not the protagonist of Book IV, but Book IV has no single protagonist: its theme requires numerous representatives of friendship, brotherhood and love, amongst whom one has the role of describing the Temple of Venus to the rest.

In the light of the criteria just mentioned, Book III stands out as the anomalous case. In neither Canto ix or x does Britomart receive a 'showing' of the nature of the moral virtue which Book III explores. For the reader, Britomart's own rapt yet heroically disciplined behaviour in the House of Busyrane episode (III. xi–xii) provides the book's most arresting example of chaste love in action against one of its subtlest psychological opponents, but nowhere in Book III does the protagonist see an allegorical or mythical spectacle which displays the inner nature of her own virtue. The Garden of Adonis, we need perhaps to remind ourselves, is not concerned with a moral virtue but with a natural principle which operates throughout the organic world. Spenser here investigates, and embodies in a mythic garden, the process by which the physical world is constantly re-stocked, mutable creatures steadily replaced, through the endless re-imposition of form upon substance. The Garden is the seedbed or storehouse where forms wait to be impressed upon matter. Plants, fishes, birds, animals, human beings, all participate in the generative process, and for most of these groups their participation depends on the sexual instinct. Hence in the very 'middest' of the Garden Spenser portrays Venus and Adonis enjoying each other eternally, in an image which represents all sexual union. The poet has looked behind the human realm to the vast animal realm of which the human is in this respect a part; and by affirming that Amoret, human sexual or married love, was brought up in this Garden he provides a crucial reminder that married love has a place in a far wider natural context, and participates in the universal process of generation. The naturalness of the sexual instinct is strongly asserted in this philosophical but also at times vividly concrete episode. Nevertheless, biology and instinct are a beginning not an end; Spenser in this section of his poem is looking at natural origins, not at the use made of instinct in the complicated situations of human life, where base individuals characteristically misuse their erotic drive while 'braue sprites' channel it towards creative and virtuous action (III. v. 1).

Hence the Garden of Adonis is not analogous to the episodes I listed earlier either in its position within the book, its theme, or its mode of presentation. Instead we may note that the sixth or seventh cantos of books of *The Faerie Queene* often contain, as one would expect at the mid-point of a twelve-canto structure, particularly important material in relation to the unfolding narrative (the Redcross Knight's bondage at I. vii, Guyon's visit to the Cave of Mammon at II. vii, the Garden of Adonis at III. vi, Britomart's betrothal to Artegall at IV. vi, her sojourn in the Temple of Isis at V. vii, Timias's and Serena's cure at the Hermitage at VI. vi) without constituting that revelation of the nature of a book's moral virtue which is bestowed on the protagonist comparatively late in his or her quest. Book III does not possess a 'canto of instruction and vision' if a strict definition is maintained. In the present chapter I shall be considering these cantos in particular, and especially the possibility that one of their functions is to remind the protagonist and the reader that the moral virtues possess a divine as well as a secular meaning.

At the start of Book II the temperate knight lacks the self-mastery which is necessary for the fulfilment of his quest, the binding of Acrasia. Since he is neither a personification of Temperance nor a psychologically complex 'character', he is subject to just those normative tendencies to passion which the temperate or continent man must learn to bridle.[5] Deceived by Archimago he is briefly 'inflam'd with wrathfulnesse' (i. 25), and faced with the anguish of Amavia he feels an intense pity which for a moment causes him to exclaim against fortune and 'too cruell fate' (i. 56). In Canto iv the assault of Furor brings his heart temporarily to boiling point (iv. 9). But an increase of 'warie gouernaunce' during this canto and Canto v allows him to meet the frantic attack of Pyrochles with the necessary self-control ('*Guyon*, in the heat of all his strife, / Was warie wise', v. 9), and to refuse, subsequently, to be 'inflamed' by 'vaine occasions' (v. 21). He is ready, in fact, to move on to the exploration of other areas of experience, the concupiscible in place of the irascible passions. The first of these, the foolish and excessive mirth of Phaedria in Canto vi, possesses an initial appeal ('Sometimes she sung, as loud as larke in aire') which quite soon betrays its potential tediousness. Guyon feels the attraction of what Phaedria offers to the extent of entering her 'flit barke'; but his mastery of this impulse towards an idle and sensual frivolity is reflected by the way in which he successfully frees himself from his hostess without offending against courtesy.

At this point Spenser begins to complicate the sequence of episodes. The protagonist has certainly shown 'goodly maisteries' in relation to 'griefe and wrath' (vi. 1) and in his polite victory over Phaedria; but the opening stanzas of Canto vii introduce a note of fascinating equivocation. The simile of the expert pilot who has lost sight of the star by which he navigated applies aptly to Guyon who has acquired distinct expertise during his travels and yet has lost his guide, the Palmer. But what is not quite certain is whether the thought upon which the knight now chooses to rely in the absence of the Palmer is to be trusted:

> As Pilot well expert in perilous waue,
>   That to a stedfast starre his course hath bent,
> When foggy mistes, or cloudy tempests haue
>   The faithfull light of that faire lampe yblent,
> And couer'd heauen with hideous dreriment,

Vpon his card and compas firmes his eye,
  The maisters of his long experiment,
  And to them does the steddy helme apply,
Bidding his winged vessell fairely forward fly:
So *Guyon* hauing lost his trusty guide,
  Late left beyond that *Ydle lake*, proceedes
  Yet on his way, of none accompanide;
  And euermore himselfe with comfort feedes,
  Of his owne vertues, and prayse-worthy deedes.
  So long he yode, yet no aduenture found,
  Which fame of her shrill trompet worthy reedes:
  For still he traueild through wide wastfull ground,
That nought but desert wildernesse shew'd all around.

(vii. 1–2)

In the first stanza the narrator clearly approves of the pilot's use of
a compass when the North Star is obliterated by clouds; but in
the second stanza he makes no comment on the particular 'card and
compas' which Guyon has selected to assist his navigation, that is
to say, the thought of 'his owne vertues, and prayse-worthy deedes'.
The tone of approval grows fainter as the second stanza unfolds, and
the reader becomes uncertain whether a pilot whose 'winged vessell'
flies 'fairely forward' is adequately replaced by a traveller who feeds
himself with comfortable memories of his own virtuous achievements – a retrospective rather than a forward-looking activity.
Nothing is clear-cut as yet; the reader is just alerted to the possibility
that the morally successful Guyon may be in a new kind of danger.

The knight's state of mind at the time of his entry into Mammon's
Cave has become a famous crux in Spenser criticism. Does he show
an heroic, even Christ-like virtue in facing and overcoming
temptation – or is he to be regarded as in some way culpable?[6] In
his debate with the 'God of the world and worldlings' Guyon's grasp
of the ethically correct view of riches certainly remains secure. He
knows that regard for 'worldly mucke' is damaging to the spirit,
knows that riches are the cause of unquietness and bloodshed, and
understands that the basic needs of men are few. He gives expression
to much of the common wisdom, classical and Christian, on the
subject. But at the same time there is audible in his speech a note
of exuberant self-congulation:

Me ill besits, that in der-doing armes,
  And honours suit my vowed dayes do spend,
  Vnto thy bounteous baytes, and pleasing charmes,
  With which weake men thou witchest, to attend:

> Regard of worldly mucke doth fowly blend,
> And low abase the high heroicke spright,
> That ioyes for crownes and kingdomes to contend;
> Faire shields, gay steedes, bright armes be my delight:
> Those be the riches fit for an aduent'rous knight.
>
> (vii. 10)

He rightly rejects the offer of money, but he takes the opportunity to refer to his own 'high heroicke spright', and, indeed, in the exultation of the moment even speaks of contending for 'crownes' and 'kingdomes', a glamorous occupation not much connected with the task of binding Acrasia. He takes pleasure in the image of himself as 'an aduent'rous knight' whose 'bright' arms form a gratifying spectacle. Mammon at once identifies the impulse latent in his companion's words: 'Vaine glorious Elfe (said he)...' (vii. 11). Guyon's view of riches is sound; but Spenser hints that something is awry in his assessment of himself.

What Mammon proceeds to offer the knight is the experience of visiting a region which no human being has penetrated before, and which is beyond the reach of even heaven's gaze:

> Perdy (quoth he) yet neuer eye did vew,
> Ne toung did tell, ne hand these handled not,
> But safe I haue them kept in secret mew,
> From heauens sight, and powre of all which them pursew.
>
> What secret place (quoth he) can safely hold
> So huge a masse, and hide from heauens eye?
> Or where hast thou thy wonne, that so much gold
> Thou canst preserue from wrong and robbery?
> Come thou (quoth he) and see.
>
> (vii. 19–20)

The proposed adventure is a descent into the underworld, a literary topic regularly associated with grave danger and the possibility of no-return for human characters who attempt it. Aeneas undertakes such an adventure only after dutiful preparations (*Aeneid* vi. 156–263); the narrator–protagonist in Sackville's 'Induction' to the *Mirror for Magistrates* expresses horror and reluctance at Sorrow's invitation to him ('"Come, come," quod she, "and see what I shall show"') to follow her into the underworld:

> half distraught, unto the ground I fell,
> Besought return, and not to visit hell.
>
> (stanza 28)

The narrator of *The Faerie Queene*, describing the visit to the underworld made by Duessa and Night in I. v, explicitly refers to the extreme peril of the place for human beings:

> By that same hole an entrance darke and bace
> With smoake and sulphure hiding all the place,
> Descends to hell: there creature neuer past,
> That backe returned without heauenly grace.
>
> (I. v. 31)

But Guyon, for his part, enters a realm which no human being has ever previously explored, without a moment's self-questioning. Inside the Cave of Mammon he continues to show both a steady indifference to riches and considerable courage in the face of darkness, dead men's bones, and attendant fiends; but his speeches in reply to Mammon's temptations retain that note of self-satisfaction audible in the earlier debate:

> To them, that list, these base regardes I lend:
> But I in armes, and in atchieuements braue,
> Do rather choose my flitting houres to spend.
>
> (vii. 33)

The reader's response to Guyon's courage is qualified by the suspicion that he is remarkably pleased with his own moral and chivalric stature. Only in one speech does the knight refer to the fact of inherent human frailty — and the irony is that he does so merely in order to provide himself with an escape route from the offer of Philotime's hand in marriage:

> Gramercy *Mammon* (said the gentle knight)
> For so great grace and offred high estate;
> But I, that am fraile flesh and earthly wight,
> Vnworthy match for such immortall mate
> My selfe well wote, and mine vnequall fate.
>
> (vii. 50)

The self-deprecating words slip out easily to meet the emergency, without in fact modifying the high view of his own worth which Guyon had taken earlier in the episode. It is only at the end of the adventure that he will genuinely discover what it means to be 'fraile flesh and earthly wight'.

During his visit to the Garden of Proserpina[7] Guyon remains as free as before from intemperate desires, and as 'warie wise' (vii. 64) as he had been in dealing with Pyrochles and with Phaedria (vi. 26). But the serene self-confidence with which he embarked on this journey is found at last to have been misplaced. His catastrophic faint on returning to the upper air is irrefutable evidence of his condition as 'fraile flesh and earthly wight', a condition he had forgotten when he savoured the thought of 'his owne vertues', and boasted to Mammon about his 'high heroicke spright'. He now discovers what it means to possess an 'enfeebled spright' (vii. 66) rather than an heroic one. The adventure which was to have been worthy of fame's shrill trumpet ends much less gloriously:

> And now he has so long remained there,
>   That vitall powres gan wexe both weake and wan,
>   For want of food, and sleepe, which two vpbeare,
>   Like mightie pillours, this fraile life of man,
>   That none without the same enduren can.
>   For now three dayes of men were full outwrought,
>   Since he this hardie enterprize began:
>   For thy great *Mammon* fairely he besought,
> Into the world to guide him backe, as he him brought.
>
> The God, though loth, yet was constrained t'obay,
>   For lenger time, then that, no liuing wight
>   Below the earth, might suffred be to stay:
>   So backe againe, him brought to liuing light.
>   But all so soone as his enfeebled spright
>   Gan sucke this vitall aire into his brest,
>   As ouercome with too exceeding might,
>   The life did flit away out of her nest,
> And all his senses were with deadly fit opprest.
>
>   (vii. 65–6)

The adjective 'hardie' in the phrase with which the narrator sums up the episode, 'this hardie enterprize', is richly ambiguous: it means brave, but it also means foolhardy. Mammon had employed the word in the latter sense at the very beginning of their conversation when he named Guyon, 'Hardy Elfe':

> In great disdaine, he answerd; Hardy Elfe,
> That darest vew my direfull countenaunce,
> I read thee rash, and heedlesse of thy selfe.
>
>   (vii. 7)

The adjective recurs in the formula 'that hardy guest' (vii. 27) which places Guyon in relationship to the attendant fiend. Here both the knight's bravery and his rashness are registered. In the final occurrence of the word in this canto (stanza 65, quoted above) the narrator acknowledges a remarkable display of fortitude yet simultaneously judges the 'enterprize' to have been a foolhardy undertaking which derived from self-trust and forgetfulness of human frailty.

Elizabethan Protestant divines often warned their hearers or readers of a mental state similar to Guyon's during this episode. The regenerate man who begins to attain successive virtues may find himself in a new danger, that of a self-confident belief in his own strength which can variously be labelled vainglory, pride, self-trust, or presumption (in the special sense of presuming upon a man's own deserts – illustrated in some of the quotations below). Arthur Golding in a 1576 translation of a handbook on spiritual warfare explained that when the devil fails to overthrow a man with vices he labours instead to overcome him by the thought of 'his owne vertues':

To be shorte, whom he cannot catch with sweetenesse and delight, him he compasseth with the conceyte and wel lyking of his owne vertues.

Neither can wee hope for any victory against the Diuel by reason of the feeblenesse and infirmitie of our owne strength: vnlesse God helpe vs.

And whom he could not perchaunce driue to dispayre, him he stirreth vp to a certaine vngodly self-trust, and to a presuming vpon his own desertes.[8]

A famous biblical example of such self-trust was St Peter when he boasted to Christ of his unswerving loyalty:

The second braunch of Peters presumption, consisteth in this, that hee sayth: I am ready to goe with thee into prison and vnto death. Peter thought he was stronge inough to be a Martyr, when in deed he had scarce learned the principles of his faith, nor that which is moste necessary for all men to know: namely, his own power and hability, and how he must learne to stand before the Lord. Here you see Peter thinking him selfe a valiant souldier, and yet is not so, out of which we note the pride of mans hearte, and confidence that flesh and bloud conceiueth of himselfe.[9]

Christians should preserve a humility of spirit through 'the considera-tion of our estate by nature':

as namely the mettal wher of we be made. It is not onely earth, which we dayly treade vnder our feet, but euen the very dust and slime of the earth...

beholde then in [Peter] thy owne frailtie.[10]

The self-trusting man thinks himself a valiant soldier, forgetting his own frailty and the fact that he is made of earth. Guyon's state of mind is the same: pleased with his own virtues he ignores his true condition as 'fraile flesh and earthly wight', with the result that the humbling reality needs to be exposed in the final stanzas.

This reading of the Cave of Mammon episode obviously makes no claim for any resemblance between Guyon and Christ. I, for one, do not see the episode as based on the temptation of Christ at all. The scholarly effort to find Christ's three temptations in Mammon's Cave has proved rather inconclusive. One critic argues that the lust of the flesh is dealt with in the Phaedria episode, while the Cave of Mammon canto is concerned with wealth, honour and vain learning; two other critics find wealth, honour and physical hunger in the present episode, while another identifies wealth, honour and the lust of the flesh.[11] Christ's threefold temptation was all-inclusive, whereas Guyon's experience in Canto vii is narrower and more specific, I would argue. Since he is being tempted by the 'God of the world and worldlings' the revelations which Mammon makes to him are necessarily concerned with the true nature of worldliness, rather than ranging over the whole spectrum of temptation. Nor does the rescue of the knight by an angel at the end of the adventure seem to me to allude to the angelic ministrations received by Christ at the end of his ordeal in the wilderness and recorded by St Matthew in the words 'beholde the Angels came: and ministred vnto him' (Matthew 4.11). Spenser's language and tone at the opening of Canto viii point in a different direction, I think. It is not simply the fact that among the many verbs which the poet uses to define the activities of angels in relation to man ('serue to', 'succour', 'aide', 'fight', 'watch', 'ward') he surprisingly never echoes the verb 'minister'. More fundamentally, it is a matter of the narrator's mood and tone as he describes the angelic rescue. With extraordinary fervour he turns from the contemplation of Guyon's helpless body – 'And all his senses were with deadly fit opprest' – to the thought of divine care and divine love for undeserving man:

> And is there care in heauen? and is there loue
> In heauenly spirits to these creatures bace,
> That may compassion of their euils moue?
> There is: else much more wretched were the cace
> Of men, then beasts. But O th'exceeding grace

Of highest God, that loues his creatures so,
And all his workes with mercy doth embrace,
That blessed Angels, he sends to and fro,
To serue to wicked man, to serue his wicked foe.

(viii. 1)

The stress is on the miraculous fact of heavenly care for human beings
who are 'bace' and, indeed, 'wicked'. If the reader at the end of
Canto vii has been regarding Guyon as an example of heroic virtue
and of Christ-like ability to resist temptation, the change of attitude
required by this adjoining stanza is jarringly abrupt. It is true that
within the Christian worldview all men are sinners, and therefore
that even a triumphant hero needs divine aid; but for the narrator
to present Guyon's achievement as Christ-like in one stanza and then
to label him 'wicked' in the next would be gauche rather than
judicious. The intimate link between Cantos vii and viii is marked
by the unusual use of 'And' quoted above. If Guyon's very human
but culpable self-trust in the Cave of Mammon episode has been
imaginatively understood, his acute need for divine aid follows with
true poetic logic.

The words and phrases which Spenser employs in viii. 1 and 2
to describe the angelic aid bestowed on Guyon belong not to the
scriptural account of Christ's temptation but to the language of
Protestant divines when they spoke of the angels' defence of
Christian believers. A full discussion of the activities of angels is to
be found in *An Homely or Sermon of Good and Euill Angels* (1590)
translated from the Latin of the Lutheran theologian, Urbanus
Rhegius, by Richard Robinson, a vigorously Protestant citizen of
London to whom we shall refer again in Chapter 7. In the following
passage the characteristic vocabulary and imagery of Protestant
writing on angels make their appearance, together with the allusion
to Psalm 34.7 which was frequent in this context ('The Angell of
the Lord pitched rounde about them, that feare him, and deliuereth
them'):

Here we learne that Angels are Ambassadors and messengers sent from
heauen, euen from God vnto true beleeuers, to serue and to attend vppon
them, and in all assaies to bee present with them, to succour them, [and] helpe
them...Here are their hearts manifest known to vs, how sincere, how godly,
how welwilling and how ready they are to do vs good, yea how feruently
they loue vs, and how faithfuly they embrace vs.

O, that wee could see with corporall eies, with how firme and strong sauegard and succour of his Angels, God gardeth, preserueth, defendeth, and protecteth vs from all daungers...

So lykewise also with vs and rounde aboute vs, there are alwaies holie Angels, nightes and dayes protecting and keeping vs, least we shoulde be hurt by Sathan, and wicked men his members.

Which thinge, Dauid acknowledgeth in 34. Psal. with great thankfulnes, thus singing. The Angell of the Lorde pitcheth his tent, about them that feare him and deliuereth them.[12]

The angels' protection of Christian men is defined in the verbs 'serue', 'attend', 'succour', 'helpe', 'loue', 'embrace', 'protect' and 'keep'. Significantly, the whole passage is informed by a mood of intense gratitude for the divine love which sends angels to assist believers when they are in danger. Spenser draws on the same stock of verbs, and remembers the same quotation from Psalm 34 towards the end of his second stanza ('And their bright Squadrons round about vs plant'). This time I quote both stanzas:

> And is there care in heauen? and is there loue
>   In heauenly spirits to these creatures bace,
>   That may compassion of their euils moue?
>   There is: else much more wretched were the cace
>   Of men, then beasts. But O th'exceeding grace
>   Of highest God, that loues his creatures so,
>   And all his workes with mercy doth embrace,
>   That blessed Angels, he sends to and fro,
> To serue to wicked man, to serue his wicked foe.
>
> How oft do they, their siluer bowers leaue,
>   To come to succour vs, that succour want?
>   How oft do they with golden pineons, cleaue
>   The flitting skyes, like flying Pursuiuant,
>   Against foule feends to aide vs millitant?
>   They for vs fight, they watch and dewly ward,
>   And their bright Squadrons round about vs plant,
>   And all for loue, and nothing for reward:
> O why should heauenly God to men haue such regard?
>
> (viii. 1–2)

The poet's imagination is occupied not with the angels' ministration to Christ but with the remarkable fact of God's love for and protection of sinful men through the agency of heavenly spirits. The sermon idiom is heightened by the impassioned sequence of questions and exclamations, by the poignant juxtaposition of 'heauenly spirits' and 'creatures bace' in line 2, and by the sensuous glimpses of light and motion which transform the pitched tents of Psalm 34 into 'bright Squadrons', and endow the skies themselves with the 'flitting' character of the messengers.

Guyon, the self-trusting adventurer in need of rescue, is accurately described by the narrator as a 'wicked man'; but it is worth pausing a moment over the question of whether he is also described as God's 'wicked foe' (viii. 1, final line). The usual reading assumes that the two phrases 'To serue to wicked man' and 'to serue his wicked foe' stand in apposition. However, the verbs in the two halves of the line are differentiated in a way which may be important. When in stanza 8 the angel describes his own role (using again the language of the sermons and of Spenser's opening stanzas) he refers to Guyon's infernal enemy as 'his foe'. The Cupid-like visitant is addressing the Palmer:

> The charge, which God doth vnto me arret,
> Of his deare safetie, I to thee commend;
> Yet will I not forgoe, ne yet forget
> The care thereof my selfe vnto the end,
> But euermore him succour, and defend
> Against his foe and mine.
>
> (viii. 8)

The 'foe' of both God and man is of course the Devil. It seems to me probable that when Spenser employed the word 'foe' only seven stanzas previously he had the same meaning in mind. Angels 'serue to' (minister to) 'wicked man', but they 'serue' (serve as he deserves, punish) 'his wicked foe' – the wicked foe of both man and God, the Devil himself.

The progress of Guyon during the first six cantos of Book II was in the direction of increasing self-mastery. The Cave of Mammon episode, we have suggested, represents a disturbance in this moral progress, arising from the fault common among virtuous men of too great a liking for their own virtues. This mistaken self-trust may lead a human being into dangers from which only God's mercy can extricate him, mercy which in Guyon's case employs first an angel, then the Palmer, and then Prince Arthur to restore the knight to his interrupted journey. The insights into human nature implicit in the adventures of Cantos vii and viii are made explicit, and extended, in Canto ix: the Castle of Alma episode, as a canto of instruction and vision, reminds Guyon of fundamental facts about the human condition. The castle which he and Arthur come upon one evening – and which they only gradually understand to be an allegorical representation of the human body – is constantly under siege from passions and temptations which assail the five senses. This fact, easily neglected by the self-trusting man, cannot now be overlooked by the travellers. Nor can the fact that the human frame is composed of 'earth' and 'slime' (ix. 21), since this is the first point to which their attention is drawn when they begin their sight-seeing. Nevertheless, it is also a fact that there is no creation of God's which is 'more faire and excellent' than the human body when it is kept under wise government (ix. 1). The canto reveals both the permanent dangers to which human nature is subject and the potential beauty and worth of the body if it is rightly used.

Spenser's decision to portray the temperate body by means of an elaborately worked out analogy between the parts of a castle and the parts of the human frame was doubtless influenced by literary analogues (perhaps the sixth day of the first of du Bartas's Divine Weeks was the most important); but some engaging effects could be attained by the chosen method. While the reader's mind is occupied in identifying the sections of the face and body denoted by the castle images, a pleasure created both by the experience of recognition and by the writer's ingenuity accompanies the survey. Very familiar features are in this way made new, and a delight stirred by poetic invention is attached to the contemplation of what are otherwise extremely well-known facts. The poet's ingenuity often takes an amusing form, so that we read with a mixture of satisfaction and laughter. The talkative tongue is praised for the resonance of the sound it makes, but also teased by means of a compliment which is all too often undeserved:

> His larumbell might lowd and wide be hard,
> When cause requird, but neuer out of time.

> (ix. 25)

The marvels of human digestion are brought into view by images of cauldrons, cooks and ladles; in particular the neatness of the arrangement for the disposal of waste matter is celebrated by a pun which again causes a mixture of amusement and admiration: unserviceable material is conveyed by secret ways to the backgate, 'and throwne out priuily'. The overall effect of the poet's verbal inventiveness is to draw attention to God's supreme inventiveness in the creation of so adroit a system:

> Which goodly order, and great workmans skill
> Whenas those knights beheld, with rare delight,
> And gazing wonder they their minds did fill;
> For neuer had they seene so straunge a sight.
>
> (ix. 33)

The goodly order of the body reminds the two knightly visitors of the great workman, God; but it is not this fact alone which gives the canto its visionary aspect. It is, I think, in the description of Alma, who issues forth with graceful poise immediately after the disturbing portrayal of the 'troublous rout', that the poet chiefly reminds us of the reality of the spiritual world. Alma, the soul, is projected as a figure of extraordinary charm, whether or not the reader notices more specific allusions:

> *Alma* she called was, a virgin bright;
> That had not yet felt *Cupides* wanton rage,
> Yet was she woo'd of many a gentle knight,
> And many a Lord of noble parentage,
> That sought with her to lincke in marriage:
> For she was faire, as faire mote euer bee,
> And in the flowre now of her freshest age;
> Yet full of grace and goodly modestee,
> That euen heauen reioyced her sweete face to see.
>
> (ix. 18)

Spenser communicates a sense of the soul's beauty; but his conception of her predicament — that of a virgin approached by numerous suitors — and his description in the following stanza of her dress and crown are profoundly informed by biblical and homiletic tradition. Henry Smith had reminded his listeners that the human heart has many suitors, some indeed of distinguished parentage, but that it belongs nevertheless to God:

Thus doth man hang in a ballance, like a yong virgin which hath manie sutors: some she fancieth for parentage, some for personage, some for friends, some for wealth, some for wit, some for vertue...so the heart hath so many suters besides God.[13]

Spenser conceives the situation of the soul in similar terms. Alma belongs to God. Moreover the long white robe which she is wearing reveals that she is clothed in Christ's righteousness. Smith's sermon on 'The Wedding Garment' elaborates the familiar metaphor in a way which throws light on Spenser's poem:

wee must put on his Garment, that is, his righteousnesse, his merites, and his death...and much adoo wee haue to put it on, and when it is on, there is great cunning to weare it cleanly and comely from soyling and renting, that such a precious Garment bee not taken from vs againe.[14]

The preacher stresses the care with which the precious garment must be worn, an emphasis which clarifies the function of the two Damsels who carry Alma's train in Spenser's stanza:

> In robe of lilly white she was arayd,
>   That from her shoulder to her heele downe raught,
>   The traine whereof loose far behind her strayd,
>   Braunched with gold and pearle, most richly wrought,
>   And borne of two faire Damsels, which were taught
>   That seruice well. Her yellow golden heare
>   Was trimly wouen, and in tresses wrought,
>   Ne other tyre she on her head did weare,
> But crowned with a garland of sweete Rosiere.
>
> (ix. 19)

The poet remembers not only the homiletic expositions of the subject but goes back directly to the bible in the opening line of the stanza: 'In robe of lilly white she was arayd.' Among several passages which he may be echoing, Revelation 7.13 probably constitutes the primary source: 'And one of the Elders spake, saying vnto me, What are these which are araied in long white robes?' The reply comes that they are souls who have made their long robes white in the blood of the Lamb. Spenser's use of the biblical words 'robe', 'white' and 'arayd' establishes the particular allusion, while the remaining biblical adjective, 'long', is amplified in the following line, 'That from her shoulder to her heele downe raught'.

If Alma is clothed in Christ's righteousness, there is a strong possibility that the crown she wears belongs to the same cluster of ideas and images. If this 'faire' maiden appeared in some other context in the poem, the garland 'of sweete Rosiere' on her head would almost certainly link her with Venus (the usual interpretation at this point as Hamilton's edition shows), just as Colin's damsel, 'crownd with a rosie girlond' (VI. x. 14), is as it were a second Venus. But with Spenser context is all. In the tradition of 'clothing the soul',

Christ becomes not only a garment but, as Henry Smith put it, 'an eternall crowne of beautie to their heades'.[15] For those who are clothed in Christ, 'there shall be no neede of Wyres, nor curles, nor perriwigs'.[16] The biblical character of the present stanza prompts me to argue that the crown of 'sweete Rosiere' worn by Alma is biblical too. Chief among biblical roses was the rose of Sharon, regularly interpreted by sixteenth-century Protestants as a metaphor for Christ, as Thomas Wilcox's commentary of 1585 demonstrates:

I am the rose of Sharon.) I take these to be the wordes of the spouse, commending him selfe, for his moste excellent sweete vertue... So that when Christ resembleth him selfe to the rose of *Sharon*, hee meaneth nothing els, but that he was well coloured, fruitful and of verye good sauor, able inough thorow his sweetnesse, and the aboundance of his giftes and graces, to allure and drawe his Churche to him selfe.[17]

In the Geneva Bible the phrase used by the translator for the verse in question (Song of Solomon 2.1) was 'the rose of the field': 'I am the rose of the field, (and) the lilie of the valleis.' Although modern scholarship indicates that the relevant flower was not in fact a rose at all but perhaps a crocus or narcissus, sixteenth-century readers took the plant to be a rose in the familiar sense, and the formula employed in the Geneva Bible suggests that they envisaged a *wild* rose. Spenser's choice of the word 'Rosiere' may be worth pondering in this connection. *The Oxford English Dictionary* gives its meaning as 'a rose-tree, rose-bush', but since the word was a sixteenth-century borrowing from French a glance at a Renaissance French dictionary will not come amiss. Randle Cotgrave in his *A Dictionarie of the French and English Tongues* (London, 1611) defined 'Rosier: m' as 'A Rose-tree, Rose-bush, Rose-brier'. The rose-brier was a wild rose, which could often possess an exceedingly sweet smell. Alma, crowned with a garland of 'sweete Rosiere', is crowned, I think, with wild roses; symbolically she is crowned with Christ and his 'moste excellent sweete vertue'.

Guyon, then, receives a vision of the Christian soul, dedicated to God despite external pressures, clothed and crowned in the merits of the Redeemer, and also of the temperate body which in its order and beauty is recognised as a supreme work of the greatest workman. The vision is a reminder to the moral knight that he depends on and belongs to his Creator. When he rises the next morning to continue his journey, it is with a freshness and vigour which the reader experiences as though it were the direct result of the vision ('Early before the Morne...Vprose Sir *Guyon*, in bright armour clad'). Meanwhile, Arthur's battle with Maleger further extends our understanding of the plight of body and soul assailed by 'strong affections' under the captaincy of the pale villain whose name means 'evil' and 'sick'. It is probably a mistake to regard Maleger as an embodiment of original sin itself, as A. S. P. Woodhouse suggested; rather, the grimly persistent enemy represents that continuing 'infection of nature' which survives in believers after baptism, and to which Article ix of the Thirty-nine Articles refers: 'this infection of nature doth remain, yea in them that are regenerated',[18] as, of course, Alma is. For this reason the 'standing lake' into which Arthur throws Maleger's 'carrion corse' in stanza 46 cannot represent baptism in any unqualified sense, because the poet is concerned with the corruption or sickness of nature which persists after baptism. Besides, if the poetry is allowed to speak for itself, it is clear that the description of the lake lacks the vitality which Spenser unerringly gives to images of present spiritual power:

> Tho vp he caught him twixt his puissant hands,
> And hauing scruzd out of his carrion corse
> The lothfull life, now loosd from sinfull bands,
> Vpon his shoulders carried him perforse
> Aboue three furlongs, taking his full course,
> Vntill he came vnto a standing lake;
> Him thereinto he threw without remorse,
> Ne stird, till hope of life did him forsake;
> So end of that Carles dayes, and his owne paines did make.
>
> (xi. 46)

The poet emphasises the journey which Arthur deliberately makes to the lake, and in previous stanzas stress was placed on the knight's thoughts and memories ('For thy he gan some other wayes aduize, / How to take life from that dead-liuing swaine' and 'He then remembred well, that had bene sayd, / How th'Earth his mother was, and first him bore'). Perhaps what William Perkins has to say about the 'right vse' of baptism on the part of adults who received it long ago is relevant:

baptisme is of great force, to releeue the heart in distresse. For when any child of God, feeles himselfe loden with the burden of his sinnes; the consideration and remembrance thereof, that God hath pardoned them all, and giuen him a speciall, and certaine pledge of his pardon in baptisme; will serue to stay and support his soule.[19]

Arthur carries the burdensome Maleger to a lake which has been 'standing' unchanged for a period of time. The static quality of the lake proves not to be a momentary lapse of Spenserian art but a major signal about the lake's nature as an image of the knight's remembrance of his baptism.

In Books III and IV of the poem the area of human experience under investigation shifts to the emotion of love in its multifarious forms. Book III is especially concerned with the individual's response to the onset of erotic passion symbolised in Cupid's arrows. The response may be nobly active or merely lustful, as v. 1 explains; but in this book the experience of love tends to leave individuals isolated, seeking or bewailing an absent lover (this is the case for Britomart, Amoret and Florimell) or striving to control a hopeless desire (Timias's plight). Book IV, in contrast, portrays the resolution of emotional discords into lasting friendships and marriages. Although Spenser's inclusive art celebrates both virginity and marriage, friendship and sexual love, it is notable that his Protestant epic contains a distinctively Protestant mythologisation of marriage. The 'goodly storie' of the birth of Belphoebe and Amoret makes a subtle yet at the same time lucid statement about the nature and worth of Christian virginity and Christian marriage, as Thomas P. Roche, Jr, has rightly shown.[20] My own concern is briefly to extend Roche's discussion by means of a comparison between a mediaeval Catholic account of the subject and Spenser's narrative, in order to point up the characteristically Protestant nature of the Elizabethan poet's vision. Gower in his *Mirour de l'Omme*, an allegorical poem on the virtues and vices, had presented among the virtues 'Dame Chasteté' with her five daughters. Her second daughter is Virginity ('Sur toutes autres la plus gente / De son fait et de son entente'),[21] and her third daughter is Matrimony. The fact that Spenser invents a myth in which virginity and marriage are not merely sisters as in Gower's poem but 'twinnes', who 'twixt them two did share / The heritage of all celestiall grace' (vi. 4), is a striking indication of his sense of their equality in dignity and status. His myth-making genius, we should note also, transforms the simple personification Chastity into a fictional figure, 'the faire Chrysogonee', whose name – borrowed from Theocritus's Epigrams – brings with it some apt associations. In Theocritus's Epigram xiii chaste Chrysogone lived platonically with her husband Amphicles but nevertheless bore him children.[22] Spenser invents a new myth of Chrysogone who conceives her twin daughters in a miraculously chaste way, through the action of sunbeams on her moist body. Hence Amoret, who is to typify the faithful married woman, like Belphoebe the virgin huntress, is totally pure in origin and nature, and she is equal to her twin sister in status. The Protestant affirmation of marriage acquires its own myth.

The narration of this myth at III. vi. 4–10 does not constitute a canto of instruction and vision, however. It is in Book IV, Canto x, that the reader is shown the nature of the love which has been drawing characters into harmonious relationships in the course of the book despite the efforts of Ate. Since this is the legend 'Of Friendship' the narrative has activated all the Elizabethan senses of the word 'friend', which could denote a lover, a brother or sister, or a friend of the same gender. The word has echoed throughout the book, along with other key words used to mark the achievement of relationship between successive pairs or groups, that is to say the words 'concord', 'accord', 'band' and 'bands'. 'Accord' is established at the unnamed castle in i. 15; Britomart and Artegall reach 'accord' in vi. 41; Belphoebe and Timias are restored to 'good accord' in viii. 18. Ate's dwelling is hung with the 'broken bandes' of friends, brethren and lovers who have become enemies (i. 24); love is defined as 'the band / Of noble minds deriued from aboue' (vi. 31) and friendship is defined in the same way at ix. 1 as 'the band of vertuous mind'. The episode which presents the two characters named on the book's title page ends with the creation of an emotional and social harmony in which love, friendship and kinship all play a part, celebrated in two stanzas containing the key words:

> Thus when they all accorded goodly were,
>   The trumpets sounded, and they all arose,
>   Thence to depart with glee and gladsome chere...
>
> Where making ioyous feast theire daies they spent
>   In perfect loue, deuoide of hatefull strife,
>   Allide with bands of mutuall couplement...
>
> (iii. 51, 52)

Spenser's notable ability to draw variety into artistic unity receives remarkable illustration in the present book where the vision canto concerns itself with the harmony possible for both lovers and friends (x. 25–7). The recurrent terms 'accord', 'band' and 'bands' are now objectified in the personification, Dame Concord, who sits in the porch of the Temple of Venus and compels Love and Hate to join in 'louely band'. The personification had a long history. She had been worshipped by the Romans, had been given a prominent place among the virtues by Prudentius in the *Psychomachia*, and had appeared in schemes of mediaeval religious sculpture, for example at Paris, Amiens and Chartres.[23] Expositions of her meaning declared that one and the same principle of concord was involved in the creation of mutual agreement among animals, between human beings, in kingdoms, and between the four elements which compose the universe.[24] Her meaning, in fact, overlapped with that of Love understood as a cosmic principle and celebrated for example by Boethius in the *Consolatio* Book II, poem 8, and by Boccaccio in *Il Filostrato* Canto iii.

Nevertheless, although the concept of Concord was familiar, Spenser attained a powerful effect by placing this 'sober' personification at the entrance to the Temple of Venus. Other lovers in other mediaeval and Renaissance poems had approached temples dedicated to Venus, but none had met the personification of Concord at the door. The nearest analogue, probably, is the temple in Chaucer's *Parlement of Foules*,[25] where the door is kept by the at first seemingly similar 'Dame Pees'. Spenser knew the poem well; and it is possible that at this moment he was deliberately rewriting it to gain a significantly different effect. Chaucer for his part had been rewriting, and subtly altering, a passage in Boccaccio's *Teseida* Book VII, 58 ff., with a view to the evocation of a temple which is 'more sultry, more sinister, and at the same time more voluptuous' than Boccaccio's.[26] Spenser was working in a different direction. His Temple of Venus possessed a religious dimension not present in his models. Scudamour, the representative lover, and the interested reader, expecting the door of the Temple to be kept by Idleness perhaps – as is the gate of the garden in the *Roman de la Rose* – or by Chaucer's Dame Peace whose meaning in context is clearly that of the leisure or seclusion needed for a possibly illicit love affair, find instead that love depends upon a profound principle of mutual harmony. The description of this personification is given an extraordinary weight and tranquillity, developing without strain into a moment of religious vision:

> *Concord* she cleeped was in common reed,
>   Mother of blessed *Peace* and *Friendship* trew;
>   They both her twins, both borne of heauenly seed,
>   And she her selfe likewise diuinely grew;
>   The which right well her workes diuine did shew:
>   For strength, and wealth, and happinesse she lends,
>   And strife, and warre, and anger does subdew:
>   Of litle much, of foes she maketh frends,
> And to afflicted minds sweet rest and quiet sends.
>
> By her the heauen is in his course contained,
>   And all the world in state vnmoued stands,
>   As their Almightie maker first ordained,
>   And bound them with inuiolable bands;
>   Else would the waters ouerflow the lands,
>   And fire deuoure the ayre, and hell them quight,
>   But that she holds them with her blessed hands.
>   She is the nourse of pleasure and delight,
> And vnto *Venus* grace the gate doth open right.
>
> (x. 34–5)

The traditional functions of Concord as source of personal, political and elemental peace are all included, but the reader receives in addition a glimpse of the divinely ordered universe, by means of the dense and symmetrical patterning of consonants in the first four lines of stanza 35. Concord is perceived as the agent who strongly but paradoxically gently sustains the divine will. Near the centre of this religious vision occurs the word 'bands' which figured so largely in the preceding narrative of human adventures, and whose presence in this stanza reveals that the bands between human beings and the 'inuiolable bands' of the cosmos derive from a single principle.

Spenser carries us effortlessly back into the human world with a reference to the fact that mutual agreement and mutual acceptance form the necessary basis for the pleasure and delight that Venus bestows. Few effects are more Spenserian than the mingling of religious reverberation and human enjoyment in stanza 35.

In recounting his adventure at the Temple of Venus Scudamour reminds himself and his seven listeners of many crucial aspects of the nature of love. The cantos of instruction and vision in *The Faerie*

Queene have the function, it seems, of providing knowledge to those who are, tentatively or increasingly successfully, practising the titular virtues. In some cases the knowledge may come as a reminder of what has been in part forgotten; in others the episode brings a new influx of understanding to a protagonist whose knowledge is recognisably incomplete.This was the case for the Redcross Knight at the House of Holiness and on the Mount of Contemplation. It is also the case for Artegall at the Court of Mercilla in Book v. In this episode (v. ix) the poet again creates an impressive spectacle of the full nature of the book's virtue, and in doing so provides a particular revelation for Artegall about an aspect of justice which he has not yet understood. In Cantos i, ii and iii Artegall administers one form of justice quite correctly, judging accurately and punishing decisively (even ruthlessly, we may feel) in a manner which the narrator approves. Sir Sanglier, Pollente, Munera, the Giant, Braggadochio, all receive appropriate treatment.[27] This is not to deny, though, that Artegall's temperament is marked by a certain harshness. He is quick to anger: Sir Sanglier's crime makes the judge flame 'with zeale of vengeance inwardly' (i. 14); the 'villaine's' demand at ii. 11 produces instantaneous 'wroth'; Braggadochio's insults arouse him to a 'choler' which it takes Guyon to pacify (iii. 36). Spenser is maintaining the characterisation of Artegall which was established in the previous book, where the armour and motto ('Saluagesse sans finesse') which he chose for Satyrane's tournament hinted at an aspect of his temperament. There is a streak of fierceness in Artegall; but in the early cantos of Book v this energy is directed towards a necessary social purpose, the castigation of the unjust.

A stern justice is presented as both useful and worthy of admiration, but it is not applicable in all circumstances. The canto of instruction and vision will include among its parts the description of an occasion where another form of justice will be appropriate. But Spenser's probing of the subject begins earlier: Britomart's visit to the Temple of Isis in Canto vii introduces and celebrates the new theme, that of equity, which is also 'part of Iustice' (vii. 3). In Canto ix the two themes of justice absolute and of equity will be woven together. Although several studies of the poem have demonstrated this,[28] there is a recurrent critical tendency to allow an accurate interpretation to slip out of sight because of a preference for the Temple of Isis episode, which is taken to be the book's true

centre or 'allegorical core' as C. S. Lewis claimed.[29] If we remain
in touch with the conception of cantos of instruction and vision put
forward at the beginning of this chapter, we may be able to hold
the two episodes in a thematically and artistically satisfactory
relationship.

The statue in the Temple represents the Egyptian and Roman
goddess Isis, whose allegorical meaning, the poet tells us, is equity,
while in planetary terms she is associated with the moon. Like many
allegorical or mythic figures in the poem Isis keeps a watchful
control over a dangerous animal; and again the poet provides an
interpretation:

> One foote was set vppon the Crocodile,
>   And on the ground the other fast did stand,
>   So meaning to suppresse both forged guile,
>   And open force.
>
> (vii. 7)

Equity rightly functions to suppress fraud and force; but a second
and deeper meaning for the image is disclosed as a result of
Britomart's dream: equity is seen to restrain the principle of stern
justice itself, because the crocodile is now interpreted as a meta-
morphosis of Osiris, the god of justice absolute:

> For that same Crocodile *Osyris* is,
>   That vnder *Isis* feete doth sleepe for euer:
>   To shew that clemence oft in things amis,
>   Restraines those sterne behests, and cruell doomes of his.
>
> (vii. 22)

Jane Aptekar in an iconographical study of the episode has drawn
attention to several Renaissance emblems of a young hero or god
standing with a foot on a crocodile's back; but she remarks that
'none of these explains why the crocodile should be subjected to
Isis' in Spenser's poem.[30] There is, however, a classical precedent
for Spenser's image which I do not think has previously been noted:
two wall paintings at Pompeii show the goddess Isis seated with her
feet resting on a crocodile. One is to be found in the Temple of
Isis, the other in the room north of the atrium in the House of the
Duke of Aumale.[31] Clearly the iconographical tradition of which
these two Pompeian paintings were part (they themselves having
been lost to view) reached the Renaissance and Spenser through some

visual or verbal medium, although I cannot locate this. It would be fascinating to know what allegorical meanings had attached themselves by the sixteenth century to the inherited image of the goddess Isis with her feet on a crocodile (and perhaps future research will uncover this). One or possibly both of Spenser's allegorical interpretations may have been present in his source; but we may be confident that no future discovery will lessen our regard for the skill with which the poet progressively extends and deepens the implications of the episode.

Britomart's dream, as she sleeps near the base of the statue, communicates two sorts of prophetic information – first, a prophecy of her own future life in its personal and political aspects, and second, a hint about the resolution of what may seem to be a conflict in the book's ethical concerns. True to the character of the dream world, in this prophetic dream identities shift, moods change quite suddenly, images are puzzling or sometimes frightening. In stanza 13 Britomart's discovery that she is wearing a scarlet robe and royal crown is accompanied by an innocent delight which foreshadows her own joy when she succeeds to the throne of Wales:

> Her seem'd, as she was doing sacrifize
> To *Isis*, deckt with Mitre on her hed,
> And linnen stole after those Priestes guize,
> All sodainely she saw transfigured
> Her linnen stole to robe of scarlet red,
> And Moone-like Mitre to a Crowne of gold,
> That euen she her selfe much wondered
> At such a chaunge, and ioyed to behold
> Her selfe, adorn'd with gems and iewels manifold.
>
> (vii. 13)

In stanza 15 Artegall's prodigious achievement in devouring the flames of war which follow Britomart's accession gives him an aggressive energy which suggests simultaneously his pride in his military prowess, his political ambition in relation to Britomart's kingdom, and his triumphant masculinity:

> With that the Crocodile, which sleeping lay
> Vnder the Idols feete in fearelesse bowre,
> Seem'd to awake in horrible dismay,
> As being troubled with that stormy stowre;
> And gaping greedy wide, did streight deuoure
> Both flames and tempest: with which growen great,

> And swolne with pride of his owne peerelesse powre,
> He gan to threaten her likewise to eat;
> But that the Goddesse with her rod him backe did beat.
>
> (vii. 15)

At this point the mood changes yet again: Artegall's approach to Britomart becomes that of the humble Petrarchan lover:

> Tho turning all his pride to humblesse meeke,
> Him selfe before her feete he lowly threw,
> And gan for grace and loue of her to seeke.
>
> (vii. 16)

But even this is not the final stage, since Britomart soon accepts him, and their relationship becomes one of equality and sexual game:

> Which she accepting, he so neare her drew,
> That of his game she soone enwombed grew,
> And forth did bring a Lion of great might.
>
> (vii. 16)

Marriage and the birth of a child produce both a personal and a dynastic solution. The image of the lion, which represents the couple's son Conan, is disturbing but at the same time potentially gratifying, because it promises Conan's future military greatness. Meanwhile the dream has also embodied an ethical revelation in so far as it has suggested, through the future marriage of Britomart and Artegall, the possibility of a union or combination of equity and justice absolute, which will replace the domination of either over the other.

In this way Britomart's dream prepares the ground for Artegall's vision in Canto ix. The two visions are not identical. Britomart at the Temple of Isis witnesses the cult of equity as a distinct principle, although in the final stage of her dream she receives a prophecy of a future union between equity and justice, whereas Artegall in Canto ix directly encounters the complex figure of Mercilla who in herself embodies a perfect combination of the two principles. The name Mercilla may tempt us to suppose that she especially represents mercy; but the images and events of the canto are a reminder that this would be a mistaken view. Mercilla holds the sceptre of 'peace and clemencie', but she also has at her disposal the sword of justice: 'at her feet her sword was likewise layde' (ix. 30). The two judgments of hers which are recorded in the canto, the stern judgment on

Malfont for the crime of slandering a prince, and the judgment on Duessa which allows for delay in the implementation of the punishment (a point I shall elaborate in a moment), exemplify justice absolute and equity respectively. Mercilla administers both justice and equity, and so fulfils the thematic prediction at the end of Britomart's dream.

Artegall, on the other hand, at this stage in his adventures still the knight of justice absolute rather than of justice-and-equity, regards the case of Duessa as one which calls solely for the exercise of judicial rigour:

> Artegall with constant firme intent,
> For zeale of Iustice was against her bent.
>
> (ix. 49)

Mercilla's more profound response to Duessa is a correction of Artegall's. That is to say, in the circumstances of this particular case, where the defendant's royal birth must be taken into account, Mercilla perceives that some mitigation of the sternest administration of justice is appropriate. Her personal recognition of the claims of mercy is signalled in the tears she sheds in ix. 50, and in x. 4 we learn of the form which her mitigation of the law's severity has taken: she defers Duessa's punishment until 'strong constraint' finally compels her to carry it out. The narrator's own feelings are stirred by this example of mercy or equity, so that in the opening stanzas of Canto x he celebrates first of all the divine nature of mercy itself (x. 1), then speaks of the need for both justice and mercy (x. 2), and finally praises Mercilla – his own queen – for her administration of both, although his emotions, naturally enough, are especially roused by her mercy:

> Those Nations farre thy iustice doe adore:
> But thine owne people do thy mercy prayse much more.
>
> (x. 3)

For Artegall, Mercilla's conduct in this case has provided an influx of new understanding. His former limited focus on justice absolute is replaced by an eager response to the queen's capacity for merciful, equitable, 'tempred' rule in appropriate circumstances:

> Much more it praysed was of those two knights;
> The noble Prince, and righteous Artegall,
> When they had seene and heard her doome a rights

Against *Duessa*, damned by them all;
But by her tempred without griefe or gall,
Till strong constraint did her thereto enforce.
And yet euen then ruing her wilfull fall,
With more then needfull naturall remorse,
And yeelding the last honour to her wretched corse.

(x. 4)

The concepts to which we have been referring – justice, equity,
the ability to administer either rigorous justice or equity as occasion
required – were familiar enough to sixteenth-century readers. Protestant writings on the duties of magistrates furnished thorough
analyses of the terms. By way of a preliminary example we may
glance at what Melanchthon had to say about the rigour of the law,
and about equity, in a short work translated into English in the
mid-century:

They call that the rygore of the lawe, when the lawes be discretly / and
sencerlye vsed / withoute mitigacion of any circumstaunce / commonly they
call it in laten, strictum ius, equite of the lawe is a mittigacion of the lawe
in some circumstaunce.[32]

William Perkins clarified the circumstances in which a mitigation
of the law was appropriate:

The ground of this mitigation is, because no lawe makers beeing men, can
foresee, or set downe, all cases that may fall out. Therefore when the case
altereth, then must the discretion of the lawe maker shew itselfe, and doe that,
which the law cannot do.[33]

He went on to affirm that both modes of administration belong to
the magistrate:

This mitigation is in the hand of the Magistrate, as well as the extremitie:
nay it is a part of his dutie as well as the former: and he offends as well, that
neglects to *mitigate the extremitie*, when iust occasion is, as he that neglects to
execute the extremitie, when there is neede.

Perkins also explained the form which the mitigation of the law
might take. In appropriate cases,

the punishment prescribed in the law, is moderated, or lessened, or deferred,
or (it may be) remitted, vpon good and sufficient reason.

Failure by some modern critics to recognise that deferring the
punishment in the case of Duessa is a manifestation of equity, has

led to descriptions of Mercilla (and Elizabeth) as vacillating, and to the claim that her 'attempt to save the condemned while upholding "doome of right"...is merely a benevolent but feckless gesture'.[34] On the contrary, the equitable delay of punishment in this instance, and the rigorous punishment of Malfont earlier in the episode, are both evidence of Mercilla's worth as a magistrate or, as Perkins would say, of her 'glory'. It is

the glory of Iudges and Magistrates, thus to execute the lawes, and to temper them with such discretion, as neither too much mittigation, do abolish the law, nor too much extremitie leaue no place for mittigation.[35]

Mercilla's worth as a true magistrate receives powerful imaginative endorsement from the poet. In ix. 28–9 the description of her throne takes on a visionary quality, a fact which intimates to the reader that it is Mercilla, not Isis, who embodies the full nature of the book's virtue.

> All ouer her a cloth of state was spred,
>   Not of rich tissew, nor of cloth of gold,
>   Nor of ought else, that may be richest red,
>   But like a cloud, as likest may be told,
>   That her brode spreading wings did wyde vnfold;
>   Whose skirts were bordred with bright sunny beams,
>   Glistring like gold, amongst the plights enrold,
>   And here and there shooting forth siluer streames,
> Mongst which crept litle Angels through the glittering gleames.
>
> Seemed those litle Angels did vphold
>   The cloth of state, and on their purpled wings
>   Did beare the pendants, through their nimblesse bold:
>   Besides a thousand more of such, as sings
>   Hymnes to high God, and carols heauenly things,
>   Encompassed the throne, on which she sate:
>   She Angel-like, the heyre of ancient kings
>   And mightie Conquerors, in royall state,
> Whylest kings and kesars at her feet did them prostrate.

(ix. 28–9)

The physical throne almost vanishes into the brilliance of the scriptural images which are employed to evoke it. It seems that the cloth of state is actually less like a piece of rich tissue than it is like the 'cloude vpon the Merciseat' mentioned in Leviticus 16.2. The cloud, in turn, acquires the spreading wings which cover the mercy seat in Exodus 25.20. Everywhere light streams out, and 'litle

Angels' (cherubim) uphold and encompass the throne, unmistakably indicating to Arthur, Artegall and the reader that the queen is God's representative on earth. The episode as a whole both provides necessary information about justice and equity, and for a moment offers a numinous experience.

By contrast, the account of Calidore's vision on Mount Acidale in Book VI, Canto x, does not rely on biblical allusions or direct references to angels or 'high God'. Its imagery of the three Graces dancing in a circle, with a hundred additional Graces moving round them, derives from classical iconography and from classical and Renaissance exposition of that iconography. Yet the significance of the vision in relation to Book VI is, we shall argue, nevertheless religious. Paradoxically we shall not be claiming that the 'grace' in question is theological grace, the divine grace which saves souls, nor for that matter that the three Graces are equivalent to the three Theological Virtues.[36] With Spenser, as we remarked earlier, context is all. The subject of theological grace and its power to rescue sinners from bondage was explored in Book I, the foundation of the entire poem. By the time Book VI is reached, Spenser's exploration has led him into questions of social conduct, especially that mode of conduct and speech which is gentle, affable, considerate of the feelings of others, which is called courtesy. Courteous conduct is what makes civilised social intercourse between human beings possible: it is the 'roote of ciuill conuersation' (i. 1). In characteristic fashion the poet presents successive *exempla* of courtesy and discourtesy, both male and female, well-born and rustic. But in some cases the courteous figures in the narrative possess an additional trait, a 'grace' of person and manner which makes their deeds or words particularly appealing. Calidore demonstrates the kindness, the helpfulness of the courteous man – to the Squire and his damsel, to Aladine, to Priscilla – but, more than this, his 'gracious speach, did steale mens hearts away' (i. 2), as the transformation of Briana through his influence witnesses. Clearly he is one of those who by nature are 'so goodly gratious' that everything they do is attractive (ii. 2).

This conception of an aesthetic grace or charm which wins the love of beholders probably reached Spenser chiefly through Castiglione's *Il Cortegiano*, although other writers also communicated the idea. During the first evening's discussion Count Lodovico insisted on the value of this mysterious and beguiling trait as an accompaniment to every action by a courtier:

> The Courtier therefore, beside noblenesse of birth, I will have him to bee fortunate in this behalfe, and by nature to have not onely a wit, and a comely shape of person and countenance, but also a certaine grace, and (as they say) a hewe [i.e. an air], that shall make him at first sight acceptable and loving unto who so beholdeth him. And let this bee an ornament to frame and accompany all his acts.[37]

The idea was important to Sidney in the *Arcadia*, as this passage in which Pamela describes the horsemanship of Musidorus (here called Dorus) shows:

> A few daies since, he and *Dametas* had furnished themselves very richly to run at the ring before me…But o how well it did with *Dorus*, to see with what a grace he presented him selfe before me on horseback, making majestie wait upon humblenes?…his hand and legge (with most pleasing grace) commanding without threatning, and rather remembring then chastising.[38]

Spenser's warm response to this notion of an aesthetic grace is reflected in his references in other books of *The Faerie Queene* and in other poems to the 'gifts of grace' and the mythological beings who may be said to bestow them. Belphoebe at the time of her birth received 'all the gifts of grace'…'And all the Graces rockt her cradle being borne' (III. vi. 2). When Elizabeth Boyle smiled 'with amiable cheare' it seemed that 'an hundred Graces' sat on each of her eyelids (*Amoretti* xl). In the *Epithalamion* the poet calls on the three Graces to 'helpe to addorne my beautifullest bride' (line 105). But it is in Book VI in particular that several characters, besides Calidore himself, possess the 'grace' to which Castiglione referred. Tristram possesses it, as Calidore immediately notices:

> Him stedfastly he markt, and saw to bee
> A goodly youth of amiable grace,
> Yet but a slender slip, that scarse did see
> Yet seuenteene yeares…
>
> (ii. 5)

So does the Hermit (v. 36), and so does Pastorella, whose physical beauty is increased by 'grace' or charm:

> And soothly sure she was full fayre of face,
> And perfectly well shapt in euery lim,

Which she did more augment with modest grace,
And comely carriage of her count'nance trim.

(ix. 9)

This, then, is the context in which to consider the vision of the Graces. As so often in *The Faerie Queene* the canto of instruction and vision gathers together words, images and themes which have played a key part in the narrative, in order to present a comprehensive 'showing' of the relevant virtue, and to offer some insight into its mysterious origin. Among the protagonists of the various books Calidore is perhaps the knight who is most completely in possession of his virtue from the start of his adventures, although he has not yet practised it among 'the lowest and the least' (xii. 2) and needs to learn how to modify his courtly manners in humble circumstances. The pastoral episode provides the necessary opportunity for this. But there is something else about which Calidore is uninformed: he knows nothing of the source of his own virtue. In the vision of the Graces dancing in concentric circles round Colin Clout's lady, he sees the elusive figures who bestow graces of body and mind – especially the ability to perform courteous actions gracefully – on certain human beings:

> These three on men all gracious gifts bestow,
> Which decke the body or adorne the mynde,
> To make them louely or well fauoured show,
> As comely carriage, entertainement kynde,
> Sweete semblaunt, friendly offices that bynde,
> And all the complements of curtesie:
> They teach vs, how to each degree and kynde
> We should our selues demeane, to low, to hie;
> To friends, to foes, which skill men call Ciuility.

(x. 23)

The Graces, indeed, are seen in the very act of bestowing gifts on the woman in their midst.

Spenser rises superbly to the occasion in the presentation of a spectacle which he himself promises in advance will surpass the glittering shows of court life: 'For what hath all that goodly glorious gaze / Like to one sight, which *Calidore* did view?' The knight is peculiarly privileged in seeing what he sees. Only those who are permitted by guardian nymphs to cross the protective river can reach

139

the earthly paradise on a mountain top (x. 7). The vision itself engages the senses, the mind and the imagination of both Calidore and the reader, while also finding room for a touch of human comedy: the courteous knight's response to the naked maidens contains at first an entirely natural element of sensuality which the narrator registers with tolerant amusement:

> There he did see, that pleased much his sight,
> That euen he him selfe his eyes enuyde,
> An hundred naked maidens lilly white.

(x. 11)

But as he takes in the beauty and 'order excellent' of the dance, his response becomes one of wonder, and of that 'rapture' which in Neoplatonic thought is the appropriate reaction to images of heavenly beauty:

> Much wondred *Calidore* at this straunge sight,
>   Whose like before his eye had neuer seene,
> And standing long astonished in spright,
>   And rapt with pleasaunce, wist not what to weene.

(x. 17)

Critical discussion of this section of the canto tends to focus on the action which follows – Calidore's interruption of the blissful dance. He has been regarded as a more or less bumbling intruder because he steps forward to discover the meaning of the spectacle.[39] Our enquiry into the subject may be helped by a couple of literary analogues, in both of which a protagonist who witnesses a mysterious dance in a remote place moves towards it and causes the dancers to vanish. The knight in *The Wife of Bath's Tale* (often and rightly cited in this context) draws eagerly towards the dance 'In hope that som wysdom sholde he lerne' (line 994), and in fact he does learn precisely what he needs to know from the 'oldewyf' sitting on the grass. Calidore, also, possesses a strong desire for knowledge ('Therefore resoluing, what it was, to know...'). Protagonists in Spenser's poem are required both to exercise their virtue and, sooner or later, to understand it. The evidence of successive books of *The Faerie Queene* suggests that the poet was deeply committed to a concept not only of virtuous action but of personal knowledge. The Redcross Knight needs both to see and to understand the meaning of the heavenly city which is shown to him, just as Calidore needs to comprehend the significance of the group of circling maidens. There is a further reason, I think, why Calidore must move towards the dancers. The world of the poem is a world in which enchanted shows can easily delude the unwary spectator. At Archimago's hermitage the Redcross Knight lacks just this wariness in relation to the false shows put on for his benefit by the 'guilefull great Enchaunter'; the False Florimell who deceives so many characters in the central books – including, poignantly, Marinell himself – is in fact the product of the Witch's magical powers (III. viii. 4–5). In the *Gerusalemme Liberata* Rinaldo alone in a forest (this is the second of the literary analogues I had in mind) finds himself surrounded by a ring of beguiling dancers who prove to have been called into activity by the enchantress Armida.[40] He marches boldly forward and ends the deceptive performance by striking a myrtle tree. As Calidore gazes at the dance of the Graces he is aware that he may be witnessing a genuine manifestation of 'the traine of beauties Queene' or, equally possibly, an 'enchaunted show, / With which his eyes mote haue deluded beene'. He has two motives, therefore, for stepping forward – a desire for knowledge and a desire to avoid delusion. This time we quote the whole stanza:

> Much wondred *Calidore* at this straunge sight,
>   Whose like before his eye had neuer seene,
>   And standing long astonished in spright,
>   And rapt with pleasaunce, wist not what to weene;
>   Whether it were the traine of beauties Queene,
>   Or Nymphes, or Faeries, or enchaunted show,
>   With which his eyes mote haue deluded beene.
>   Therefore resoluing, what it was, to know,
> Out of the wood he rose, and toward them did go.
>
> (x. 17)

His motives, I think, are not reprehensible. But there still remains the question of whether his manners are adequate to the occasion when he sees the distress which his intrusion has caused to Colin Clout. The scene is parallel to that earlier scene in which he had intruded upon Calepine's and Serena's lovemaking in a wood. In each case there is an element of bad luck on Calidore's side: he had not intended to disturb the lovers but had 'chaunst' to do so (iii. 20), and in Canto x he did not realise that the dancers would vanish when he stepped forward (although he was aware that he might 'break' the dance, x. 11). In each case the knight expresses his sorrow at the harm caused by 'fortune' (iii. 21) or 'ill fortune' (x. 20), but then goes further and accepts blame for what he has done, speaking of his 'rash default' (iii. 21) or his rashness (x. 29), even though it is uncertain whether blame is appropriate for an effect which has been brought about unintentionally. The fact that Calidore twice takes the blame upon himself suggests that Spenser regards this as characteristic of the truly courteous man – and certainly in each case the act of taking the blame heals the breach between human beings. In Canto iii with 'his gentle words and goodly wit/ He soone allayd that Knights conceiu'd displeasure' (stanza 22), and in Canto x the narrator ends the relevant stanza with an explicit comment on the protagonist's courtesy and his use of 'all comely meanes' to 'recomfort' the shepherd (x. 29).

As the character in Book VI who most completely possesses a Castiglionian grace of manner, a courtesy made beautiful by grace, Calidore fittingly receives a vision of the nature and source of his own virtue. As Colin Clout explains, the pleasant smiles and the nakedness of the Graces indicate the gentleness and openness which are essential aspects of courtesy itself. But it is not through the content of the vision but through the mode of its arrival and departure that Calidore learns perhaps the most important fact of all about the 'gifts of grace' – the fact that they cannot be commanded but are unpredictably bestowed by the Graces themselves on such individuals as they choose to favour:

> For being gone, none can them bring in place,
> But whom they of them selues list so to grace.
>
> (x. 20)

The Graces in this respect are the representatives of the bounty of Nature and of God. Count Lodovico had more than once affirmed that the 'grace' of the courtier was 'the gift of nature and of the heavens'[41] rather than the product of human effort. Spenser transforms this abstract concept into a poetic and mythological episode in which the bounty of the heavens is concretely embodied in the three Graces and their generous gifts. Through the vision and Colin's exposition of it Calidore learns what he had never known, the divine source of his virtue. In this way the episode of the dance of the Graces introduces an element of religious strangeness into the book of sociable actions.

Spenser deepens and complicates this remarkable tenth canto by
including in it not only the protagonist who is privileged to receive
a visionary experience, but also his own pastoral persona, Colin
Clout. It was not in fact uncommon for the Renaissance author of
a pastoral romance to introduce into it a representation of himself
in shepherd-guise – as Sannazaro had done in the *Arcadia* in the person
of Sincero, and as Sidney had done in his own *Arcadia* in the person
of Philisides – but Spenser, by giving Colin Clout the role of piper
for the climactic dance of supernatural beings, raises challenging
questions about the power of poets and the relationship between love
and poetry. However, it is worth remembering that Colin Clout
is Spenser's persona specifically in pastoral poetry: Colin is not the
epic poet, creator of *The Faerie Queene*. As a result, the epic poet
can address his pastoral counterpart with affection and a hint of
patronage:

> That iolly shepheard, which there piped, was
> Poore *Colin Clout* (who knowes not *Colin Clout?*)
> He pypt apace, whilest they him daunst about.
>
> (x. 16)

Colin is able to break his pipe in spontaneous irritation when
Calidore ends the dance (a gesture which has a deliberate half-
resemblance to his previous pipe-breaking exploit in 'Ianuarye')
without the action in some way carrying an ominous implication for
The Faerie Queene as a whole. The shepherd quickly recovers his
equanimity, and reveals his skill not only in the creation of music
but in lucid moral exposition. The experience of love which was
so disabling in his particular case in *The Shepheardes Calender* has now
become a source of creativity: Colin pipes to celebrate his lady's
beauty and she in her turn, elevated to the rank of a fourth Grace,
inspires his poetry: 'She made me often pipe and now to pipe apace.'
    During the conversation between Calidore and Colin it becomes
evident that Colin sees the Graces more frequently than does anyone
else. When they choose, they 'flocke' to him to hear his 'louely
layes' (x. 19). The poet, in fact, possesses an unusual capacity to see
visions, to perceive realities beyond the phenomenal world. Spenser
had anticipated this point in Book I, Canto x, when he stated that
the mountain on which contemplatives receive the vision of religious
mysteries is 'like' Mount Parnassus on which the Muses 'play /
Their heauenly notes'. Here in Book VI one particular poet, Colin

Clout, is found to be visited by supernatural beings who are embodiments of divine bounty and the source of all the 'gifts of grace' – including, perhaps, grace of literary style.

Spenser, the epic poet, in Books II to VI investigates large areas of moral, emotional and social experience. But he constructs *The Faerie Queene* in a way which allows neither the protagonists nor the readers to forget the continuing reality of the spiritual realm which is the source and the destiny of moral virtue.

7

Britons and Elves

The romantic epic which explores the moral virtues is also, of course, the nationalistic poem which asserts the greatness of Britain and the British monarchy. The moral virtues of the Queen are celebrated in the proems and mirrored in the fiction by Gloriana, Belphoebe, Mercilla and sometimes other figures; but perhaps the most fundamental compliment paid to her by Spenser was that of making Arthur, the most illustrious of her alleged ancestors, the supreme hero of a poem which would ultimately have had twelve other protagonists. Virgil and Ariosto had shown how a patron could be complimented through a narrative of the achievements of a mythical or fictional ancestor. Spenser the Protestant nationalist resolved to engage with the story of Arthur, but he did so, I shall suggest, in a remarkably considered and original way. My argument will be that his attitude to the Arthurian material led directly to his invention of the distinction between Britons and Elves, a subject of great interest and one which I am in any case under an obligation to tackle because in Chapter 4 I challenged the widely held view that Elves are essentially non-Christian, when I stated that the Elf Guyon must be regarded as a Christian knight.

Before going any further I should perhaps summarise and briefly comment on twentieth-century opinions about the Briton/Elf distinction, starting with Greenlaw's claim that 'By *Fairy* Spenser means *Welsh*, or, more accurately, *Tudor*, as distinguished from the general term British.'[1] Since the poet's concern, however, was to establish the unbroken continuity between the British kings and the Tudor princes, it seems unlikely that he would have chosen to drive a verbal wedge between them as Greenlaw's theory alleges. Janet Spens, on the other hand, argued that 'Faery Land then is the mind, the inner experience of each of us.'[2] Clearly many of the Faery figures exemplify virtues whose seat is 'deepe within the mynd', but so for that matter do British figures. The Elf Guyon who typifies

145

the temperate man does not differ in this respect from the British Artegall who typifies the just man. Spens's theory is too vague to be useful. Isabel Rathborne in 1937, recognising the importance of the pursuit of honour for virtuous deeds in *The Faerie Queene*, stated that Spenser's Faeryland is a 'land of fame', where departed heroes dwell – a version of the classical Elysium. Elves and Britons belong to the same race but with this distinction, that Britons are alive in the present, while Faeries belong to the past or the future.[3] The theory makes Britons and Elves share the same family tree, and therefore fails to explain Spenser's emphasis on the difference between his earthy, 'terrestriall' Britons and his Elfin figures.

Literary criticism since the 1960s has rightly seen that the contrasted histories of the British race and the Elfin race in Book II, Canto x must indicate some fundamental difference in nature between Britons and Elves. Harry Berger, Jr, stresses the 'Original Excellence, harmony and power of Elfin man';[4] Elves are pagans, possessing an 'Aristotelian sophrosyne' (p. 109), whereas Arthur is a Briton whose ancestors 'came by suffering to knowledge and by sin to salvation' (p. 107). Hence Book II, Canto x juxtaposes 'myth and history, poetry and politics, fable and theology' (p. 111). There is a great deal of insight in this final formulation, except perhaps in its insistence on the non-Christian status of Elves. Thomas P. Roche, Jr, speaks of 'the ideal world of Faeryland', which contains in particular 'the ideal of civil life'.[5] The chronicle of British kings, by way of contrast, is 'a history of an individual nation within the Providential scheme of Christian history'. Faeryland is outside space and time, and 'it is non-Christian' (p. 45). Berger and Roche are surely right to point to Faeryland's association with the ideal world and with fable, balanced against the British chronicle's concern with history, suffering and the real world. Their views, which have led to something near to a critical consensus on this subject, have much to recommend them, except perhaps in the following respects: they do not explain Spenser's specific decisions about which characters in his poem should be Britons and which Elves; they do not sufficiently relate the distinction to any historical (or, more precisely, historiographical) context within which Spenser was working in the 1580s; and, as I have already mentioned, they have difficulty in accommodating Christian Elves in their scheme. In the present chapter I shall hope to grasp some of these nettles.

Modern readers are familiar with the fact that propaganda on behalf of the House of Tudor claimed that the Tudor monarchs were direct descendants of the line of British kings which stretched from the Trojan Brutus, through King Arthur, to Cadwallader, and which had reappeared on the national throne in the person of Henry VII. The most active exponents of this claim were often also dedicated Protestants: in the 1540s Leland and Bale, both Protestants and both antiquaries, strongly asserted the Arthurian descent of the Tudors,[6] while Arthur Kelton's *A Chronycle with a Genealogie declaryng that the Brittons and Welshemen are lineallye dyscended from Brute* (London, 1547) gave fervent expression to Protestant, nationalistic and Arthurian convictions. A similar note was struck in the 1580s, when Richard Robinson, eager if unsophisticated Protestant and nationalist, translated Leland's Latin *Assertio*, and Warner and Churchyard produced poems in praise of England and Wales respectively, well supplied with Protestant and Arthurian propaganda.[7]

But the claim of Tudor descent from Arthur was subject, of course, to deflating criticism. The question of the historicity of King Arthur himself – the question of what deeds he had actually performed, and even the question of whether a British monarch of that name had ever in fact existed – had been raised many times both in the past and more recently. Geoffrey of Monmouth's richly inventive account of Arthur's adventures in the *Historia Regum Britanniae* had been absorbed into various English chronicles, but Ralph Higden in the fourteenth century and Robert Fabyan at the end of the fifteenth century had taken a sceptical view of Geoffrey's material. Polydore Virgil in 1534 followed Fabyan's lead, and after referring briefly to Arthur's reign indicated that the legends about him were simply a tradition among the common people.[8] The fact that Polydore was a foreigner made his comments especially unpalatable: it was Polydore who stimulated the Protestant 'assertions' of Arthur in the 1540s which we mentioned a moment ago.

In the third quarter of the sixteenth century the chroniclers Grafton and Holinshed tried to combine a degree of necessary reserve about the more extravagant legends with a continuing belief in Arthur's greatness as a British monarch. Grafton, for example, in 1569 concluded:

though of him [Arthur] be written many things in the Englishe Chronicle of small credence, and farre discordant from other writers, yet all agree in this, that he was a noble and victorious Prince in all his deedes, and testifie that he fought. xij. notable battayles against the Saxons, and had alwayes the vpper hande.[9]

Holinshed in 1577 strongly expressed the wish that it were possible to separate the 'mere fables' which had become attached to King Arthur from the 'true matter' which deserved to be affirmed. After noting the claims in British histories that Arthur conquered Gothland, Iceland and parts of France, he declared:

but for so muche as there is not anye approued authour dothe speake of any suche doings, the Britons are thoughte to haue registred mere fables in stede of true matter, vpon a vayne desire to aduaunce more than reason woulde, thys Arthur theyr noble champion, as the Frenchemen haue doone by their Roulande, and others.[10]

Subsequently he referred again to trifling tales, and went on:

but worthie was he doubtlesse of whome feigned fables shoulde not haue so dreamed, but rather that true Historyes myghte haue sette foorth hys woorthye prayses, as he that dyd for a long season susteyne and holde vp hys Countrey that was readie to goe to vtter ruyne and decaye.[11]

Grafton and Holinshed shared the view that Arthur, despite all the fables, had genuinely reigned as a British king who fought twelve victorious battles against the Saxons and protected his country for a long period against its enemies. In contrast, William Camden, the learned but tactful antiquary, avoided historical assertions about the controversial figure in the *Britannia* of 1586, although he commended his valour as a warrior.

Spenser therefore, at work on the first three books of *The Faerie Queene* between 1580 and 1589, was writing at a moment of considerable significance for the Arthurian material. He had chosen to make Arthur the hero of his poem in compliment to the Queen, but he was well aware, as was any reader of Fabyan, of Polydore Virgil, of Grafton, of Holinshed, that a vast proportion of the adventures attributed to the British king were inventions. I suggest that he devised the distinction between Britons and Elves as a means of coping with exactly this problem. He wished to assert that Arthur and some of his contemporaries had had an historical existence – were part of British history, were 'Britons', in fact – while he also wanted the freedom to introduce multifarious persons and adventures frankly created by the imagination. 'British' characters in the poem were historical beings who had existed at a specific period in time, that is to say during the reign of Uther Pendragon, shortly before Arthur succeeded to his father's throne, whereas 'Elves' and 'Fays' belonged to the realm of fiction, fable, invention, romance. The ingenious distinction allowed him to achieve the fullness and variety essential to his chosen genre and to his inclusive moral theme, without endangering the historicity of Arthur and the British line. By setting the poem in Faeryland, the world of fiction and fable, instead of in Uther Pendragon's historical Britain, the Elizabethan poet could invent any episode he chose for the young Arthur without claiming that it portrayed a real action of the future British king. At some point at the end of the poem, or after its conclusion, Arthur would return from Faeryland to Britain to ascend his historic throne in the year AD 516 (or AD 517 if the authority of Grafton is preferred to that of Holinshed). But within the body of the poem, located in Faeryland, Arthur could share in the various, the 'marvellous' escapades of invented knights. By means of the Briton/Elf distinction, Spenser endowed himself with the freedom to combine history and romance.

It is true that several other long poems of the Renaissance combined elements of historical fact with a proliferation of fable – *Orlando Furioso, Gerusalemme Liberata, Poly-Olbion* in different ways are examples. Tasso, indeed, in one of his *Discorsi del Poema Eroico* declared that an heroic poem should contain both historical material and new stories;[12] and in his own major romantic epic linked the authentic figure of Godfrey of Bouillon, besieger of Jerusalem, with fictional beings appropriate to romance like the enchantress Armida and the Amazon Clorinda. If the blending of history and fiction was a currently fashionable mode it is proper to ask why Spenser should have felt obliged to make a distinction between characters where other poets made none. The answer, I think, is that the intellectual problems attached to the Arthurian material in the 1570s and 1580s in England were urgent enough to require a deliberate response. Educated Elizabethans could not fail to be aware that the status of King Arthur was under attack; at the same time nationalists set a high value on the 'British History' for the dignity and legitimacy it gave to the House of Tudor. Italian poets could interlace the acts of Charlemagne or Godfrey of Bouillon with the adventures of imaginary beings without imperilling the former; but Arthur's standing was far less secure. The historicity of the British king needed protection from the surrounding world of legend.

Having invented a way of distinguishing historical figures from fictional ones, Spenser found the device provided him with an opportunity to explore the difference between history and fiction as modes of discourse, and he exploited the opportunity in Book II, Canto x and elsewhere. I shall discuss this topic in the second half of the present chapter, but our first concern must be a scrutiny of the 'British' characters in the narrative in the light of the claims made in previous paragraphs. The position which Spenser took up in relation to King Arthur's existence and adventures seems to me to be very similar to that of Grafton and Holinshed. There was a relatively small amount of 'true matter' which needed to be affirmed: Arthur, the son of Uther Pendragon and Igrayne, ascended the throne in AD 516 or 517, and thereafter fought successfully against the Saxons, although he was unable to drive them from the realm entirely. But the story, for example, of his conception (found in Geoffrey), which involved a magical change of appearance on the part of Uther as well as adultery, had already been pared down by Holinshed. Spenser neatly avoids saying anything at all on the subject by bringing the British chronicle in II. x to an abrupt and dramatic end with the accession of Uther to the throne. It is obvious to the reader that Prince Arthur is Uther's son, but that is the limit of what we know or need to know. In the matter of Arthur's upbringing, however, Spenser makes use of the 'Faery' category which allows for free, unhistorical invention. The Prince was educated, we are told, by a 'Faery knight' named Timon:

> From mothers pap I taken was vnfit:
> And streight deliuered to a Faery knight,
> To be vpbrought in gentle thewes and martiall might.
>
> (I. ix. 3)

If, as I am suggesting, a 'Faery knight' is a fictional knight, Spenser is making the point that in the absence of historical information about Arthur's upbringing he himself has created a tutor for him. No reputable chronicler said anything about the Prince's education, but the romance writers did, Malory for example declaring that the boy was reared by Sir Ector. Spenser was free to supply an equally fictional tutor, the Faery Timon.

Arthur's love for and pursuit of Gloriana is similarly an invention of Spenser's. If the chroniclers mention a wife for Arthur at all – and Holinshed does – it is Guinevere. But while Arthur resides in Faeryland he seeks a Faery queen without prejudice to any subsequent historical marriage. The relationship is a fiction which gives a forward-impulse to the total narrative yet in no way claims to be part of the 'true matter' which history records about the British monarch. The years 'before he was king' (the phrase comes from the *Letter to Raleigh*) provided Spenser with an ideal temporal space for the creation of adventures for Prince Arthur, adventures which took place in Faeryland, fiction-land, not in historical Britain.

Almost equal to Arthur in status and military prowess, his name suggests, is the British knight Artegall. Artegall may seem to belong essentially to the world of fiction, but in fact he had a place in some of the chronicles.[13] Grafton in his *Chronicle* of 1569, immediately after the paragraphs affirming that Arthur was a victorious British Prince, stated:

In this tyme also I finde mencion made of a noble and valiant man called Arthgall, and he was the first Erle of Warwike, and he was one of the knightes of the round Table of King Arthure.[14]

Artegall was an 'historical' figure, belonging to time and process, who participated in the reigns of Uther and Arthur. But as nothing was known of his childhood or young manhood Spenser could frankly invent a life-story for him and could acknowledge that he was doing so. Artegall was born into history, but during *The Faerie Queene* he is to be found in Faeryland:

> He wonneth in the land of *Fayeree*,
> Yet is no *Fary* borne, ne sib at all
> To Elfes, but sprong of seed terrestriall,
> And whilome by false *Faries* stolne away,
> Whiles yet in infant cradle he did crall;
> Ne other to himselfe is knowne this day,
> But that he by an Elfe was gotten of a *Fay*.
>
> (III. iii. 26)

At some later date, like Arthur, he would return to historical Britain to fight against 'forrein Paynims' (III. iii. 27).

It was legitimate to assume that the first Earl of Warwick had possessed a wife. To fill this role Spenser created Britomart, probably the most richly imagined figure in the entire poem yet still justifiably described as a Briton on the grounds that the woman whom Artegall, Knight of the Round Table, married must have had an historical existence early in the sixth century. Within the world of Faeryland the poet had a licence to depict her love for and search for her future husband, in such a way as to exemplify many of the pains and pleasures, absurdities and achievements of romantic lovers. This is the most important of the love affairs in the poem, forming a major strand in the interwoven narrative from Book III to Book V, and destined to culminate in a marriage of profound dynastic significance. Britomart, like Arthur and Artegall, would at the appropriate moment return from Faeryland where her adventures take place to Britain, land of historical fact.

Spenser had a special need in the world of his poem for the historical Artegall and his wife, because they could be employed to strengthen a weak link in the royal succession. In the additions which he here made to chronicle history the poet was undoubtedly adjusting facts in a manner which may strike us as dangerously close to fiction; but it is interesting to note that his additions remain within the bounds of what, in chronicle terms, was historically possible. The problem with which Spenser had to cope was a seeming break, or, to put it another way, an uncertain connection in the line of British kings shortly after the death of King Arthur. The chronicles indicated that Arthur, who had no legitimate children, was succeeded by his nephew Constantius (also referred to as Constantine), son of his half-brother Cador. Constantius, however, was soon deposed by his 'kinsman' Conan. Conan passed the crown to his own son, Vortipore, from whom the line of British kings descended. For the nationalist poet, the seeming usurpation by Conan was a blemish in the British history which called for careful treatment.[15] The chroniclers described Conan as the 'cousin' (Hardyng's word but not a very precise one) or 'kinsman' (Grafton's and Holinshed's term) of Constantius, but no chronicler gave the name of Conan's father. It was here that Spenser made two additions to the recorded facts: he presented Artegall not merely as the historical companion of Arthur but as his half-brother; and he defined Conan not merely as the 'kinsman' of Constantius but as the son of Artegall and hence the cousin, in the modern sense, of Constantius and the nephew of Arthur. As a result, the succession moved from King Arthur to one of Arthur's nephews, Constantius,

to another of Arthur's nephews, Conan, and thence to Conan's son,
Vortipore (III. iii. 27–31). The blood-relationship of Arthur's
successors was brought more clearly into view.

Spenser could have defended his two modifications of the
chronicles without very much difficulty. The historical Artegall is
mentioned by Grafton in the closest possible proximity to the
historical Arthur, in a manner which could imply family relationship
as well as friendship; and the name 'Arthgall' seems to signal some
especially intimate link between the two men. Equally, the historical
Conan, 'kinsman' to the family of Arthur, could perfectly possibly
have been Artegall's son and Arthur's nephew. The poet transposed
the possible into the historical, but he did not travel very far from
his copy of Hardyng or Grafton in doing so. As the name of Conan
was associated with usurpation in the minds of those who had read
the chronicles, Spenser wisely avoided it, and referred to the future
king in heroic terms simply as a 'Lyon' (III. iii. 30) and 'Lion-like'
(v. vii. 23). He had removed a blemish from the Arthurian succession
without defying historical possibility.

The remaining major British figure in the poem is Tristram, who
informs Calidore, 'I am a Briton borne, / Sonne of a King'
(VI. ii. 27). Like all the other Britons in *The Faerie Queene* he early
left the land of his birth, Cornwall or Lionesse, a tributary kingdom
of Britain, and was brought to Faeryland where any adventure the
poet might wish to devise could befall him. His mother, Queen of
Cornwall, sent the youth

> Out of the countrie, wherein I was bred,
> The which the fertile *Lionesse* is hight,
> Into the land of *Faerie*, where no wight
> Should weet of me, nor worke me any wrong.

(VI. ii. 30)

Tristram of course figured largely in romances, for example in
Malory and in the Italian *Tristano*, so that we may well wonder why
Spenser claimed a 'British' rather than simply a fictional status for
him. I think the answer may lie in a quasi-historical list of the
Knights of the Round Table published during the 1580s, with a page
devoted to each knight and a description of his coat of arms. The
author was Richard Robinson who translated Leland's *Assertio*.
Among the knights listed is 'Messyr Tristran de Lyonis' with his
'Sheeld all Greene', who is 'no lesse worthy...Of fame, then others

are'.[16] The book presented itself with the air of a document rather than of a romance; and I think it is possible that this or some similar work suggested to Spenser that Tristram had an historical existence, quite apart from the legends which romance-writers chose to add to his name. Because his poem was set in Faeryland, fiction-land, Spenser could freely amplify the young knight's story.

Spenser's standards of what constitutes history are not ours. But in every case he could cite a printed 'authority' of one kind or another for the claim that his Britons were historical beings. He was writing at a moment when the difference between 'mere fables' and 'true matter' in the story of King Arthur was becoming an urgent question, yet he did not live quite late enough in time to benefit from a more developed sense of what constitutes a reliable authority. The date of the first edition of Camden's *Britannia* is important in this context: 1586. That the first three books of *The Faerie Queene* were well advanced by then is demonstrated by the fact that in 1588 Abraham Fraunce could quote some lines (in the *Arcadian Rhetorike*) from Book II of Spenser's poem with their precise canto and stanza number. During the following year, 1589, Spenser brought the finished manuscript from Ireland to England. C. A. Harper in her invaluable study has shown that the influence of Camden on the passages of British chronicle history in *The Faerie Queene* is slight, whereas by the mid 1590s Camden's influence on the *View of the Present State of Ireland* is unmistakable.[17] Spenser's major sources for the Book II chronicle were Geoffrey of Monmouth, Hardyng, Stow, the *Mirror for Magistrates*, and Holinshed,[18] rather than Camden. There is evidence that he was deeply interested in history and that he enjoyed comparing the conflicting versions of events in the chronicles; but there is no sign that in the 1580s he attempted to cultivate the 'new' historian's discrimination between the validity of one authority and another. As C. A. Harper put it: 'Spenser was no whit in advance of his times in his historical methods. He did not consistently reject such statements as were without a firm foundation of contemporary records. He was credulous of the printed word' (p. 21). All the characters whom he chose to call 'Britons' had a place in quasi-historical publications.

The Redcross Knight is not a Briton but he is not an Elf either. He learns from the hermit Contemplation that he has 'sprong out from English race, / How euer now accompted Elfins sonne' (I. x. 60).

According to the argument we have been putting forward, if St George is not an Elf he is not a fictional figure but a participant in English history, the descendant of an 'ancient race / Of *Saxon* kings' (x. 65). In making this claim Spenser is turning aside from the more usual account of St George's background, which stated that he was born in Cappadocia, and giving preference to the alternative account which roundly declared that his mother was the daughter of a king of England. A printed version of this story exists in a volume published in 1608, Richard Johnson's *The Most Famous History of the seuen Champions of Christendome*, but undoubtedly there had been earlier printed books containing the same legend. In Johnson's text St George's mother is said to be 'by birth the King of Englands daughter'.[19] Spenser was certainly taking risks in giving weight to this version of the story. As the sceptical John Selden wrote in 1613, even the Cappadocian legend was open to serious objection, 'but you may better beleeue the Legend, then that he was a *Couentry* man borne, with his *Caleb* Lady of the woods, or that he descended from the *Saxon* race, and such like; which some *English* fictions deliuer'.[20] But Spenser's temperament, as we argued in the previous paragraph, was quite unlike Selden's. It seems that the poet wanted to embed the national hero, the future patron saint of England, securely in English history, and that he was willing to regard a popular version of the St George story as his authority for doing so. In defiance of sceptics he declared that St George was not fictional but was part of Saxon and English history. The knight's adventures in Faeryland, however, to which he was carried off in infancy (I. x. 65–6) were poetic images of the human spiritual journey and made no claim to be historical facts.

Balanced against the Britons and the Englishman are the Elves and Fays – Guyon, Calidore, Triamond, Satyrane, Timon, Gloriana, Belphoebe, Amoret and Cambina, for example – who are all named as Faeries, as well as by implication most of the other persons in the poem. The Elves and Fays have no place in history, but they are as essential as the Britons to Spenser's scheme, since through them he can attain the variety necessary to romantic epic which would have been out of his reach if he had confined himself to the 'historical' acts of Arthur and the Knights of the Round Table mentioned in Holinshed. Through the Faery figures the poet can explore the subtly different manifestations of virtues and vices which contribute to the world as we know it. The British Tristram exemplifies a youthful, impulsive courtesy, but he is not alone: the Elves Calidore, Aldus, Calepine, the Hermit, Meliboe, even the Salvage Man, all exhibit variant forms of courtesy and hospitality depending on their age, experience and temperament.

The 'faery' tradition which Spenser inherited came to him not so much from folklore – whose mischievous beings tended to visit human dwellings at night in order to eat and drink, dance and gambol – as from mediaeval romance. But the fays of mediaeval romance themselves often possessed malignant traits, despite their beauty and their skill as healers. Morgan le Fay is the outstanding example. Nevertheless in a few romances the reader comes upon faery beings who are entirely virtuous in their activities,[21] and among these romances probably *Huon of Bordeaux* is the most relevant to our discussion. There the faery king, Oberon, who assists Huon of Bordeaux in the fulfilment of his quest, is not only noble and handsome but, interestingly, a devout Christian. Spenser alludes directly to *Huon of Bordeaux* at II. i. 6, and inherits, I think, its Christian faeries. As we have seen, he presented the Elf Guyon undoubtedly as a Christian. The Elizabethan poet's Elves and Fays, like those in *Huon of Bordeaux*, inhabit a territory called Faeryland to which visitors may travel on foot or horseback from named geographical regions in its vicinity, although the exact position of its boundaries is never defined. But Spenser made bold adjustments to his model: in *The Faerie Queene* Elves and Fays become a majority not a minority of the characters; almost all the action takes place in Faeryland instead of in the European countries nearby; and the magical powers of Faery figures are in the main removed. Elfin protagonists in Spenser's poem possess no magical resources to differentiate them from British ones – it is Britomart in fact who carries an enchanted spear not Guyon – and the adventures of Arthur and Guyon in the final cantos of Book II or of Calidore and Tristram in the early cantos of Book VI reveal how much they have in common.

The similarity between Britons and Elves within the narrative of the poem does not extend to the histories of the British and Elfin monarchies, however. In juxtaposing the two sets of antiquities in Book II, Canto x, Spenser takes the opportunity of pointing up the profound difference between history and poetry as literary modes, the one all too often troubled and violent, the other potentially harmonious and exemplary. The 'Briton moniments' have the double function of establishing the British ancestry of Prince Arthur (and hence of Queen Elizabeth I), and of illustrating the nature of human history, whereas the ideally valiant and wise Elfin monarchs in the 'Antiquitie of Faerie lond' provide 'braue ensample, both of martiall, / And ciuill rule to kings and states imperiall' (II. x. 74). This contrast between poetry and history was familiar to readers of Sidney's *Apologie for Poetrie*:

For indeede Poetrie euer setteth vertue so out in her best cullours, making Fortune her wel-wayting hand-mayd, that one must needs be enamored of her. Well may you see *Vlisses* in a storme, and in other hard plights; but they are but exercises of patience and magnanimitie, to make them shine the more in the neere-following prosperitie...But the Historian, beeing captiued to the trueth of a foolish world, is many times a terror from well dooing, and an incouragement to vnbrideled wickednes.[22]

The Sidneian concepts are transposed in Canto x into sequences of vivid examples. Spenser's distinction between Britons and Elves, product of the debate about the historicity of King Arthur in the second half of the sixteenth century, opened up this remarkable opportunity to show rather than simply define the contrasted materials of history and poetry.

In order to draw attention to the quintessentially fictive nature of the Elfin race, Spenser gave its earliest kings activities which transparently belonged to romance. Elfiline 'enclosed' Cleopolis 'with a golden wall', more for beauty than for fortification we feel, unlike the historical walls of London in the British history which fell into ruin and needed to be rebuilt by Lud 'gainst force of enimy' (x. 46). Elfinor created something even more wonderful, by means of magic powers:

> He built by art vpon the glassy See
> A bridge of bras, whose sound heauens thunder seem'd to bee.
>
> (x. 73)

This impressive achievement resembles other magical projects in fictional works: Friar Bacon in Greene's play of c. 1590, for example, planned to surround 'fair England with a wall of brass'.[23] But such projects belong to the world of the imagination and fiction, not to history. In their combats, too, the Elfin kings perform feats

which are characteristic of romance. Giant-slaying plays a part both
in the history of Britain and the history of Faeryland; but whereas
Brutus and his followers, Corineus, Debon and Canutus, slay giants
whom Spenser takes care to make sufficiently credible by equating
them with savages – 'hideous Giants, and halfe beastly men, / That
neuer tasted grace, nor goodnesse felt' (x. 7) – in contrast Elfar kills
two giants 'the one of which had two heads, th'other three' (x. 73).
These are the giants of poetry not of history.

The first Elf of all, Spenser states at II. x. 70, was created by
Prometheus. The stanza offers a version of the familiar classical
creation myth which is found in *Metamorphoses* 1 and elsewhere.
Renaissance commentators (Golding and Lodge will do as examples)[24]
often explained the Prometheus story as a fictional, pagan version
of the true biblical history of the creation of man. Classical myths
could parallel biblical records because pagan poets were thought to
have gathered ideas from the Old Testament, but the classical forms
of the stories were essentially fictional. Hence Spenser starts his
history of Faeryland with an account of the creation of man which
everyone knew to be the invention of poets. Similarly, in place of
the Garden of Eden, he refers to a garden from within his own poetic
world, 'the gardins of *Adonis*', as the location in which the first Fay
was found. He could hardly link the origins of the Faery race more
pointedly with fiction and poetry.

The last three monarchs in the Elfin line, leading up to and
including Gloriana, possess a special interest. Quite obviously they
function in some way as equivalents to the major Tudor monarchs,
Henry VII, Henry VIII and Elizabeth, but this fact can make for
critical confusion about the 'then' and 'now' of *The Faerie Queene*.
Guyon is reading about Gloriana, who occupies the Faery throne in
his own era, yet modern readers may well feel that Gloriana 'is'
Queen Elizabeth I who occupies the throne of England in the poet's
era. Spenser gives the key to this puzzle in a word which he uses
in the Proem to Book 1. Addressing Elizabeth, 'Great Lady of the
greatest Isle', he asks for her help in writing about

> that true glorious type of thine,
> The argument of mine afflicted stile.
>
> (1 Proem 4)

Gloriana, his 'argument', is a 'type' of Elizabeth, that is to say she prefigures the Tudor queen, and exists well before her in time as types by definition must. Gloriana's grandfather, 'the wise *Elficleos*', and her father, 'the mightie *Oberon*', are types in the same way of Henry VII and Henry VIII respectively. They constitute part of the recent history of Faeryland, seen from Guyon's perspective; in addition they prefigure the Tudor monarchs who will come into existence centuries later. The compliment which Spenser has devised here for the Tudor sovereigns is that of saying that they are actual historical manifestations of ideal fictional rulers in the poem. His use of the word 'type' is particularly illuminating because it explains a relationship in time: the type precedes its fulfilment. The poet also, of course, employs a variety of other terms more familiar in Renaissance literary theory to refer to the relationship between Gloriana and Elizabeth – the poem is a 'mirrhour' in which the Queen will find an 'Image' and 'shadowes' (II Proem 4–5) or 'colourd showes' representing herself (III Proem 3) – but the special advantage of the theological term 'type' is that it establishes a temporal distance between the 'Image' and the living monarch.

In any discussion of the relationship between fiction and reality in *The Faerie Queene* the Proem to Book II invites particular attention. A note of serene confidence and suppressed amusement is audible as the poet talks about 'that happy land of Faery, / Which I so much do vaunt, yet no where show':

> Right well I wote most mighty Soueraine,
>   That all this famous antique history,
>   Of some th'aboundance of an idle braine
>   Will iudged be, and painted forgery,
>   Rather then matter of iust memory,
>   Sith none, that breatheth liuing aire, does know,
>   Where is that happy land of Faery,
>   Which I so much do vaunt, yet no where show,
> But vouch antiquities, which no body can know.
>
> (II Proem 1)

It seems to me that Spenser can afford to be confident because he has so firm a grasp of the meaning of Faeryland. As it is fiction-land he can indeed 'vaunt' it and invent 'antiquities' for it, especially the history of the Elfin monarchs, without needing to rely on printed chronicles which his readers could consult or 'know'. The world of the imagination needs no geographical location either, but the poet in these stanzas can enjoy the joke of suggesting that it *might* one day be discovered through the enterprise of explorers, just as the River Amazon and Virginia have been:

> But let that man with better sence aduize,
>   That of the world least part to vs is red:
>   And dayly how through hardy enterprize,
>   Many great Regions are discouered,
>   Which to late age were neuer mentioned.
>   Who euer heard of th'Indian *Peru*?
>   Or who in venturous vessell measured
>   The *Amazons* huge riuer now found trew?
> Or fruitfullest *Virginia* who did euer vew?
>
> Yet all these were, when no man did them know;
>   Yet haue from wisest ages hidden beene:
>   And later times things more vnknowne shall show.
>   Why then should witlesse man so much misweene
>   That nothing is, but that which he hath seene?
>   What if within the Moones faire shining spheare?
>   What if in euery other starre vnseene
>   Of other worldes he happily should heare?
> He wonder would much more: yet such to some appeare.
>
> (II Proem 2–3)

Men are pleasantly absurd in asking to 'see' with their physical eyes the world created by poetry, when it is only to be seen by the imagination, but the poet can make fun of them by pretending that maybe they will stumble on it some day. In the fourth stanza he alters his tone, and soberly tells the Queen where Faeryland can be found. Since it is an invented world, which contains images of actual human experience, the thoughtful observer will recognise that it reflects the world he knows 'here' in England. Its images are heightened representations of familiar phenomena; hence the Queen will be able to see her 'owne realmes in lond of Faery' when she looks in the mirror provided by fiction.

Spenser's opportunity to investigate the difference between poetry and historical fact, in this Proem, in the two sets of antiquities, or elsewhere, came to him, I have suggested, through his initial distinction between Britons and Elves made necessary by the current debate about the historicity of the Arthurian material. The distinction proved to be an extraordinarily happy one. It gave him the freedom to invent a whole fictive world whose ways were 'so exceeding spacious and wyde, / And sprinckled with such sweet variety' (vi Proem 1); yet at the same time it allowed him to assert quite firmly that the Queen was the descendant of the historic British monarch, Arthur. The poem could be a romance yet deal at times with historical fact; it could be mainly located in Faeryland yet make frequent references to British topography – the Roman Wall, the springs of Bath, Ludgate in London, Arlo Hill near Kilcolman, the almost innumerable rivers of England and Ireland. The poet's creative freedom was assured, but so was his chance to indulge, like another Holinshed or another Leland, his nationalistic passion for history and geography. His patriotism was voiced by Arthur:

> At last quite rauisht with delight, to heare
>   The royall Ofspring of his natiue land,
>   Cryde out, Deare countrey, O how dearely deare
>   Ought thy remembraunce, and perpetuall band
>   Be to thy foster Childe, that from thy hand
>   Did commun breath and nouriture receaue?
>   How brutish is it not to vnderstand,
>   How much to her we owe, that all vs gaue,
> That gaue vnto vs all, what euer good we haue.
>
> (II. x. 69)

8

Secret Wisdom?

I have left until the end of the book a fundamental critical question
which continues to provoke sharp disagreement among Spenserians:
should Spenser be regarded, at least in part, as an esoteric poet?
Several distinguished modern critics have argued that he should. A
theory of poetry still available in England at the end of the sixteenth
century would certainly permit such a view of this Elizabethan
writer. Renaissance Neoplatonism had given renewed prestige to the
belief that poetry contained secret wisdom to be hidden from the
multitude. The case for regarding certain episodes of *The Faerie
Queene* as deliberately obscure (for example, the Cave of Mammon,
the Garden of Adonis, and the Temple of Isis) has been argued by
Frank Kermode in an influential essay on the Cave of Mammon:

> [Spenser] is, in his way, an esoteric poet; like all poets in the Neo-Platonic
> tradition, not only the guardian of secrets but the creator of new secret
> wisdom. The position is one that was so familiar to Renaissance poets that
> to put it out of one's mind is almost certainly to distort one's reading not
> only of a Chapman or a Spenser but even in some degree of Shakespeare;
> for it was taken for granted that one of the properties of a fiction, however
> exoteric it might appear, was the possession of occult significance.[1]

Since 1960 when the essay was first published a split between
Spenserians on the issue has become quite visible. As Kermode
summed it up in a later essay, 'on the one hand we have a new
interest in occult aspects of structure and imagery, on the other, a
strong distaste for such matters accompanied by new definitions and
valuations of allegory'.[2]

The question is especially intractable because Spenser's own
contemporaries differed from each other both in their poetic theory
and in their practice. Chapman, for one, certainly boasted of the
esoteric meanings hidden in his work,[3] whereas Sidney did not.
Spenser himself described *The Faerie Queene* in the *Letter to Raleigh*

as 'a continued Allegory, or darke conceit', but this does not really help the debate since the meaning of the word 'darke' in such a context is by no means easy to establish, as we shall indicate below. Individual episodes in the poem have received interpretations both esoteric and comparatively plain, without settling the theoretical issue. I intend to debate the question afresh, first by a consideration of rival sixteenth-century poetic theories,[4] then by looking at some of the statements Spenser made about his own conception of the purpose of poetry, and then by studying episodes of the poem itself.

More than one theory about how, and to whom, narrative poems communicated was available to Spenser as he planned and wrote *The Faerie Queene*. A substantial line of poets and scholars from fourteenth-century and fifteenth-century Italy to sixteenth-century England claimed that some poems, at least, contained secret wisdom deliberately veiled by the poet in order to protect it from the gaze of the multitude. The fourteenth book of Boccaccio's *De Genealogia Deorum Gentilium* was profoundly influential in this context. Defending poetry against a variety of opponents, Boccaccio tackled amongst others those who complained of the frequent obscurity of poetic works. He replied that in some cases the alleged obscurity may be the beholder's fault because the poem itself is perfectly clear. In other cases the poet's subject may be so profound that not even the keenest intellect can comprehend it without great difficulty. In yet other cases, the material is deliberately veiled and hidden by the poet's skill, to protect it from the irreverent. I quote the passage dealing with this third category:

some things, though naturally clear perhaps, are so veiled by the artist's skill that scarcely anyone could by mental effort derive sense from them; as the immense body of the sun when hidden in clouds cannot be exactly located by the eye of the most learned astronomer. That some of the prophetic poems are in this class, I do not deny.

Yet not by this token is it fair to condemn them; for surely it is not one of the poet's various functions to rip up and lay bare the meaning which lies hidden in his inventions. Rather where matters truly solemn and memorable are too much exposed, it is his office by every effort to protect as well as he can and remove them from the gaze of the irreverent, that they cheapen not by too common familiarity. So when he discharges this duty and does it ingeniously, the poet earns commendation, not anathema.[5]

One of the purposes, then, of this deliberate obscurity is to protect the material from the unworthy; but there is a second purpose also, which is to stimulate the intellects of the few. The poet aims

> to make truths which would otherwise cheapen by exposure the object of strong intellectual effort and various interpretation, that in ultimate discovery they shall be more precious.
>
> (p. 60)

With the authority of St Augustine behind him, Boccaccio argued that the same kind of obscurity is to be found in scripture, although with this difference: scripture is 'addressed to all nations' whereas poetry 'is addressed to the few' (p. 61).

The concepts and key terms in Boccaccio's discussion – truths deliberately 'veiled' or 'hidden', for the benefit of the 'few' – were frequently repeated by Elizabethan poets in their prefaces and apologias. Richard Stanyhurst, who translated the first four books of the *Aeneid* into English quantitative verse, firmly asserted in his dedication that Virgil had sealed up 'hydden secrets' regarding the physical world in his poem, and that the inner meaning of the work was intended only for the 'diuing searcher':

> What deepe and rare poynctes of hydden secrets *Virgil* hath sealed vp in his twelue bookes of *Aeneis* may easelye appeere too such reaching wyts as bend theyre endewours too thee vnfolding thereof, not onlye by gnibling vpon thee outward ryne of a supposed historie, but also by groaping thee pyth that is shrind vp wythin thee barck and bodye of so exquisit and singular a discourse. For where as thee chiefe prayse of a wryter consisteth in thee enterlacing of pleasure wyth profit, oure author hath so wiselye alayed thee one wyth thee oother as thee shallow reader may bee delighted wyth a smooth tale, and thee diuing searcher may bee aduantaged by sowning a pretiouse treatise.[6]

The familiar rind-and-pith metaphor (found also in Boccaccio and in Erasmus's *Enchiridion*, for example) re-occurs in Sir John Harington's preface to his translation of *Orlando Furioso* (1591). He is writing a defence of poetry, relying in this passage on the Italian commentators on Ariosto. His account is particularly useful because it explains the various layers of meaning which can be found in poetry:

> The ancient Poets haue indeed wrapped as it were in their writings diuers and sundry meanings, which they call the senses or mysteries thereof. First of all for the literall sence (as it were the vtmost barke or ryne) they set downe in manner of an historie the acts and notable exploits of some persons worthy

memorie: then in the same fiction, as a second rine and somewhat more fine, as it were nearer to the pith and marrow, they place the Morall sence profitable for the actiue life of man, approuing vertuous actions and condemning the contrarie. Manie times also vnder the selfesame words they comprehend some true vnderstandingof natural Philosophie, or somtimes of politike gouernement, and now and then of diuinitie: and these same sences that comprehend so excellent knowledge we call the Allegorie.[7]

He goes on to state, as we might anticipate, that one purpose of the concealment of 'deepe mysteries of learning' under the 'vaile of fables' was 'that they might not be rashly abused by prophane wits, in whom science is corrupted, like good wine in a bad vessell' (p. 203). Another, and chief, purpose is that poetry with its layers of meaning will be able to satisfy different sorts of readers:

a principall cause of all, is to be able with one kinde of meate and one dish (as I may so call it) to feed diuers tastes. For the weaker capacities will feede themselues with the pleasantnes of the historie and sweetnes of the verse, some that haue stronger stomackes will as it were take a further taste of the Morall sence, a third sort, more high conceited then they, will digest the Allegorie: so as indeed it hath bene thought by men of verie good iudgement, such manner of Poetical writing was an excellent way to preserue all kinde of learning from that corruption which now it is come to since they left that mysticall writing of verse.

(p. 203)

Poetry may be read by many, but its deepest and most valuable meanings are deliberately preserved for the 'more high conceited'.

Harington makes a useful spokesman for what may be loosely called the 'secret wisdom' tradition. Nevertheless the tradition was being undermined during the same period by opponents who felt the claim that poetry contained secrets for the few was untrue or even absurd. Sidney's *Apologie for Poetrie* is crucial in this respect. His case for poetry is that it supremely possesses the power to delight, to teach, and to move the feelings, thereby surpassing both philosophy and history. The poet creates images which 'strike', 'pierce' and 'possesse the sight of the soule'. Significantly, the audience for whom the poet does this is not composed only of the learned, as is the case with the philosopher, but includes even 'the tenderest stomacks':

For conclusion, I say that the Philosopher teacheth, but he teacheth obscurely, so as the learned onely can vnderstande him, that is to say, he teacheth them that are already taught; but the Poet is the foode for the tenderest stomacks, the Poet is indeed the right Popular Philosopher, whereof *Esops* tales giue good proofe: whose pretty Allegories, stealing vnder the formall tales of Beastes, make many, more beastly then Beasts, begin to heare the sound of vertue from these dumbe speakers.[8]

The idea of the 'tenderest stomacks' went back to Plutarch; but Sidney's affirmation of it is fundamental to his whole case. Poetry creates images which move men to a desire for virtuous action; and evidently it is characteristic of poetry that it moves not the few but 'any man' who listens to it. The poet 'dooth not only show the way, but giueth so sweete a prospect into the way, as will intice any man to enter into it' (p. 172). Indeed, the fact that poetry teaches in a 'familiar' fashion is near the heart of its value:

and so a conclusion not vnfitlie ensueth, that as vertue is the most excellent resting place for all worldlie learning to make his end of, so Poetrie, beeing the most familiar to teach it, and most princelie to moue towards it, in the most excellent work is the most excellent workman.

(p. 175)

The only occasion on which Sidney refers to the 'secret wisdom' argument in defence of poetry is in the final section of the *Apologie*, the 'peroratio'. As tone is the all-important consideration here, it is as well to remind ourselves of K. O. Myrick's point made years ago that this section is coloured with an urbane and light-hearted irony.[9] Sidney regales the reader with an impressive collection of authorities and opinions, including the opinion that there are 'many misteries contained in Poetrie':

I coniure you all that haue had the euill lucke to reade this incke-wasting toy of mine, euen in the name of the nyne Muses, no more to scorne the sacred misteries of Poesie, no more to laugh at the name of Poets...but to beleeue, with *Aristotle*, that they were the auncient Treasurers of the Graecians Diuinity...To beleeue, with *Clauserus*, the Translator of *Cornutus*, that it pleased the heauenly Deitie, by *Hesiod* and *Homer*, vnder the vayle of fables, to giue vs all knowledge, Logick, Rethorick, Philosophy, naturall and morall; and *Quid non*? To beleeue, with me, that there are many misteries contained in Poetrie, which of purpose were written darkely, least by prophane wits it should bee abused. To beleeue, with *Landin*, that they are so beloued of the Gods that whatsoeuer they write proceeds of a diuine fury. Lastly, to beleeue themselues, when they tell you they will make you immortall by their verses.

(pp. 205–6)

The claims of the authorities grow increasingly grandiose. Poor Clauserus's inflated view of the contents of Hesiod and Homer is put down with the mocking phrase: 'and *Quid non?*' Landino's belief that poets are inspired by a divine 'furor' is cheerfully endorsed despite the fact that Sidney has personally denied it earlier in the present work (p. 192). The notion that 'there are many misteries contained in Poetrie, which of purpose were written darkly, least by prophane wits it should bee abused', wittily placed between the extravagant claims of Clauserus and Landino, is in open contradiction to the view which Sidney has urged throughout the *Apologie*.

Certainly the secret wisdom theory faded in the following century (Henry Reynolds, to whom I shall refer later on, was probably its last major spokesman). Of considerable interest, I think, are the causes which were working to undermine the theory during the sixteenth century. The influence of Aristotle's *Poetics*, or, more precisely, of a combination of Aristotle and Horace, on sixteenth-century criticism operated against esoteric theories. Aristotle was concerned with imitation, with the general truths of poetry as opposed to the particular truths of history, with questions of structure and unity, not with mysteries. Among other causes, the influence of Protestant thought on sixteenth-century ideas about allegory and hence about poetry is especially relevant in the context of the present book. Renaissance humanists – Boccaccio, Pico della Mirandola, Erasmus, for example – frequently pointed to an analogy between the methods of the poets and the methods of scripture: both tended to be obscure, both needed to be read allegorically. But Protestant thinkers, led by Luther, vehemently denied the relevance of allegorical interpretation in the case of many biblical books where it had previously been customary. Genesis was a particularly important instance. Luther declared that to make Moses so mystical and allegorical was not helpful, since Moses spoke in the literal sense, about the real world. He roundly called the ideas of Origen, Jerome and other allegorical interpreters 'silly'.[10] However, this is not to say that Protestant commentators denied the presence of allegory in the bible altogether. Obviously scripture contained many allegorical passages and indeed entire allegorical books, above all the Song of Solomon and Revelation. It is in the discussion of these books by certain Protestants that one may note some changes going on in the conception of the *purpose* of allegory. Familiar statements

about the uses of allegory continue to recur, of course: we still find
that allegory exists to hide the truth from the wicked, and sometimes
that it exists in order to give valuable exercise to the minds of the
elect. But we also find a quite different type of statement, which
maintains that biblical allegory is not obscure at all but exists in order
to 'unfold' and clarify matters, not to 'darken' them. The following
passage from Bullinger's sermons on Revelation, although lengthy,
deserves to be quoted:

Now all these matters are set forth and handled after the Apostolicke maner,
and accustomed facion of holy scripture, playne and ful of perspicuitie. At
the beginning God propounded diuine matters, and the which concerned our
saluation, as it were vnder a veale, and vnder figures, not to thintente to darken
or obscure them: but rather to vnfolde them and set them foorth. For this
maner of declaryng inuisible thyngs, by visible, is more fit to teache, more
mete to moue, more apt for perspicuitie, and most conuenient and fitting,
that things may be more depely imprinted in minde, and the lesse fall out of
the same. And therfore we rede that sondry visions, were exhibited to the
Patriarches, as to Abraham, Israell, Ioseph, Moses and others. Certes yf you
take from the bokes of the Prophetes, the visions, parables, and sundry figures
of speache, how much, I pray you, shall you leaue of theyr doctryne? emongs
these, be more notable in visions, Ezechiel, Daniel, and Zacharie. Neyther
is thys maner of teachyng by visions, parables, and sundry figures, taken away
in the new testament, lyke as I haue shewed els where. The very story of the
Gospel doth figurate and teache most thinges by parables. And. S. Iohn
himself in his Gospel, is veri much in the mention of light, darknes, of bread,
water, of a Shepherd, and shepe, and suche other lyke. In the meane while
I am not ignorant, howe great a difference, there is betwene parables,
Metaphores or Allegories, and visions: But who agayne knoweth not, that in
teaching, and setting forth of matters the maner of either to be after a sort
al one, and of the same effect? For they serue for plainnes and perspicuitie.[11]

(A marginal note remarks: 'The boke is plaine and may be
vnderstand.') Bullinger evidently is quite aware of other points of
view about allegory. Reversing Boccaccio's position he says that
scripture is not 'obscure' but 'playne', that the 'veale' is not
intended to 'darken' or conceal God's meaning, that the function
of allegory is effective communication. Bullinger knows perfectly
well that rhetorical handbooks distinguish between allegories,
parables, visions, and so on, but he believes that they all 'serue for
plainnes and perspicuitie'.

A brief passage from the Puritan Dudley Fenner's commentary

on the Song of Solomon contains, I think, the same assumption – that
a biblical allegory exists in order to make 'great and heauenlye
misteries' comprehensible and moving:

> Solomon was indued not onley with a great measure of spirituall vnder-
> standing, necessarie for the matter, but with the knovveledge of the natures
> of all creatures: whereby so great and heauenlye misteries might be made
> more easie and plaine to our vnderstanding, when similitudes are aptlie
> drawne from them, and with the special grace of sounges, which he atteyned
> by great practise: By all which giftes he was able to frame suche a sounge,
> as the grace whereof might worke in our hartes a most heauenly melodie.[12]

Solomon's use of 'similitudes' has the effect of making mysteries
'more easie and plaine to our vnderstanding', and of moving our
'hartes' or feelings, just as Bullinger found allegory 'more fit to
teache, more mete to moue'.

The role of Protestantism in undermining the notion that allegory
is essentially concerned to hide truths cannot readily be doubted. But
we still need to ask where Spenser stood in relation to current
theories of poetry – that is to say, in relation to Harington's esoteric
theory or Sidney's non-esoteric one. In the *Letter to Raleigh* the poet
described *The Faerie Queene* as 'a continued Allegory, or darke
conceit', a definition which might raise hopes of answering the
question of the degree of obscurity intended in the poem. Actually
the word 'darke' does not provide the answer, for this reason: it
is certainly the adjective used by Richard Sherry in *A treatise of
Schemes and Tropes* (1550) and by Henry Peacham in *The Garden of
Eloquence* (1593) to describe a particular kind of allegory, 'Enigma',
employed especially in the presentation of dreams and intended to
be hard to interpret; but it is also the adjective used by Puttenham
in *The Arte of English Poesie* (1589) when referring to allegory in
general, without the implication that all allegories are intended to
be obscure.[13] Hence Spenser in his use of the phrase 'darke conceit'
might be claiming that his whole poem belongs to the category of
'Enigma', or he might simply be using the conventional epithet for
allegory in general. This phrase of Spenser's will not give us much
help, I think, but the way in which he employs the metaphor 'covert
veil' in connection with his poetry may prove more illuminating.

Only once does Spenser use the 'veil' metaphor in a way which
suggests that his poem has been devised to hide its deeper meanings

from 'comune vew', and that is in his dedicatory sonnet to Lord
Burleigh:

> To you right noble Lord, whose carefull brest
> To menage of most graue affaires is bent,
> And on whose mightie shoulders most doth rest
> The burdein of this kingdomes gouernement,
> As the wide compasse of the firmament,
> On *Atlas* mighty shoulders is vpstayd;
> Vnfitly I these ydle rimes present,
> The labor of lost time, and wit vnstayd:
> Yet if their deeper sence be inly wayd,
> And the dim vele, with which from comune vew
> Their fairer parts are hid, aside be layd.
> Perhaps not vaine they may appeare to you.
> Such as they be, vouchsafe them to receaue,
> And wipe their faults out of your censure graue.

This indeed might suggest that Spenser subscribed to the esoteric
theory, if it were not for the fact that the statesman to whom the
sonnet was addressed was the public figure whom he most disliked,
and whom he regarded as least capable of understanding his poem.
The Proem to Book IV makes plain that in Spenser's opinion, as Paul
J. Alpers has remarked, Burleigh 'does not know what it is like to
love or to read a poem'.[14] Spenser boldly concludes the Proem by
saying that Burleigh is not a reader whom he values: 'To such
therefore I do not sing at all.' If we turn back to the dedicatory
sonnet, it becomes highly significant that it is only to Burleigh that
Spenser offers the secret wisdom formula as a justification for the
poem. The proposition that the 'deeper sence' of the rhymes will
be intelligible to Burleigh, while a 'dim vele' will hide their 'fairer
parts' from 'comune vew', is extremely flattering to the statesman,
but it is unlikely that Spenser would reserve a true description of his
art for Burleigh of all people.

The other important occurrence of the veil metaphor is in a
context where Spenser is writing with more commitment. It is the
final stanza of the Proem to Book II. The earlier stanzas, as we noted
in Chapter 7, contain some subtle teasing, but stanza 4 quietly
informs the Queen that Faeryland constitutes a mirror of her realm.
In stanza 5 Spenser changes the metaphor for the poem from mirror
to 'couert vele', and asks the Queen's pardon for enfolding herself
and her ancestry in it:

> The which O pardon me thus to enfold
> In couert vele, and wrap in shadowes light,
> That feeble eyes your glory may behold,
> Which else couid not endure those beames bright,
> But would be dazled with exceeding light.
>
> (II Proem 5)

Certainly the poem acts as a veil, but the crucial point here is that the purpose of the veil is not to hide, not to conceal, but to make the Queen's glory visible to 'feeble eyes'. The Queen's supreme worth, itself a manifestation of the divine, is to be shown to readers who, far from being notable for their high conceits (Harington's phrase), possess only 'feeble eyes'. The veil has not been created by the poet to 'remove' serious matters 'from the gaze of the irreverent' (Boccaccio), nor to exercise the riddle-solving powers of the few, but for the purpose of communication with the many. The veil of allegory is (Bullinger's words this time) 'more fit to teache, more mete to moue, more apt for perspicuitie'.

The brief passages we have quoted from Spenser could not of course settle questions of poetic theory on their own. Much more important are the methods he uses in some of the great episodes of *The Faerie Queene* which have received celebrated esoteric interpretations in the twentieth century and on which modern esoteric critics rest their case. I shall look at three such episodes in the hope of finding whether the 'enigmatic' readings are truly compatible with the poetic evidence. The first is the Mordant and Amavia episode (II. i–ii), in which Guyon witnesses the fate of a fresh young sensualist, victim of Acrasia, and a desperately grieving woman. Since Mordant dies at a fountain, and the infant Ruddymane is (unsuccessfully) washed at a fountain, the episode is interpreted by Alastair Fowler as being allegorically concerned 'with baptismal regeneration and with sanctification'. He acknowledges his esoteric perspective when he states that some of the images in the episode 'were probably intended from the beginning as mysteries of poetic theology'.[15] Noting that Mordant's name means 'death-giving' and that Amavia says of him, 'he was flesh: (all flesh doth frailtie breed)', Fowler concludes that Mordant represents 'the flesh', the 'outward man', in the theological sense – and that Amavia therefore represents 'the inward man or conscience'. Perhaps the danger of imposing a schematic reading is visible here. Every detail in the narrative stresses

Amavia's role as a passionately loving woman driven to suicidal grief. Her name, included like Mordant's in Acrasia's riddle ('*Sad verse, giue death to him that death does giue / And losse of loue, to her that loues to liue*'), reveals that she in effect loves in order to live, because the process of loving is life itself to her. Her rhetorically patterned description of her husband, 'My Lord my loue; my deare Lord, my deare loue', indicates the intensity of her feeling for him. After his death she gives herself up to an extreme grief which moves both Guyon and the reader. Between them the married pair foreshadow the two major types of passion to be explored in Book II, the concupiscible and the irascible, summed up by Guyon in the single line, 'The strong through pleasure soonest falles, the weake through smart' (i. 57). The one thing the wretched Amavia does not suggest is 'the inward man or conscience'.

The fountain in which Guyon tries unsuccessfully to wash Ruddymane's hands free of Amavia's blood is interpreted by Fowler as an image of 'regenerating grace' and 'baptism' (pp. 96–7). He explains the temperate knight's failure to cleanse the hands in any way whatever by reminding us that 'baptism removed the guilt of original sin but not the infection itself, concupiscence' (p. 100). Although this is theologically true, we may feel that a well which has no cleansing properties at all – Guyon washed the child's hands 'oft and oft, yet nought they beene/ For all his washing cleaner' (ii. 3) – is in poetic terms a very odd image of baptism. In any case shortly afterwards, as Lewis H. Miller, Jr has pointed out,[16] the Palmer quite explicitly tells Guyon to put aside theological speculation about the fountain and the bloodstained hands. The knight has been wondering

> whether blot of foule offence
> Might not be purgd with water nor with bath;
> Or that high God, in lieu of innocence,
> Imprinted had that token of his wrath,
> To shew how sore bloudguiltinesse he hat'th...
>
> (ii. 4)

but the Palmer replies with 'goodly reason':

> Ye bene right hard amated, gratious Lord,
> And of your ignorance great maruell make,
> Whiles cause not well conceiued ye mistake.
>
> (ii. 5)

The fountain, he explains, springs from the 'cold', 'chast' tears (stanza 9) of a nymph whom we recognise as a thematic opposite of the warm, sensual Mordant. Besides, Ruddymane's hands must remain unwashed for a reason which has some poignancy within the fiction: the child's destiny is to act, in his own body, as a reminder of the duty of revenge – a human equivalent of the 'bloody napkin' in *The Spanish Tragedy* of which Hieronimo says:

> Horatio, this was thine,
> And when I dy'd it in thy dearest blood,
> This was a token 'twixt thy soul and me
> That of thy death revenged I should be.[17]

Amavia's blood must not be washed from Ruddymane's hands,

> That as a sacred Symbole it may dwell
> In her sonnes flesh, to minde reuengement.
>
> (ii. 10)

A wry contrast is achieved by the poet, if we let the narrative speak for itself, between the baby's innocent unawareness – 'Who with sweet pleasance and bold blandishment / Gan smyle on them' (ii. 1) – and his strange plight as a living symbol of revenge. An interpretation based on the 'outward' and 'inward' man, and on baptism, really does seem to defy linguistic, thematic and narrative effects.

The second episode we might look at is that of the Garden of Proserpina, of which Frank Kermode proposed an esoteric reading in the course of his celebrated essay on the Cave of Mammon from which we quoted at the beginning of this chapter. He argues that Guyon in II. vii undergoes an 'initiatory ordeal' like Christ and Hercules, and that having resisted the temptations of wealth and honour the knight is faced in the Garden of Proserpina with the temptation of vain learning and forbidden knowledge. The Garden, he suggests, is the most difficult part of an episode which 'labours to be shadowed with obscurity'.[18] In Chapter 6 I gave my reasons for thinking that Guyon does not in fact resemble Christ in this episode and indeed should not have entered Mammon's underworld at all; but now the moment has come to examine the imagery of that underworld, or at least the images which help to define the nature of the Garden of Proserpina.

Mammon shows Guyon the infernal origins of wealth in the hall of the sweating fiends, and gives him a glimpse of the quality of life at the court of Philotime where human beings have only one goal, the achievement of worldly honour. He then leads him 'through griesly shadowes by a beaten path' (vii. 51) into a garden which is evidently a kind of hell, near the centre of which grows a tree laden with golden apples. The adjectives used to describe the apples, 'golden', 'glistring', 'goodly' (the characteristic Spenserian equivocation),

> Their fruit were golden apples glistring bright,
> That goodly was their glory to behold,
>
> (vii. 54)

together with the phrase 'rich fee' in stanza 56 ('his broad braunches, laden with rich fee') set up strong suggestions that this is a tree of wealth, of money, of desirable but ultimately treacherous riches. Mythologically, the apples are linked by the poet with those of the Hesperides, of Atalanta, of Acontius and of Ate. Kermode's interpretation of the apples is categorical: 'Whatever they signify it is not avarice, as the commentators say; we have left that behind. The apples of the Hesperides were emblems of astronomical knowledge' (p. 72). However, as we have often remarked, with Spenser context is all, and since mythological images usually possess more than one meaning the context will play a crucial part in determining the relevance of any interpretation. If it is not too flippant an argument, one might note that in *Amoretti* lxxvii the 'twoo golden apples' mentioned by the poet, although linked once again with those of the Hesperides and those which enticed Atalanta, are not emblems of astronomical knowledge but symbolise the breasts of the poet's lady. In the case of the golden apples in the Garden of Proserpina, the opinion of any Renaissance authority whom we wish to invoke – Natalis Comes or any other – will need to be relevant to a context in which the apples have been verbally associated with glittering 'fee' and with the inexorable creation of discord. This latter point emerges from the last and longest of the mythological allusions:

> Here eke that famous golden Apple grew,
> The which emongst the gods false *Ate* threw;
> For which th'*Idaean* Ladies disagreed,

Till partiall *Paris* dempt it *Venus* dew,
And had of her, faire *Helen* for his meed,
That many noble *Greekes* and *Troians* made to bleed.

(vii. 55)

If we glance at another though less fashionable Renaissance authority, Henry Smith, we find that in a sermon on the subject of worldliness he uses the golden apple as a symbol of the worldly wealth which creates conflict between neighbours and brothers. The world strives for the world, says Smith,

like beggers thrusting at a dole, Lawyer against Lawyer, brother against brother, neighbour against neighbour, for the golden Apple.[19]

Smith does not pause to explain the classical allusion because its meaning is established by the context.

Beside the tree laden with golden apples stands 'a siluer seat', for which neither Kermode (nor I) nor any other commentator has found a really satisfactory literary analogue, although Kermode would like to link it with 'the forbidden seat in the Eleusinian mysteries' if it were not for the fact that the standard work on the subject is too late in date to be known to Spenser (pp. 74–5). We are thrown back on Spenser's own words about seats and chairs in relevant contexts. Proserpina, Queen of hell and owner of this silver seat, is the mother of Lucifera (I. iv. 11), the personification of pride. When Lucifera sets out in the procession of sins, her 'glorious glitterand light' amazing the spectators, her coach strives 'to match, in royall rich array, / Great *Iunoes* golden chaire' (I. iv. 17). Mother and daughter have silver and golden chairs respectively, and the latter chair, certainly, is an emblem of pride and ambition. It may be that in the hell of the worldly – and I shall argue that this is what the Garden of Proserpina represents – Spenser sums up his two themes of the avarice which lives for wealth and the ambition which lives for honour in the climactic images of golden apples and silver stool.

Among the souls tormented in the River Cocytus which surrounds the garden only Tantalus and Pilate are named, the former regularly found in classical hells, the other a superb example of Spenser's ability to perceive and establish connections. Of Tantalus Kermode writes: 'He is normally taken as a type of avarice, not without support from mythographers; but he is much more certainly a type of blasphemous or intemperate knowledge' (p. 73). Rival Renaissance interpretations of the figure can be piled up on either side of the argument: Paul J. Alpers has effectively summed up in a few sentences the massive weight of evidence, from Erasmus, Alciati, Whitney, Harington and Sidney, for example, that Tantalus in the river of hell is an emblem of avarice.[20] As usual the context will have to settle the question, and since the figure of Pilate is clearly linked with, or balanced against, that of Tantalus, Pilate may provide the illumination we need. Kermode remarks that in the case of Pilate 'one confesses to feeling less certain', but he suggests that Pilate's question 'what is truth?' would be an instance of Augustinian *curiositas* (pp. 73–4). Spenser, however, does not once allude to Pilate's question; instead he focuses on his activities as 'the falsest Iudge' and 'most vniust', who 'deliuered vp the Lord of life to die'. It is worth looking at what the sixteenth-century commentaries on the gospels have to say on the subject of Pilate's behaviour as a judge. Calvin in his commentary on St John had written:

> Nowe we see in Pilate an image of a proude man, whom his owne ambition maketh mad. For whilest that he will extoll his power, he depriueth himselfe of the prayse and fame of iustice.

> Pilate dooth not behaue himselfe couragiously, and is ruled rather with ambition, then with desire of iustice.[21]

The key to Pilate's behaviour is ambition. Marlorat, whose commentaries are compilations from earlier works including Calvin's, reiterates the point about ambition and stresses Pilate's unrighteousness, his unjust decision, his wickedness, and the hopelessness of his hand washing:

> Pilate...is more led by ambition than by the loue of righteousnes.

> Hee vniustlye condemned the Iuste, againste his owne conscience, whome he knewe oughte to haue beene defended. And as for the childishe ceremony which he vseth, it dothe nothynge at all mittigate the falte: For howe coulde a fewe droppes of water washe awaye the spotte of wyckednes whyche no satisfaction coulde blotte oute?...Pilate saythe that he killeth not Christe and yet he condemneth hym, and deliuereth him to be killed: in the meane time washeth his handes as one that is innocente.[22]

Spenser's Pilate uses a vocabulary of self-condemnation very similar to the vocabulary in the commentaries. Guyon asks the wretch in the water who he is, and receives this answer:

I *Pilate* am the falsest Iudge, alas,
And most vniust, that by vnrighteous
And wicked doome, to Iewes despiteous
Deliuered vp the Lord of life to die,
And did acquite a murdrer felonous;
The whiles my hands I washt in puritie,
The whiles my soule was soyld with foule iniquitie.

(vii. 62)

The tragic paradoxes in the situation presented by the commentaries are compressed and heightened in the poem: Pilate delivered 'the Lord of life' to 'die'; he 'washt' his hands and simultaneously 'soyld' his soul. The regret of the man who sought 'the fame and praise of a iust Iudge' (Marlorat, p. 705) but actually became 'the falsest' and 'most vniust' judge (Spenser) finds expression in the terse lament, 'alas'.

In the River Cocytus Spenser depicts the unjust judge who has reached this place of torment because of the ambition which motivated his life. Pilate, embodiment of ambition, is linked with Tantalus, traditional 'ensample' of avarice, of greed, who 'gaped still, as coueting to drinke' (vii. 58). The two preoccupations of worldlings, avarice and ambition, are finally revealed through their consequences: their representatives suffer endlessly in the river of hell. In the course of the episode Spenser uncovers the true nature, which means the true ugliness, of a love of riches – money chests in Mammon's Cave have skulls and dead men's bones as their accompaniment – and of a life dedicated to desire for worldly honour, sharply focused in the court of Philotime. As we have already suggested, the two themes are summed up in the golden apples and silver stool in Proserpina's arbour; and the fatal consequences of self-surrender to these two desires emerge in the sufferings of Tantalus and Pilate. The Garden of Proserpina is an extraordinary mythic creation of Spenser's – a specialised hell of the worldly.

The shape of the Cave of Mammon episode as a whole has much in common with that of the House of Pride, where, equally, the true nature of pride is progressively revealed through the character of the palace itself, the throne and the manners of its chief occupant, the lifestyle of those who choose to dwell there, and finally the discovery that behind the palace lies a dungeon crowded with 'caytiue wretched thrals, that wayled night and day'. Interestingly, the victims of Lucifera include both classical and biblical figures as Mammon's victims do. For the reader, the fascination of the episodes resides both in the inexorable exposure of the meaning of particular sins and in the by no means unambiguous behaviour of the knights who visit these dwellings. The Redcross Knight dislikes the vanity of Lucifera's courtiers even as he becomes deeply tainted by it; Guyon steadily rejects the temptations of wealth and honour even while his words in reply to Mammon and his very presence in the Cave reveal his presumptuous self-trust. The episodes are luminous rather than problematic in their overall design, I would argue; but that does not lessen the interest of their disturbing, psychologically subtle and sometimes strikingly original detail. Spenser brings together Tantalus and Pilate not only because of their thematic significance but also because his eclectic imagination perceives the resemblance between the two in their frantic, hopeless activity in water. One of them strives in vain to drink 'the cold liquor' which he wades in, the other strives in vain to wash his soiled hands.

The third esoteric reading of a Spenserian episode which invites attention is Thomas P. Roche's interpretation of the Cambell and Triamond conflict (IV. ii–iii). Just as Fowler prefaced his interpretation of II. i–ii with a reference to the 'mysteries of poetic theology', and Kermode his interpretation of II. vii with the claim that Spenser was 'in his way, an esoteric poet' in the intellectual tradition of Boccaccio, Erasmus and Chapman, so Roche bases his account of Cambell and Triamond on the poetic theory of Harington. Harington's exposition of the various layers of meaning in the myth of Perseus and Gorgon, culminating in the 'more high and heauenly Allegorie' intended for the few, seems to provide the necessary precedent for an esoteric reading of Spenser's episode. All three critics invoke the secret wisdom tradition as a theoretical framework for their particular analyses; but I have already called in question the assumption that Spenser chose to work within this tradition. I also question the accuracy of the interpretations which issue from the theory.

Roche sees the allegorical technique in the Cambell and Triamond episode as one pole or extreme of Spenser's narrative method. At the other pole is to be found, for example, the opening episode of Book III. Here Roche stresses the need for the reader to be 'patient' and to avoid trying 'to assign meanings to Florimell until the poem warrants it'.[23] In my opinion this is a most valuable emphasis; it is only in connection with the very different method of interpretation used for the Book IV episode that questions need to be raised. Roche argues that the name Agape, the Greek term for Christian love, and the names of her three sons Priamond, Diamond and Triamond (this last occurring on the title page though not in the narrative as Telamond) are an allusion to the fact that 'Love' created 'the three worlds: terrestrial, celestial, and supercelestial' (pp. 15–16). Hence Cambell's struggle, supported by the magic ring given him by Canacee, against the three brothers is to be interpreted as follows:

> Let us postulate that Cambell is man and that his name represents the warring elements of *bellum intestinum* and that Canacee represents those human elements that sustain man in his battle against himself and the world, whether we call this mind or soul or reason. The magic ring then would become the sustaining link between the two. Cambell's battle with the three brothers figures man's battle with the three worlds to find his place in the universe, to establish harmony in God's creation, and ultimately to achieve salvation.
>
> (p. 30)

We may wonder why 'man' should not only fight but actually kill the terrestrial and celestial worlds in order 'to find his place in the universe', why 'man' is to be regarded as the agent who establishes 'harmony in God's creation', and why a Protestant poet should show an individual achieving 'salvation' by his own efforts. It is doubtful whether the grim battle between Cambell and the brothers suggests any of these things. Roche might reply that the esoteric tradition does not require 'easy leaps between tenor and vehicle' (p. 30), but some relationship between the two would give the reader confidence.

Roche is surely right to point out that the name Agape indicates the presence of an allegorical statement. However, the names of her sons are less transparent: it is as likely that they refer to the identity of each individual as a 'little world' as that they signal an equivalence with the 'three worlds' of Neoplatonic cosmology. As always the reader must attend to the vocabulary and rhetorical figures employed by the poet to communicate the nature of new characters:

> Amongst those knights there were three brethren bold,
>   Three bolder brethren neuer were yborne,
>   Borne of one mother in one happie mold,

Borne at one burden in one happie morne,
Thrise happie mother, and thrise happie morne,
That bore three such, three such not to be fond;
Her name was *Agape* whose children werne
All three as one, the first hight *Priamond*,
The second *Dyamond*, the youngest *Triamond*.

Stout *Priamond*, but not so strong to strike,
Strong *Diamond*, but not so stout a knight,
But *Triamond* was stout and strong alike:
On horsebacke vsed *Triamond* to fight,
And *Priamond* on foote had more delight,
But horse and foote knew *Diamond* to wield:
With curtaxe vsed *Diamond* to smite,
And *Triamond* to handle speare and shield,
But speare and curtaxe both vsd *Priamond* in field.

These three did loue each other dearely well,
And with so firme affection were allyde,
As if but one soule in them all did dwell,
Which did her powre into three parts diuyde.

(IV. ii. 41–3)

The particularly emphatic use of repetition and parallelism clearly establishes the unity of the brothers and their equality in physical prowess. In the third stanza the poet refers to the love which unites them, and in the climactic line, 'As if but one soule in them all did dwell', makes an affirmation of central relevance to this book of *The Faerie Queene*: their brotherly love constitutes a profound form of friendship. The familiar phrase 'one soul in bodies twain' regularly appeared in Renaissance discussions of friendship, of which Lodowick Bryskett's is representative. Friendship, he writes,

bindeth mens minds so fast together, and breedeth so firme a consent in them, that they become as one; in so much as it seemeth that one mind dwelleth in two bodies to guide and rule them.[24]

Spenser's rhetorical figures, his deployment of traditional phrases (not only 'As if but one soule in them all did dwell' but also 'All three as one' in stanza 41), and the narrative which he develops in Canto iii in which the brothers' souls pass from one of their bodies to the next, could hardly indicate more clearly that his theme is brotherly love as a form of friendship. The origin or 'roote' (ii. 43) of this love is Agape. The poet seems to be making a biblical point of a kind much repeated in the First Epistle of John, that Christian love, love of God, is the true source of the love of brother for brother. 'And this commandement haue we of him that he whiche loueth God, shulde loue hys brother also' (1 John 4.21). Spenser frequently draws attention to the origin of virtues and vices through the parents he assigns to his characters; in the present case having made his point about love he is free to put it aside and allow the Fay, Agape, to function simply as a devoted mother who rather misguidedly (iii. 2) attempts to secure long life for her sons. This reading is far from revolutionary, but it seems to explain the name Agape more satisfactorily than does the esoteric interpretation.

On the basis of the arguments I have put forward in this chapter concerning Spenser's poetic theory and his practice in these three episodes, I conclude that it was not his intention in *The Faerie Queene* to create narratives which would contain secret wisdom for the few, deliberately veiled from the many. Indeed I would argue that a peculiar feature of Spenser's art is the commitment it shows to a recurrent process of gradual clarification. Whether we look at small units or large – single stanzas and pairs of stanzas, or whole episodes – we find a characteristic movement through a dense net of details, physical, moral, psychological, sombre or comic, to a final word or passage which explicitly confirms the meaning which the reader has slowly or rapidly been discovering. Some examples of single stanzas or pairs of stanzas which work in this way were mentioned above on pp. 81–2, although the stanzas just quoted about Agape and her sons would provide an equally useful instance. A. C. Hamilton has rightly pointed to the way in which Spenser refrains from naming the 'sad house of *Pride*' until the very end of that episode.[25] Especially interesting is the poet's almost invariable procedure when presenting visionary tableaux. After he has described a climactic spectacle he follows it with an explanatory discourse which ensures that the main points are not lost on the reader. Britomart's dream in the Temple of Isis is expounded by the gravest of the priests; Calidore's vision of the dance of the Graces is expounded by Colin Clout in a fashion which delights his visitor (VI. x. 30). In IV. x. 41 the priests who attend the veiled statue of Venus seen by Scudamour evidently favour the notion of secret wisdom, but Spenser through the mouth of his character arranges that the meaning of this central figure should be communicated to the reader:

> The cause why she was couered with a vele,
> Was hard to know, for that her Priests the same
> From peoples knowledge labour'd to concele.
> But sooth it was not sure for womanish shame,
> Nor any blemish, which the worke mote blame;
> But for, they say, she hath both kinds in one,
> Both male and female, both vnder one name:
> She syre and mother is her selfe alone,
> Begets and eke conceiues, ne needeth other none.
>
> (IV. X. 41)

In the case of the Garden of Adonis, exposition is not reserved to the end but mingled with the description. Needless to say we are not implying that the explanations are substitutes for the poetic images, or encompass more than a small part of the total sensuous and spiritual experience created by the images, but the aim of the explanations is to make sure that the reader comprehends the main thrust of the episode and is not left to stray in bewildered speculation.

Two seventeenth-century readers of *The Faerie Queene* provide interesting confirmation of this view of the poet. The first is Henry Reynolds, whose *Mythomystes* (1632) is an impassioned affirmation of the esoteric tradition. He quotes Pico on the subject of the 'secreter Mysteries' of the Pentateuch 'hidden and concealed vnder the barke, and rude couer of the words'.[26] He then pours scorn on 'our Modernes', especially poets, because they clearly 'possesse the knowledge of no such mysteries as deserue the vse of any art at all for their concealing' (pp. 43–4). All they have is 'Morall doctrine' (p. 45) which 'needes no fiction to clothe or conceale it in' (p. 48). These statements establish the necessary context for understanding what he has to say about Spenser. Although he praises him and acknowledges his learning, he wishes he had not been 'so close riuetted to his Morall':

Next, I must approue the learned *Spencer*, in the rest of his Poems, no lesse then his *Fairy Queene*, an exact body of the *Ethicke* doctrine: though some good iudgments haue wisht (and perhaps not without cause) that he had therein beene a little freer of his fiction, and not so close riuetted to his Morall.

(p. 8)

'Morall doctrine' or as he calls it here 'Ethicke doctrine' is not an adequate subject, Reynolds stresses throughout the book, for great poetry. He wishes that Spenser had invented fictions more freely because fictions are capable of containing secret wisdom, and that he had not been so exclusively preoccupied with moral issues. From the point of view of the esoteric tradition the poet of *The Faerie Queene* must be seen as defective.

The other seventeenth-century reader I have in mind is Sir Kenelm Digby. Digby's short book devoted to one particular stanza of *The Faerie Queene* contains an arresting statement about what he regards as Spenser's usual manner of proceeding throughout the poem. He makes an exception of only one stanza (II. ix. 22), which he will be concerned to interpret during his treatise. In the whole of the rest of the work Spenser's method is gradually to uncover what may at first appear obscure until it becomes accessible 'to any ordinarie capacitie'. Digby begins by referring to the one problematic stanza or 'Staffe' (and he refers to it again with the phrase 'But in this' half-way through the passage):

In this Staffe the Author seems to me to proceed in a different manner from what he doth elsewhere generally through his whole Book. For in other places, although the beginning of his Allegory or mysticall sense, may be obscure, yet in the process of it, he doth himself declare his own conceptions in such sort as they are obvious to any ordinarie capacitie: But in this, he seems only to glance at the profoundest notions that any Science can deliver us, and then on a sudden (as it were) recalling himself out of an Enthusiasme, he returns to the gentle Relation of the Allegoricall History he had begun, leaving his Readers to wander up and down in much obscuritie, and to come within much danger of erring at his Intention in these lines?[27]

In this one stanza the reader is left to wander in obscurity; elsewhere through 'the processe' of the allegory the meaning is revealed 'to any ordinarie capacitie'. This significant phrase is intended, I think, to contrast with formulations like Harington's reference to the 'more high conceited', for whom the most valuable meanings are reserved in the esoteric tradition. Digby finds no intention on Spenser's part to withhold wisdom.

Both Reynolds and Digby recognise Spenser's remarkable learning. The poet was familiar with an impressive range of literature, history, philosophy of various kinds, mythography and iconography, not to mention biblical commentaries and religious works; and some of this material was available only to a truly learned individual. But in Spenser's case obscurity of sources is not at all the same thing as an intentionally obscure effect. He characteristically transforms learned materials into accessible poetic experiences. In *The Faerie Queene* the abstract becomes concrete, the remote becomes imaginatively available.

Throughout the present study we have had frequent occasion to refer to the Spenserian synthesis of divergent materials. In conclusion it is important to emphasise what has been implicit or explicit at every stage, that with this artist juxtaposition and combination do not indicate that ambivalence lies at the centre of his work. Spenser's procedures are inclusive, and his attitudes generous, tolerant and sympathetic, despite some moments in Book v. But this does not make him a pluralist or a relativist. His peculiarity is that he unites a wide-ranging eclecticism with a strong sense of direction. In *The Shepheardes Calender* he juxtaposes the satirical mode of Mantuanesque pastoral with the lyrical charm and 'soft' pastoral of the opening stanzas of 'Iune', for example. But as the work proceeds its consistent allegiance to an ideal of dedicated clergy and of poets who delight and instruct the community through their verses emerges steadily from the patterned and contrasted eclogues. In *The Faerie Queene* the interwoven romance narratives with all their comedy and pathos unfold a vision of human life as a journey which begins with unmerited salvation and moves forward from virtue to virtue towards an eternal kingdom. The Protestant poet's profound and unselfconscious assumptions give an underlying certainty of direction to a work of extraordinary scale and variety. Spenser knows what it is all for, and this gives ease and assurance to his writing. We have argued this case without turning to the *Mutabilitie Cantos*; but there can be little doubt that the cantos reinforce an interpretation which sees the poem as essentially concerned with growth and development. The poem which is about a journey finally reveals that Change, for all 'her cruell sports', is to be understood as the necessary condition of the process by which creatures move towards their perfection.

Notes

I INTRODUCTION

1 Lilian Winstanley, 'Spenser and Puritanism – 1', *Modern Language Quarterly*, iii (1900), 6–16; J. J. Higginson, *Spenser's Shepherd's Calender in Relation to Contemporary Affairs* (New York, 1912); F. M. Padelford, 'Spenser and the Puritan Propaganda', *Modern Philology*, xi (1913), 85–106; F. M. Padelford, 'Spenser and the Theology of Calvin', *M. P.*, xii (1914), 1–18.

2 W. L. Renwick (ed.), *The Shepherd's Calendar* (London, 1930).

3 Virgil K. Whitaker, *The Religious Basis of Spenser's Thought*, Stanford University Publications in Language and Literature, vii, no. 3 (Stanford, 1950), pp. 3, 23, 69.

4 P. E. McLane, *Spenser's Shepheardes Calender: A Study in Elizabethan Allegory* (Notre Dame, 1961), pp. 117, 118, 130n.

5 William Nelson, *The Poetry of Edmund Spenser* (New York, 1963), p. 23.

6 Peter Bayley, *Edmund Spenser: Prince of Poets* (London, 1971), p. 52.

7 Rosemond Tuve, *Allegorical Imagery* (Princeton, 1966), p. 418n.

8 John Whitgift, *The Defense of the Aunswere to the Admonition, against the Replie of T. C.* (London, 1574), p. 4.

9 Ibid., pp. 11, 80, 145, and *passim*.

10 *Certayne Sermons appoynted by the Quenes Maiestie* (London, 1560), sig. C4^v.

11 P. M. Dawley, *John Whitgift and the Reformation* (London, 1955), pp. 206–8.

12 Horton Davies, *Worship and Theology in England* (Princeton, 1970), i, 4.

13 See Patrick Collinson, *The Elizabethan Puritan Movement* (London, 1967), p. 27.

14 Ibid., pp. 120–1. See also the same author's 'John Field and Elizabethan Puritanism', in *Elizabethan Government and Society: Essays Presented to Sir John Neale* (London, 1961), pp. 136–7.

15 Claire Cross, *The Puritan Earl: The Life of Henry Hastings, Third Earl of Huntingdon* (London, 1966), pp. 131–5.

16 Collinson, *The Elizabethan Puritan Movement*, p. 105.

17 M. M. Knappen, *Tudor Puritanism* (Chicago, 1939), p. 262.

18 Collinson, *The Elizabethan Puritan Movement*, p. 179.

19 Eleanor Rosenberg, *Leicester, Patron of Letters* (New York, 1955), pp. 243–56.

20 Patrick Collinson (ed.), *Letters of Thomas Wood, Puritan, 1566–1577*, Bulletin of the Institute of Historical Research, Special Supplement, no. 5 (London, 1960), p. xxxvii.

21 Conyers Read, *Mr Secretary Walsingham and the Policy of Queen Elizabeth* (Oxford, 1925), ii, 261.

22 Ibid., ii, 264–5.

23 A. C. Judson, *A Biographical Sketch of John Young, Bishop of Rochester*, Indiana University Studies, no. 103 (1934), pp. 16–18.

24 H. J. Byrom, 'Edmund Spenser's First Printer, Hugh Singleton', *The Library*, 4th Series, xiv (1933), 121–56.

25 Arthur Lord Grey of Wilton, *A Commentary, etc.*, ed. Sir Philip de Malpas Grey Egerton (Camden Society, 1847), pp. 66, 68.

26 W. L. Renwick (ed.), *A View of the Present State of Ireland* (Oxford, 1970), pp. 19–20.

27 A. G. Dickens, *The English Reformation* (London, 1967), p. 426.

28 Collinson, *The Elizabethan Puritan Movement*, p. 434. See also pp. 385–7.

2 'MAYE', 'IULYE' AND 'SEPTEMBER'

1 William Webbe, *A Discourse of English Poetrie*, in *Elizabethan Critical Essays*, ed. G. Gregory Smith (Oxford, 1904), i, 262–4.

2 William Nelson, *The Poetry of Edmund Spenser* (New York, 1963), p. 46; Patrick Cullen, *Spenser, Marvell, and Renaissance Pastoral* (Cambridge, Mass., 1970).

3 Nancy Jo Hoffman, *Spenser's Pastorals: The Shepheardes Calender and 'Colin Clout'* (Baltimore, 1977), p. 118.

4 *Animadversions*, in *The Works of John Milton* (New York, 1931), iii, 165–6.

5 Patrick Cullen, *Spenser, Marvell, and Renaissance Pastoral*, p. 26.

6 Ibid., p. 42.

7 Edward Dering, *A Sermon preached before the Quenes Maiestie, the. 25. day of February. Anno 1569* (1570?), sig. E4^v.

8 Paul S. Seaver, *The Puritan Lectureships* (Stanford, 1970), p. 17.

9 Edmund Grindal, *The Remains* (Parker Society, 1843), pp. 123, 130.

10 *A Seconde admonition to the Parliament* (1572), sig. C3.

11 Walter Travers, *A full and plaine declaration of Ecclesiastical Discipline* (1574), sig. O4.

12 John Field and Thomas Wilcox, *An Admonition to the Parliament* (1572), sig. A3.

13 Sir Philip Sidney, *The Prose Works*, ed. Albert Feuillerat (Cambridge, 1963), i, 405.

14 John Whitgift, *The Defense of the Aunswere* (London, 1574), sigs. A2, B3, B4^v.

15 Anthony Gilby, *A Pleasaunt Dialogue, Betweene a Souldior of Barwicke, and an English Chaplaine* (1581), sigs. E3^v–E4.

16 Harold Stein, 'Spenser and William Turner', *Modern Language Notes*, li (1936), 345–51.

17 *A Pleasaunt Dialogue*, sigs. D7–D7^v.
18 Ibid., sig. A3.
19 *The Fables of Esope in Englishe* (printed by Henry Wykes, London, 1570?), sigs. F6–F6^v.
20 E.K., on the other hand, declares that the Fox represents 'the false and faithlesse Papistes'. But E.K. is notable for his caution (see p. 26). Modern scholars who endorse E.K.'s statements, e.g. D. Douglas Waters, 'Spenser and Symbolic Witchcraft in *The Shepheardes Calender*', *Studies in English Literature*, xiv (1974), 3–15, will need to find an explanation for Spenser's substitution of a Fox for Aesop's Wolf.
21 *An Admonition to the Parliament* (second edition, 1572), sig. B8^v.
22 Ibid., sig. D3.
23 *A Pleasaunt Dialogue*, sigs. F8^v, G7, L7, M5^v.
24 Ibid., sig. A2^v.
25 Ibid., sigs. M2^v–M3, M3^v.
26 Robert Crowley, *A briefe discourse against the outwarde apparell and Ministring garmentes of the popishe church* (1566), sig. A4^v.
27 *A Pleasaunt Dialogue*, sigs. H7^v, I7.
28 J. J. Higginson, *Spenser's Shepherd's Calender in Relation to Contemporary Affairs* (New York, 1912), p. 86.
29 *A Pleasaunt Dialogue*, sig. F6.
30 Thomas White, *A Sermon Preached at Pawles Crosse on Sunday the thirde of Nouember 1577. in the time of the Plague* (London, 1578), sigs. B7–C1.
31 *A Seconde admonition to the Parliament* (1572), sig. D4^v.
32 William Tyndale, *The obedience of a Christen man* (1528), in *The Whole workes of W. Tyndall, Iohn Frith, and Doct. Barnes* (John Daye, 1573), sig. Y4. I cite Daye's folio because this was the edition in which Elizabethans generally read Tyndale.
33 Kluge was the first to note the debt to Mantuan. See *Variorum, The Minor Poems*, i, 329.
34 W. P. Mustard (ed.), *The Eclogues of Baptista Mantuanus* (Baltimore, 1911), p. 143, provides information about the monastic sites.
35 John Skelton, *The Poetical Works*, ed. Alexander Dyce (1856), ii, 135.
36 W. L. Renwick (ed.), *The Shepherd's Calendar* (London, 1930), pp. 210–11.
37 *The Poetical Works* (1856), ii, 128–36. For a thoughtful reading of *Colyn Cloute* see Stanley Eugene Fish, *John Skelton's Poetry* (New Haven, 1965), pp. 176–205.
38 H. S. V. Jones, *A Spenser Handbook* (New York, 1930), pp. 47–52; Hallett Smith, *Elizabethan Poetry* (Cambridge, Mass., 1952), p. 45n.
39 Nancy Jo Hoffman, *Spenser's Pastorals*, p. 118.
40 Walter Travers, *A full and plaine declaration*, sigs. M4^v, O4–O4^v.
41 Patrick Cullen, *Spenser, Marvell, and Renaissance Pastoral*, pp. 66 and 67.

3 PASTORS AND POETS

1 A. C. Hamilton, 'The Argument of Spenser's *Shepheardes Calender*', *ELH*, xxiii (1956), 171–82, valuably states that Spenser in the *Calender* 'explores the roles of the poet and pastor in society'. His conclusion, however, that the poem's argument is 'the rejection of the pastoral life for the truly dedicated life in the world' seems to me to be mistaken.
2 R. A. Durr, 'Spenser's Calendar of Christian Time', *ELH*, xxiv (1957), 269–95, argues that in the *Calender* earthly love is an evil.
3 *Astrophel and Stella* xlix, in *The Poems of Sir Philip Sidney*, ed. William A. Ringler, Jr (Oxford, 1962), p. 189.
4 Ibid., p. xlix.
5 Isabel G. MacCaffrey, 'Allegory and Pastoral in *The Shepheardes Calender*', in *Critical Essays on Spenser from ELH* (Baltimore, 1970), p. 133.
6 K. R. R. Gros Louis, 'The Triumph and Death of Orpheus in the English Renaissance', *S.E.L.*, ix (1969), 63–80.

4 NATURE AND GRACE RECONSIDERED

1 Isabel G. MacCaffrey, *Spenser's Allegory: The Anatomy of Imagination* (Princeton, 1976); Thomas H. Cain, *Praise in The Faerie Queene* (Lincoln, Nebraska, 1978); Alastair D. S. Fowler, 'Emanations of Glory: Neoplatonic order in Spenser's *Faerie Queen*', in *A Theatre for Spenserians*, ed. Judith M. Kennedy and James A. Reither (Toronto, 1973); Carol V. Kaske, 'Spenser's Pluralistic Universe: The View from the Mount of Contemplation', in *Contemporary Thought on Edmund Spenser*, ed. Richard C. Frushell and Bernard J. Vondersmith (Carbondale, 1975).
2 A. S. P. Woodhouse, 'Nature and Grace in *The Faerie Queene*', *ELH*, xvi (1949), 194–228. See also his later article, 'Spenser, Nature and Grace: Mr Gang's Mode of Argument Reviewed', *ELH*, xxvii (1960), 1–15.
3 Paul J. Alpers (ed.), *Elizabethan Poetry: Modern Essays in Criticism* (Oxford, 1967); Hugh Maclean (ed.), *Edmund Spenser's Poetry* (New York, 1968); *Critical Essays on Spenser from ELH* (Baltimore, 1970); A. C. Hamilton (ed.), *Essential Articles for the Study of Edmund Spenser* (Hamden, Conn., 1972).
4 Robert Hoopes, '"God Guide Thee, Guyon": Nature and Grace Reconciled in *The Faerie Queene*, Book II', *Review of English Studies*, n.s., v (1954), 14–24; Harry Berger, Jr, *The Allegorical Temper* (New Haven, 1957); Alastair D. S. Fowler, 'The Image of Mortality: *The Faerie Queene*, II, i–ii', *Huntington Library Quarterly*, xxiv (1961), 91–110.
5 *Spenser: The Faerie Queene*, ed. A. C. Hamilton (Longman Annotated English Poets, 1977), p. 163.
6 Carol V. Kaske, 'Spenser's Pluralistic Universe', p. 125.
7 St Augustine, *The City of God*, trans. Marcus Dods (Edinburgh, 1872), ii, 525–6; Calvin, *The Institution of Christian Religion* (London, 1561), Book II, fol. 11ᵛ.

8 St Thomas Aquinas, *The Summa Theologica*, trans. Fathers of the English Dominican Province (Chicago, 1952), ii. 64.
9 Calvin, *The Institution of Christian Religion*, Book II, fol. 18ᵛ.
10 Richard Hooker, *Of the Laws of Ecclesiastical Polity* (London, 1954), i, 312.
11 A. S. P. Woodhouse, 'Nature and Grace in Spenser: a Rejoinder', *R.E.S.*, n.s., vi (1955), 284–8.
12 Calvin, *The Institution of Christian Religion*, Book II, fol. 13.
13 William Perkins, *The Workes* (Cambridge, 1608–9), ii, 365–6. This is not the first edition of Perkins's works, but as it contains items not included in the earlier editions I have chosen to cite it.
14 The episode is discussed in Chapter 8.
15 William Perkins, *The Workes*, i, 269.
16 John Woolton, *The Christian Manual* (Parker Society, 1851), p. 51.
17 Robert Hoopes, '"God Guide Thee, Gyon"', pp. 15–16.
18 *Certayne Sermons appoynted by the Quenes Maiestie* (London, 1560), sig. F3ᵛ.
19 Richard Rogers, *Seven Treatises* (London, 1603), p. 72.
20 Ibid., p. 78.
21 Ibid., p. 87.
22 Henry Smith, *The Sermons of Maister Henrie Smith, Gathered into One Volume* (1593), p. 677.
23 Thomas White, *A Godlie Sermon preached the xxj. day of Iune, 1586. at Pensehurst in Kent* (London, 1586), sigs. C3–C3ᵛ.
24 I have inherited the 'baton' metaphor from an earlier generation of Spenser critics.
25 William Perkins, *The Workes*, i, 714.
26 Ibid., i, 715.
27 The seeming contrast between this line from Book II and the couplet quoted a moment ago from I. x. 1 is one of the pieces of evidence for Spenser's 'pluralism' put forward by Carol V. Kaske, 'Spenser's Pluralistic Universe', p. 124.
28 Jan van der Noodt, *A Theatre wherein be represented...the miseries and calamities that follow the voluptuous Worldlings* (London, 1569), sig. D7.
29 Ibid., sig. F3.
30 Sir Philip Sidney, *An Apologie for Poetrie*, in *Elizabethan Critical Essays*, ed. G. Gregory Smith (Oxford, 1904), i, 164.
31 Kathleen Williams, *Spenser's Faerie Queene: The World of Glass* (London, 1966), pp. 31–3.
32 George Gyffard (trans.), *Praelections vpon the Sacred and holy Reuelation of S. Iohn* (London, 1573), sig. *3.

5 BOOK I: SOLA GRATIA

1 Josephine W. Bennett, *The Evolution of 'The Faerie Queene'* (Chicago, 1942), pp. 108–19.
2 John Lydgate, *The Minor Poems*, Part I, ed. H. N. MacCracken, E.E.T.S., Extra Series, cvii (1911), p. 145.

3 David Chytraeus, *A Postil or orderly disposing of certeine Epistles vsually red in the Church of God*, trans. Arthur Golding (London, 1570), p. 54.

4 *The Image of both Churches*, in *Select Works of John Bale* (Parker Society, 1849), p. 303.

5 A. C. Hamilton, *The Structure of Allegory in The Faerie Queene* (Oxford, 1961), pp. 43, 87.

6 Katharine R. Firth, *The Apocalyptic Tradition in Reformation Britain, 1530–1645* (Oxford, 1979), pp. 6–7, 25.

7 Ibid., p. 44.

8 Josephine W. Bennett, *The Evolution of 'The Faerie Queene'*, p. 116.

9 Bale, *The Image of both Churches*, pp. 417–18.

10 *Variorum, Book One*, p. 450.

11 Bale, *The Image of both Churches*, p. 291.

12 *The Romance of Sir Beues of Hamtoun*, ed. E. Kölbing, E.E.T.S., Extra Series, xlvi, xlviii, lxv (1885–94), p. 30.

13 Bale, *The Image of both Churches*, p. 259.

14 Donald Cheney, *Spenser's Image of Nature: Wild Man and Shepherd in 'The Faerie Queene'* (New Haven, 1966), p. 50.

15 The phrase comes from Bale, *The Image of both Churches*, p. 282.

16 Ibid., pp. 416–17.

17 Sr Mary R. Falls, 'Spenser's Kirkrapine and the Elizabethans', *Studies in Philology*, 1 (1953), 457–75.

18 James Bisse, *Two Sermons preached, the one at Paules Crosse the eight of Ianuarie 1580*...(London, 1581), sigs. E1–E1ᵛ.

19 Frank Kermode, *Renaissance Essays: Shakespeare, Spenser, Donne* (London, 1973), p. 48.

20 Calvin, *The Institution of Christian Religion* (London, 1561), Book 1, fol. 3ᵛ–4.

21 See Paul J. Alpers, *The Poetry of The Faerie Queene* (Princeton, 1967), pp. 170–4. Particularly helpful is Alpers's statement, 'we cannot say how much of our response is physical experience and how much is moral awareness', p. 173.

22 William Tyndale, *An aunswere vnto Syr Thomas Mores Dialogue*, in *The Whole workes of W. Tyndall, Iohn Frith, and Doct. Barnes* (John Daye, 1573), sig. Pp1.

23 Abraham Fleming (trans.), *A Monomachie of Motives in the mind of man* (London, 1582), p. 104.

24 William Fulke, *Praelections vpon the Sacred and holy Reuelation of S. Iohn, written in latine by William Fulke Doctor of Diuinitie, and translated into English by George Gyffard* (London, 1573), sigs. M1–M1ᵛ.

25 Jan van der Noodt, *A Theatre* (London, 1569), sigs. G8ᵛ–H1.

26 William Fulke, *Praelections*, sig. Q1.

27 William Tyndale, *A Pathway into the holy Scripture*, in *The Whole workes*, sig. Tt2.

28 See William Haller, *The Rise of Puritanism* (New York, 1938), pp. 26–8 for information about Greenham's life.

29 Richard Greenham, *A Most Sweete and assured Comfort for all those that are afflicted in Conscience* (London, 1595), sigs. D2ᵛ–D3.
30 See Alpers, *The Poetry of The Faerie Queene*, pp. 36–8 for a sensitive discussion of patience in stanzas 28–9.
31 Charles E. Mounts, 'Spenser's Seven Bead-men and the Corporal Works of Mercy', *PMLA*, liv (1939), 974–80.
32 The Redcross Knight's Englishness is discussed in Chapter 7.
33 Augustine Marlorat, *A Catholike exposition vpon the Reuelation of Sainct Iohn* (London, 1574), sigs. Qq1ᵛ–Qq2.
34 Ibid., sig. Qq3.
35 Jan van der Noodt, *A Theatre*, sig. P7.
36 Bale, *The Image of both Churches*, p. 617.
37 Rosemond Tuve, *Allegorical Imagery* (Princeton, 1966), p. 404.

6 BOOKS II–VI: FROM VIRTUE TO VIRTUE

1 Giovanni Battista Giraldi, *Dialogues Philosophiques et Tres-Vtiles Italiens–Francois, touchant la vie Ciuile* (Paris, 1583), sig. D2ᵛ in the Italian text.
2 Pierre de la Primaudaye, *The French Academie, wherin is discoursed the institution of maners*, trans. T. B. (London, 1586), p. 256.
3 John Erskine Hankins, *Source and Meaning in Spenser's Allegory* (Oxford, 1971), pp. 1–16, argues that Spenser was chiefly influenced by Francesco Piccolomini, *Vniuersa Philosophia de Moribus*, but I doubt if such a pinpointing of sources is possible.
4 C. S. Lewis, *English Literature in the Sixteenth Century excluding Drama* (Oxford, 1954), p. 381.
5 Spenser does not, I think, observe a strict distinction between temperance and continence.
6 See, on the one hand, Frank Kermode, *Renaissance Essays: Shakespeare, Spenser, Donne* (London, 1973), pp. 60–83, and on the other, Harry Berger, Jr, *The Allegorical Temper* (New Haven, 1957), pp. 15–38. I am much indebted to Berger's discussion, although I am not convinced that *curiositas* is Guyon's chief motive for entering the Cave.
7 The imagery and significance of the Garden of Proserpina are discussed in Chapter 8.
8 Arthur Golding (trans.), *The Warfare of Christians: Concerning the conflict against the Fleshe, the World, and the Deuill* (London, 1576), sigs. E5ᵛ, E8ᵛ, F2ᵛ.
9 John Udall, *Peters Fall. Two Sermons vpon the Historie of Peters denying Christ* (London, 1585?), sigs. B8ᵛ–C1.
10 Ibid., sigs. C2, F1.
11 Respectively, Frank Kermode, *Renaissance Essays*, pp. 70–1; John Erskine Hankins, *Source and Meaning in Spenser's Allegory*, pp. 132–3; A. C. Hamilton in his edition of *The Faerie Queene* (London, 1977), p. 225; Patrick Cullen, *Infernal Triad: The Flesh, the World and the Devil in Spenser and Milton* (Princeton, 1974), Chapter 2.

12 Richard Robinson (trans.), *An Homely or Sermon of Good and Euill Angels* (London, 1590), sigs. D3–D3ᵛ, D4.

13 Henry Smith, *The Sermons of Maister Henrie Smith, Gathered into One Volume* (1593), pp. 267–8.

14 Ibid., p. 327.

15 Ibid., p. 336 (misnumbered 326).

16 Ibid., p. 341.

17 Thomas Wilcox, *An exposition vppon the Booke of the Canticles, otherwise called Schelomons Song* (London, 1585), p. 37.

18 Article IX is quoted by A. C. Hamilton, *The Structure of Allegory in The Faerie Queene* (Oxford, 1961), p. 115, but he nevertheless interprets Maleger as original sin, p. 114.

19 William Perkins, *The Whole Treatise of the Cases of Conscience*, in *The Workes* (Cambridge, 1608–9), ii, 92.

20 Thomas P. Roche, Jr, *The Kindly Flame* (Princeton, 1964), pp. 103–16.

21 John Gower, *The Complete Workes*, ed. G. C. Macaulay (Oxford, 1899), i, 195.

22 See John Erskine Hankins, *Source and Meaning in Spenser's Allegory*, p. 278n.

23 Emile Male, *The Gothic Image* (reprinted London, 1961), pp. 125–6.

24 Palingenius, *The Zodiake of Life*, trans. Barnabe Googe, ed. Rosemond Tuve (New York, 1947), Book IV, pp. 51–61, cited by Alastair D. S. Fowler, *Spenser and the Numbers of Time* (London, 1964), p. 26. See also Stephan Batman, *The Golden Booke of the Leaden Goddes* (London, 1577), sigs. E1–E2.

25 Alastair D. S. Fowler, *Spenser and the Numbers of Time*, p. 165n, mentions this analogue.

26 J. A. W. Bennett, *The Parlement of Foules: An Interpretation* (Oxford, 1957), p. 91.

27 However, T. K. Dunseath, *Spenser's Allegory of Justice in Book Five of The Faerie Queene* (Princeton, 1968) argues a different case.

28 E.g. William Nelson, *The Poetry of Edmund Spenser* (New York, 1963), pp. 266–71; Alastair D. S. Fowler, *Spenser and the Numbers of Time*, pp. 44–6.

29 E.g. Kathleen Williams, *Spenser's Faerie Queene: The World of Glass* (London, 1966), p. 176, who states that 'Mercilla's palace is a lesser companion piece to Isis Church'; Thomas H. Cain, *Praise in The Faerie Queene* (Lincoln, Nebraska, 1978), p. 146, who argues that 'the relation of justice and mercy in the Mercilla icon becomes problematic'.

30 Jane Aptekar, *Icons of Justice: Iconography and Thematic Imagery in Book V of The Faerie Queene* (New York, 1969), pp. 92–4.

31 John Ward-Perkins and Amanda Claridge, *Pompeii AD 79*, catalogue of the Royal Academy Exhibition (London, 1976), no. 186.

32 Melanchthon, *A ciuile nosgay wherin is contayned not onelye the offyce and dewty of all magestrates and Iudges but also of all subiectes*, trans. I. G. (London, 1550?), sig. C1.

33 William Perkins, *A Treatise of Christian Equitie and Moderation*, in *The*

Workes (Cambridge, 1608–9), ii, 503. The next two quotations also come from this page.

34 Thomas H. Cain, *Praise in The Faerie Queene*, p. 144.

35 William Perkins, *A Treatise of Christian Equitie*, ii, 504.

36 See Humphrey Tonkin, *Spenser's Courteous Pastoral* (Oxford, 1972), pp. 236, 254–7, for the contrary view.

37 Castiglione, *The Book of the Courtier*, trans. Sir Thomas Hoby (London, 1928), p. 33. I am much indebted to the late Professor Donald J. Gordon for his illuminating comments on the subject of Castiglione's influence on Book VI.

38 Sir Philip Sidney, *The Prose Works*, ed. Albert Feuillerat (Cambridge, 1963), i, 178–9.

39 Humphrey Tonkin, *Spenser's Courteous Pastoral*, p. 299.

40 Tasso, *Gerusalemme Liberata*, trans. Edward Fairfax, Book XVIII, stanzas 26–38.

41 Castiglione, *The Book of the Courtier*, pp. 43–4.

7 BRITONS AND ELVES

1 Edwin Greenlaw, *Studies in Spenser's Historical Allegory* (Baltimore, 1932), p. 198.

2 Janet Spens, *Spenser's Faerie Queene: An Interpretation* (London, 1934), p. 52.

3 Isabel E. Rathborne, *The Meaning of Spenser's Fairyland* (New York, 1937), Chapters 2 and 3.

4 Harry Berger, Jr, *The Allegorical Temper* (New Haven, 1957), p. 108.

5 Thomas P. Roche, Jr, *The Kindly Flame* (Princeton, 1964), p. 38.

6 Edwin Greenlaw, *Studies in Spenser's Historical Allegory*, pp. 11–20; Charles B. Millican, *Spenser and the Table Round* (1932, reprinted 1967), pp. 24–33.

7 William Warner, *The First and Second parts of Albions England* (London, 1589); Thomas Churchyard, *The Worthines of Wales* (1587).

8 R. H. Fletcher, *The Arthurian Material in the Chronicles* (Boston, 1906), p. 262.

9 Richard Grafton, *A Chronicle at large and meere History of the affayres of Englande and Kinges of the same* (London, 1569), p. 105.

10 Raphaell Holinshed, *The Firste volume of the Chronicles of England, Scotlande, and Irelande* (London, 1577), pp. 133–4.

11 Ibid., p. 136 (misnumbered 156).

12 Tasso, *Discourses*, in Allan H. Gilbert, *Literary Criticism: Plato to Dryden* (Detroit, 1962), pp. 479–92.

13 See *Variorum, Book Three*, p. 228.

14 Grafton, *A Chronicle at large and meere History*, p. 106.

15 Isabel Rathborne, *The Meaning of Spenser's Fairyland*, p. 228, rightly states that Spenser wished to whitewash Conan.

16 Richard Robinson, *The Auncient Order, Societie, and Vnitie Laudable, of Prince Arthure, and his Knightly Armory of the Round Table* (London, 1583), sig. B3.

17 Carrie A. Harper, *The Sources of the British Chronicle History in Spenser's Faerie Queene* (Philadelphia, 1910), pp. 16n, 177.

18 Ibid., pp. 172, 177.

19 Richard Johnson, *The Most Famous History of the seuen Champions of Christendome* (London, 1608), sig. A3^v.

20 John Selden, 'Illustrations', in Michael Drayton, *Poly-Olbion. or a Chorographicall Description of...this renowned Isle of Great Britaine* (London, 1613), p. 68.

21 See Isabel Rathborne, *The Meaning of Spenser's Fairyland*, pp. 174–7.

22 Sir Philip Sidney, *An Apologie for Poetrie*, in *Elizabethan Critical Essays*, ed. G. Gregory Smith (Oxford, 1904), i, 170.

23 Robert Greene, *Friar Bacon and Friar Bungay*, ed. Daniel Seltzer (Regents Renaissance Drama Series, 1963), xi. 20.

24 Arthur Golding, *Ovid's Metamorphoses, 1567*, ed. John F. Nims (New York, 1965), pp. 417–18; Thomas Lodge, *Defence of Poetry*, in *Elizabethan Critical Essays*, i, 65.

8 SECRET WISDOM?

1 Frank Kermode, *Renaissance Essays: Shakespeare, Spenser, Donne* (London, 1973), p. 61.

2 Ibid., p. 2.

3 E.g. in the Dedication of *The Shadow of Night*, and the Dedication of *Ovids Banquet of Sence*, in *The Poems of George Chapman*, ed. Phyllis Brooks Bartlett (New York, 1941), pp. 19, 49–50.

4 Michael Murrin, *The Veil of Allegory* (Chicago, 1969), examines some of the same material in his first chapter, but reaches a directly opposed conclusion.

5 Charles G. Osgood (trans.), *Boccaccio on Poetry* (Indianapolis, 1956), pp. 59–60.

6 Richard Stanyhurst, *Thee First Foure Bookes of Virgil his Aeneis*, in *Elizabethan Critical Essays*, ed. G. Gregory Smith (Oxford, 1904), i, 136.

7 Sir John Harington, *A Preface, or rather a Briefe Apologie of Poetrie*, in *Elizabethan Critical Essays*, ii, 201–2.

8 Sir Philip Sidney, *An Apologie for Poetrie*, in *Elizabethan Critical Essays*, i, 167.

9 Kenneth Orne Myrick, *Sir Philip Sidney as a Literary Craftsman* (Cambridge, Mass., 1935), pp. 80–1.

10 Luther, *Lectures on Genesis, Chapters 1–5*, in *Luther's Works*, ed. J. Pelikan (Concordia edition, Saint Louis), i, 91.

11 Bullinger, *A Hundred Sermons vpon the Apocalips of Iesus Christe* (1561), sigs. B3–B3^v.

12 Dudley Fenner, *The Song of Songs...translated out of the Hebrue into Englishe meeter* (Middelburgh, 1587), sig. B2^v.

13 George Puttenham, *The Arte of English Poesie*, ed. Gladys D. Willcock and Alice Walker (Cambridge, 1936), p. 154.

14 Paul J. Alpers, *The Poetry of The Faerie Queene* (Princeton, 1967), p. 282.

15 Alastair D. S. Fowler, 'The Image of Mortality: *The Faerie Queene*, II. i–ii', *H.L.Q.*, xxiv (1961), 91.

16 Lewis H. Miller, Jr, 'A Secular Reading of *The Faerie Queene*, Book II', in *Critical Essays on Spenser from ELH* (Baltimore, 1970), p. 208.

17 Thomas Kyd, *The Spanish Tragedy*, ed. Philip Edwards (The Revels Plays, 1959), III. xiii. 86–9.

18 Frank Kermode, *Renaissance Essays*, p. 83.

19 Henry Smith, *The Sermons of Maister Henrie Smith, Gathered into One Volume* (1593), p. 205.

20 Paul J. Alpers, *The Poetry of The Faerie Queene*, p. 246.

21 Calvin, *The holy Gospel of Iesus Christ, according to Iohn, with the Commentary of M. Iohn Caluine*, trans. Christopher Fetherstone (London, 1584), pp. 416, 418.

22 Augustine Marlorat, *A Catholike and Ecclesiasticall exposition of the holy Gospell after S. Mathewe*, trans. Thomas Tymme (London, 1570), pp. 706, 709.

23 Thomas P. Roche, Jr, *The Kindly Flame* (Princeton, 1964), p. 15.

24 Lodowick Bryskett, *A Discourse of Ciuill Life*, in *Literary Works*, ed. J. H. P. Pafford (1972), p. 226.

25 A. C. Hamilton, *The Structure of Allegory in The Faerie Queene* (Oxford, 1961), p. 68.

26 Henry Reynolds, *Mythomystes* (1632; Scolar Press reprint 1972), p. 42.

27 Sir Kenelm Digby, *Observations on the 22. Stanza in the 9th. Canto of the 2d. Book of Spencers Faery Queen* (London, 1643), sig. A4.

Index

Abessa, 86–7
Acidale, Mount, 137
Acrasia, 111, 113, 171–2
Admonition controversy, 5, 8, 23, 186
    n. 10, 187 n. 31
Adonis, 110; Garden of, 109–10, 158,
    162, 182
Aeneas, 113
Aesop, 22–3, 25–6
Agape, 179–81
Aladine, 137
Albigensianism, 87, 89
Alcina, 64, 95
Aldus, 156
Alençon, Duke of, 6, 8
Alma, 122–5; Castle of, 68, 107, 120–2
Alpers, Paul J., 170, 176, 190 n. 21, 191
    n. 30
Amavia, 64, 80, 111, 171–3
ambition, 175–7
Amoret, 73, 110, 126–7, 155
angels, 117–20, 136–7
Antichrist, 76, 80–1
apostasy, 75, 84, 92
Aptekar, Jane, 131
Aquinas, St Thomas, 61, 62, 101
Archimago, 77, 80, 81–3, 87, 111,
    141
Arianism, 79
Ariosto, Ludovico, 1, 145; *Orlando
    Furioso*, 95, 149, 164
Aristotle, 60, 107, 167
Armida, 141, 149
Artegall, 108, 110, 127, 130, 132–4, 137,
    146, 151–3
Arthur, 90–2, 94–6, 108, 120–2, 125–6,
    137, 145, 146, 156, 161; historicity of,
    147–51, 155; successors of, 152–3
Astrophel, 45–6
Atalanta, 174
Ate, 127, 174
Augustine, St, 61, 62, 107, 164
avarice, 174–7

Bale, John, Bishop of Ossory, 8, 72,
    74, 75, 78–80, 82, 85, 105, 147
Bancroft, Richard, 4
baptism, 104–5, 172–3; memory of,
    125–6
Barclay, Alexander, 34, 39, 41, 44
Baro, Peter, 4
Batman, Stephan, 192 n. 24
Bayley, Peter, 3
Bead-men, seven, 101
Beale, Robert, 6
Bedford, Earl of (Francis Russell), 6
beauty, heavenly, 105–6, 140
Belphoebe, 73, 126–7, 138, 145, 155
Bennett, J. A. W., 192 n. 26
Bennett, Josephine Waters, 72, 77
Berger, Harry, Jr, 59, 146, 191 n. 6
Beves, Sir, 81
Beza, Theodore, 23
bible, the, 98, 108, 136, 158, 167;
    Geneva Bible, 93, 124; Genesis, 167;
    Exodus, 136; Leviticus, 136; Psalms,
    118–20; Song of Solomon, 124, 167,
    169; Matthew, 54, 117; John, 176;
    1 Corinthians, 62, 64, 105;
    2 Corinthians, 21; Galatians, 64;
    1 Thessalonians, 108; 2 Timothy, 64;
    1 John, 181; Revelation, 72, 74–5,
    77–8, 85, 93, 95, 103–4, 123, 167–8
Bion, 44
Bisse, James, 86–7
Boccaccio, Giovanni, *De Genealogia
    Deorum Gentilium*, 163–4, 167–8, 171,
    178; *Il Filostrato*, 128; *Teseida*, 128
body, the human, 67, 68, 121–2, 124
Boethius, 128
Bower of Bliss, 81–2
Boyle, Elizabeth, 138
Braggadochio, 130
Briana, 137
Britomart, 73, 109, 110, 126, 127,
    130–4, 151–2, 156, 181

196

Index

Index

Index

Index

Morgan le Fay, 156
Morrell, 29–33, 39–40, 47
Moses, 31, 32, 167
Mounts, Charles E., 101
Munera, 130
Murrin, Michael, 194 n. 4
Muses, the, 47, 53, 143
Mustard, W. P., 187 n. 34
Myrick, K. O., 166

Nashe, Thomas, 46
nationalism, 145, 147, 149, 161
natural man, 61–66
natural religion, 88–9
nature, law of, 4, 62
Nelson, William, 3, 13, 192 n. 28
Neoplatonism, 1, 52, 140, 162
Nero, 93
new life, the, 66–69, 101, 108
Night, 81, 114

Oberon, in *Huon of Bordeaux*, 156; in
  The Faerie Queene, 159
Orgoglio, 73, 89, 91–4
Origen, 167
Orpheus, 51
Osiris, 131
Ovid, 1, 18, 158

Padelford, F. M., 3
Palingenius, *The Zodiake of Life*, 192 n.
  24
Palinode, 13, 15–16, 19–20, 27–8,
  39–40, 47
Palmer, 63–5, 111, 120, 172–3
Paris (son of Priam), 32
Parnassus, Mount, 101–2, 143
pastoral, 13, 33–4, 39, 52, 139; elegy,
  53–4; romance, 34, 49, 143
Pastorella, 138–9
Paul, St, 60, 62
Peacham, Henry, 169
Perigot, 48, 52
Perkins, William, 64, 65, 68–9, 125,
  135–6
persecution, 94–5
Peter, St, 116
Petrarch, 1, 39, 41
Phaedria, 108, 111, 115
Philotime, 114, 174, 177
Piccolomini, Francesco, 108
Pico della Mirandola, 167, 182
Piers, 13, 14, 15–19, 21, 27–8, 39, 42,
  47, 50–3

Pilate, 175–8
Plato, 60, 69, 107
Plutarch, 69, 166
poetic theory, Renaissance, 159, 162–71,
  178
Pollente, 130
Polydore Virgil, 147–8
Pompeii, 131
Pope, the, 80, 93, 94
predestination, 4
Presbyterianism, 4, 5, 6, 8
Priamond, 179
pride, 83–4, 93; self-trust or vainglory,
  113, 116–17, 118, 120–1
primitive church, the, 18, 93
Priscilla, 137
Prometheus, 158
Proserpina, 175; Garden of, 114, 173–8
providence, divine, 88
Prudentius, 128
Puritanism, 3–9, 14–15, 17–27, 32, 36,
  38–40, 99; defined, 4–5; moderate
  episcopalian Puritans, 5–6, 7, 9;
  Puritan views on church
  government, 5; in the 1590s, 9
Puttenham, George, 169
Pyrochles, 111, 115

Rathborne, Isabel E., 146, 193 n. 15,
  194 n. 21
Read, Conyers, 186 n. 21, 186 n. 22
Redcross Knight, 61–5, 69, 70–1, 72–85,
  89–92, 96–106, 110, 130, 140–1,
  154–5, 178
Renwick, W. L., 3, 15, 36
repentance, 97, 101
Reynolds, Henry, 167, 182–3
Reynolds, John, 6
Rhegius, Urbanus, 118
Rinaldo, 141
Robinson, Richard, 118, 147, 153
Roche, Thomas P., Jr, 126, 146,
  178–81
Rogers, Richard, 66–7
Roman Catholicism, 5, 6, 7, 9, 18, 21,
  23–6, 30–3, 35, 75, 82–4, 92–6;
  seminary priests, 37, 40, 50
Roman de la Rose, 128
Roman Empire, 93, 94
Rome, 33, 34, 35, 37, 41, 93
Rosalind, 42, 44, 47
Rosenberg, Eleanor, 185 n. 19
Rosiere, garland of, 123–4
Ruddymane, 171–3

Index

Sackville, Thomas, 113
saints, 15, 26, 27, 29, 33; Protestant
    attitude to, 30, 108; Protestant use of
    word, 70–1
Salvage Man, 156
Sampson, Thomas, 5, 7
Sanglier, 130
Sannazaro, Jacopo, *Arcadia*, 143
Sansfoy, 80–1, 83
Sansjoy, 80–1
Sansloy, 80, 87
Sardanapalus, 19
Satyrane, 87, 89, 130, 155
satyrs, in Book I, 87–9; in Book III, 88
Saxons, 150, 155
Scudamour, 109, 128, 129, 181–2
Seaver, Paul S., 186 n. 8
Selden, John, 155
Seneca, 69, 107–8
Serena, 110, 141
Seven-headed Beast, 74, 90, 92–4
Shakespeare, *The Winter's Tale*, 34, 49
Shamefastness, 107–8
Shepheardes Calender, The, 2–3, 8, 9, 10,
    13–40, 41–56, 60, 184; 'Ianuarye',
    43–4, 46, 52, 143; 'Februarie', 43–4;
    'March', 43–5; 'Aprill', 43, 45–7, 55;
    'Maye', 3, 13, 15–28, 37, 39, 40,
    46–7, 93; 'Iune', 46, 47–8, 49;
    'Iulye', 13, 28–33, 39, 40, 47;
    'August', 42, 46, 48–9; 'September',
    13, 21–3, 33–40, 42, 50, 53;
    'October', 50–3; 'Nouember', 50,
    53–5; 'December', 55; Epilogue,
    55–6; attack on ecclesiastical abuses
    in, 13–40, 47, 50; compared with
    other collections of eclogues, 41;
    theme of love and poetry in, 41–56,
    143; time in, 43, 46, 50; unity of,
    41–3, 55–6; variety in, 42; woodcuts
    in, 54–5
Sherry, Richard, 169
Sidney, Sir Henry, 7, 8, 67
Sidney, Sir Philip, 8, 51, 162, 169, 176;
    Apologie for Poetrie, 69, 157, 165–7;
    Arcadia, 19, 34, 138, 143; *Astrophel
    and Stella*, 45–6
sin, bondage to, 4, 68, 73–4, 89, 91–2
Sinai, Mount, 29–31
Singleton, Hugh, 8
Skelton, John, 14, 28; *Colyn Cloute*, 14,
    32, 36
sloth, 89
Smith, Hallett, 38

Smith, Henry, 67, 69, 122–4, 175
sorcery, 82–3
Spenser, Edmund, life, 7–8; works:
    Amoretti, 138, 174; *Colin Clouts Come
    Home Againe*, 34; 'Epigrams' and
    'Sonets' in *A Theatre for voluptuous
    Worldlings*, 1, 7; *Epithalamion*, 138;
    Letter to Raleigh, 60, 162–3, 169;
    Mother Hubberds Tale, 9, 18;
    Prothalamion, 9; *The Ruines of Time*,
    7; *A View of the Present State of
    Ireland*, 8, 154; *Visions of the Worlds
    Vanitie*, 7; see also: *The Faerie Queene,
    The Shepheardes Calender*; eclecticism
    of, 1–2, 54, 60, 72, 107, 184; poetic
    theory of, 51–2, 143–4, 169–71;
    religious beliefs of, 1–4, 8–10
Spens, Janet, 145–6
Stanyhurst, Richard, 164
Stein, Harold, 21–2
Stockwood, John, 7
Stow, John, 154
Stubbs, John, 8

Tantalus, 175–8
Tasso, Torquato, 1; *Discorsi del Poema
    Eroico*, 149; *Gerusalemme Liberata*,
    102, 141, 149
temperance, 107, 111, 124
temptation of Christ, 117–18
Thenot, 44, 45, 48, 52, 102
Theocritus, 14, 126
Theological Virtues, three, 98, 137
Thirty-nine Articles, 4, 125
Thomalin, 14, 29–33, 39, 42, 43–5, 47,
    48, 52
Timias, 110, 126, 127
Timon, 150, 155
Tityrus, 48
Tonkin, Humphrey, 193 n. 36, 193 n.
    39
Travers, Walter, 5, 18, 38
Tree of Life, 103–5
Triamond, 127, 155, 178–9
Tristram, 138, 153–4, 156
Tudors, 96, 159; claim of British and
    Arthurian descent, 147, 149, 161
Turner, William, 21–3
Tuve, Rosemond, 105, 185 n. 7
Tyndale, William, 30, 92, 97

Udall, John, 191 n. 9, 191 n. 10
Una, 72, 75, 76–7, 80–3, 85–9, 96, 98,
    101, 102, 105–6

Index

Printed in the United States
132436LV00002B/9/P